CROCK·POT.

◆ THE ORIGINAL SLOW COOKER ◆

365 Year-Round Recipes

pil

Publications International, Ltd.

Pictured on the front cover: Chili Verde *(page 65)*.
Pictured on the back cover *(clockwise from top left):* Simple Shredded Pork Tacos *(page 220)*, Braised Sea Bass with Aromatic Vegetables *(page 184)*, Greek Rice *(page 202)*, Ham and Cheddar Brunch Strata *(page 145)* and Nana's Mini Meatball Soup *(page 303)*.

table of contents

the joy of slow cooking

Slow Cooker Hints and Tips

Slow Cooker Sizes

Smaller slow cookers—such as 1- to 3½-quart models—are the perfect size for cooking for singles, a couple, or empty-nesters (and also for serving dips).

While medium-size slow cookers (those holding somewhere between 3 quarts and 5 quarts) will easily cook enough food at a time to feed a small family, they're also convenient for holiday side dishes or appetizers.

Large slow cookers are great for large family dinners, holiday entertaining, and potluck suppers. A 6-quart to 7-quart model is ideal if you like to make meals in advance, or have dinner tonight and store leftovers for another day.

Types of Slow Cookers

Current **CROCK-POT®** slow cookers come equipped with many different features and benefits, from auto cook programs to timed programming. Visit **www.crockpot.com** to find the slow cooker that best suits your needs.

How you plan to use a slow cooker may affect the model you choose to purchase. For everyday cooking, choose a size large enough to serve your family. If you plan to use the slow cooker primarily for entertaining, choose one of the larger sizes. Basic slow cookers can hold as little as 16 ounces or as much as 7 quarts. The smallest sizes are great for keeping dips hot on a buffet, while the larger sizes can more readily fit large quantities of food and larger roasts.

Cooking, Stirring, and Food Safety

CROCK-POT® slow cookers are safe to leave unattended. The outer heating base may get hot as it cooks, but it should not pose a fire hazard. The heating element in the heating base functions at a low wattage and is safe for your countertops.

Your slow cooker should be filled about one-half to three-fourths full for most recipes unless otherwise instructed. Lean meats such as chicken or pork tenderloin will cook faster than meats with more connective tissue and fat such as beef chuck or pork shoulder. Bone-in meats will take longer than boneless cuts. Typical slow cooker dishes take approximately 7 to 8 hours to reach the simmer point on LOW and about 3 to 4 hours on HIGH. Once the vegetables and meat start to simmer and braise, their flavors will fully blend and meat will become fall-off-the-bone tender.

According to the USDA, all bacteria are killed at a temperature of 165°F. It is important to follow the recommended cooking times and not to open the lid often, especially early in the cooking process when heat is building up inside the unit. If you need to open the lid to check on your food or are adding additional ingredients, remember to allow additional cooking time if necessary to ensure food is cooked through and tender.

Large slow cookers, the 6- to 7-quart sizes, may benefit with a quick stir halfway during cook time to help distribute heat and promote even cooking. It's usually unnecessary to stir at all, as even ½ cup liquid will help to distribute heat, and the crockery is the perfect medium for holding food at an even temperature throughout the cooking process.

Oven-Safe

All **CROCK-POT®** slow cooker removable crockery inserts (without their lids) may be used safely in ovens at up to 400°F. Also, all **CROCK-POT®** slow cookers are microwavable without their lids. If you own another brand slow cooker, please refer to your owner's manual for specific crockery cooking medium tolerances.

Frozen Food

Frozen food or partially frozen food can be successfully cooked in a slow cooker; however, it will require longer cooking than the same recipe made with fresh food. It's almost always preferable to thaw frozen food prior to placing it in the slow cooker. Using an instant-read thermometer is recommended to ensure meat is fully cooked through.

Pasta and Rice

If you're converting a recipe that calls for uncooked pasta, cook the pasta on the stovetop just until slightly tender before adding to the slow cooker. If you are converting a recipe that calls for cooked rice, stir in raw rice with other ingredients; add ¼ cup extra liquid per ¼ cup of raw rice.

Beans

Beans must be softened completely before combining with sugar and/or acidic foods. Sugar and acid have a hardening effect on beans and will prevent softening. Fully cooked canned beans may be used as a substitute for dried beans.

Vegetables

Root vegetables often cook more slowly than meat. Cut vegetables accordingly to cook at the same rate as meat—large or small, or lean versus marbled—and place near the sides or bottom of the stoneware to facilitate cooking.

Herbs

Fresh herbs add flavor and color when added at the end of the cooking cycle; if added at the beginning, many fresh herbs' flavor will dissipate over long cook times. Ground and/or dried herbs and spices work well in slow cooking and may be added at the beginning, and for dishes with shorter cook times, hearty fresh herbs such as rosemary and thyme hold up well. The flavor power of all herbs and spices can vary greatly depending on their particular strength and shelf life. Use chili powders and garlic powder sparingly, as these can sometimes intensify over the long cook times. Always taste dish at end of cook cycle and correct seasonings including salt and pepper.

Liquids

It is not necessary to use more than ½ to 1 cup liquid in most instances since juices in meats and vegetables are retained more in slow cooking than in conventional cooking. Excess liquid can be cooked down and concentrated after slow cooking on the stovetop or by removing meat and vegetables from stoneware, stirring in one of the following thickeners, and setting the slow cooker to HIGH. Cook on HIGH for approximately 15 minutes until juices are thickened.

Flour: All-purpose flour is often used to thicken soups or stews. Place flour in a small bowl or cup and stir in enough cold water to make a thin, lump-free mixture. With the slow cooker on HIGH, quickly stir the flour mixture into the liquid in the slow cooker. Cook, stirring frequently, until the mixture thickens.

Cornstarch: Cornstarch gives sauces a clear, shiny appearance; it is used most often for sweet dessert sauces and stir-fry sauces. Place cornstarch in a small bowl or cup and stir in cold water, stirring until the cornstarch dissolves. Quickly stir this mixture into the liquid in the slow cooker; the sauce will thicken as soon as the liquid boils. Cornstarch breaks down with too much heat, so never add it at the beginning of the slow cooking process, and turn off the heat as soon as the sauce thickens.

Arrowroot: Arrowroot (or arrowroot flour) comes from the root of a tropical plant that is dried and ground to a powder; it produces a thick clear sauce. Those who are allergic to wheat often use it in place of flour. Place arrowroot in a small bowl or cup and stir in cold water until the mixture is smooth. Quickly stir this mixture into the liquid in the slow cooker. Arrowroot thickens below the boiling point, so it even works well in a slow cooker on LOW. Too much stirring can break down an arrowroot mixture.

Tapioca: Tapioca is a starchy substance extracted from the root of the cassava plant. Its greatest advantage is that it withstands long cooking, making it an ideal choice for slow cooking. Add it at the beginning of cooking and you'll get a clear thickened sauce in the finished dish. Dishes using tapioca as a thickener are best cooked on the LOW setting; tapioca may become stringy when boiled for a long time.

Milk

Milk, cream, and sour cream break down during extended cooking. When possible, add during the last 15 to 30 minutes of cooking, until just heated through. Condensed soups may be substituted for milk and can cook for extended times.

Fish

Fish is delicate and should be stirred in gently during the last 15 to 30 minutes of cooking time. Cook until just cooked through and serve immediately.

Baked Goods

If you wish to prepare bread, cakes, or pudding cakes in a slow cooker, you may want to purchase a covered, vented metal cake pan accessory for your slow cooker. You can also use any straight-sided soufflé dish or deep cake pan that will fit into the ceramic insert of your unit. Baked goods can be prepared directly in the insert; however, they can be a little difficult to remove from the insert, so follow the recipe directions carefully.

slow cooking
the year-round

You know your **CROCK-POT®** slow cooker is the key to feeding your family great-tasting meals with a minimum of hassle. If you're like many owners of **CROCK-POT®** slow cookers, you probably have your favorite recipes memorized, you may even have a steady rotation of recipes you regularly prepare. But are you really getting the most out of this versatile appliance? Do you really get the most out of it year-round? This book will give you some of the best seasonal uses for your **CROCK-POT®** slow cooker.

winter

Holiday Entertaining

The winter holidays offer many opportunities to entertain family and friends. Use your **CROCK-POT®** slow cooker to make your next family gathering extra special without requiring extra effort.

What would the holidays be without all your favorite winter foods? The **CROCK-POT®** slow cooker can make whipping up a holiday feast easier than ever before. Preparing a side dish in it means freeing up room on your stove or in your oven. And since at least one of your recipes is slow cooked, you'll have more time to concentrate on the other dishes you're preparing.

You'll find your **CROCK-POT®** slow cooker can even make phenomenal desserts that are perfect for holiday entertaining. These cakes, quick breads, and even puddings will turn out warm, moist, and delicious every time.

The Big Game

You don't have to go to the stadium to enjoy the big game. Call the whole gang and plan a laid-back get-together to watch your favorite team from the comfort of your own home. Complete the festive atmosphere with simple but hearty food like hot appetizers, chilies, soups, or sandwiches made in your **CROCK-POT®** slow cooker. Switch it to the WARM setting and your **CROCK-POT®** slow cooker can easily keep food hot and waiting for you and your guests no matter when you want to get another bite.

Winter Warm-Ups

A steaming bowl of a hearty soup or stew is the ultimate comfort food in the cold of winter. The **CROCK-POT®** slow cooker is the key to nearly effortless cooking of soups and stews. A few simple steps in the morning and you're well on your way to a filling, comforting pot of soup for dinner.

Try **Pumpkin Soup with Crumbled Bacon and Toasted Pumpkin Seeds (page 32), Chicken and Sweet Potato Stew (page 62),** or any other great soup and stew.

spring

Springtime Traditions

Spring is full of its own traditions. Most people find time to pack up winter coats and scarves, plan any planting the yard may require, and get into spring cleaning. But there's no need to pack away your **CROCK-POT®** slow cooker just because the weather is starting to warm. Make the most of the spring season by putting your **CROCK-POT®** slow cooker to work in the kitchen so you can spend your time doing things elsewhere. A bit of prep in the morning (or even the night before) and you can set dinner to cook itself while you're called away to other chores.

Try a recipe like **Chicken Sausage Pilaf (page 124)** for an early taste of spring's great flavors. It's simple and hearty, and it practically cooks itself while you're off doing other things.

Marching to St. Patrick's Day

Your **CROCK-POT®** slow cooker is the perfect way to cook corned beef for St. Patrick's Day this spring, since corned beef is best when slowly simmered for hours. Serve it with a solid loaf of nice, crusty bread, Dijon mustard, and horseradish so your guests can dress it to their preferences. A crisp green salad and a potato side dish, and you're set to party.

Spring's First Produce

Spring brings fresh produce to your local farmers markets and grocery stores—such a welcome change from the pale, limp vegetables of winter. Your **CROCK-POT®** slow cooker offers a great, hassle-free way to take advantage of the season's fresh flavors.

Breaking for Brunches

Hosting a brunch is a great way to celebrate the fun occasions spring seems to bring, but who wants to do all the work of preparing food for a party first thing in the morning? With the help of your **CROCK-POT®** slow cooker, you don't have to.

A complete brunch menu should be built around either a rich egg dish like **Ham and Cheddar Brunch Strata (page 145)** or something hearty like **Bacon and Cheese Brunch Potatoes (page 155)**. Be sure to include a sweet dish like **Glazed Cinnamon Coffee Cake (page 140)** or **Orange Cranberry-Nut Bread (page 153)**. And don't forget a fresh and

Kale, Olive Oil and Parmesan Soup (page 122)

fruity delight like a fruit salad with ripe spring berries (maybe lashed with thick, creamy yogurt) and served with coffee, tea, and assorted juices.

You can also use a **CROCK-POT®** slow cooker to make and serve a bracing pick-me-up beverage to your guests. The temperature control allows you to make sure the coffee or cocoa is warm enough to be welcome, but not too hot to enjoy. Try **Cinnamon Latté (page 150)** or **Mucho Mocha Cocoa (page 155)** to start your party (and your day!) off right.

summer

Simple Summer Entertaining

Slow cooking and easy summer entertaining go hand-in-hand. Your **CROCK-POT®** slow cooker is just as useful for summer get-togethers as it is the rest of the year—pick a savory side, and your next barbecue is nearly complete. And with one less reason to turn on your stove, your home will stay more comfortable for your guests.

Barbecuing on the patio? Bring your **CROCK-POT®** slow cooker along to keep your hot food hot while you're finishing up at the grill. Your food will stay delicious and at the perfect temperature until you're ready to serve it.

Summer fun is so much better when you don't have to worry about what's for supper, and the **CROCK-POT®** slow cooker is a great way to take

the hassle out of slow cooking. It requires minimal attention: no stirring, no watching, no fussing. Simply prepare the ingredients, set your **CROCK-POT®** slow cooker, and turn your attention to all the great outdoor fun to be had in the summer. The **CROCK-POT®** slow cooker does the cooking while you're at work or spending quality time with family and friends.

You can even make some great tasting desserts using nothing much more than your **CROCK-POT®** slow cooker and some of the fresh flavors of the season, such as **Cherry Delight (page 218), Fresh Bosc Pear Granita (page 210)** or **Spicy Fruit Dessert (page 215)**.

autumn

Weeknight Wonders

Every fall moms and dads find themselves flustered with all the confusion and demands of the kids returning to school. Somehow, through the flurry of bus schedules and sports practices, homework assignments, and study dates, someone has to find a way to get a nutritious, filling dinner on the table.

The **CROCK-POT**® slow cooker can help you prepare healthy weeknight dinners on even the most hectic of evenings. Even better—kid-friendly favorites like **Macaroni and Cheese (page 275)** or **Harvest Ham Supper (page 222)** mean you can make one recipe the entire family can share, instead of a separate meal for each family member.

Tailgating Time

No matter the season or sport, everyone loves a great tailgate party. Follow these suggestions for a better tailgate:

• **Organize!** Take the time to make sure you have everything you need. Set important items together (a large plastic storage container is perfect for this). Be sure to include paper towels, trash bags, utensils, charcoal, matches, and any other important things that you don't want to forget, but won't have to repack every time you tailgate.

• **Invest!** Quality tailgating equipment and furniture is totally worth a little extra money. Folding tables and chairs, tents, tarps, and portable grills that you can rely on help ensure your tailgate goes off without a hitch.

• **Decorate!** Decorate with the colors of your favorite team, driver, or personality. You'll not only support your team, you'll be easier for your guests to locate.

• **Prepare!** Marinate meats, chop vegetables, and do anything else possible to prepare ahead of time in order to maximize the time you have for socializing and decrease the number of tools and ingredients you have to pack. Your **CROCK-POT**® slow cooker is perfect for cooking ahead.

You don't have to have a grill to have a great tailgate party—but every perfect tailgate has at least one **CROCK-POT**® slow cooker filled with the spicy, hearty, full-flavored foods sports fans love. Chili or Jambalaya are perfect to fuel your fans before the big game. Using your **CROCK-POT**® slow cooker simplifies your pre-game routine, too, since you can complete the cooking at home before you leave or finish it once you get there. Cleanup is easier too, so you can tear down your tailgate and get into the game in record time.

Food Safety

Whether on a buffet table in your dining room or tailgate party at the stadium, always keep hot foods hot (above 140°F) and cold foods cold (below 40°F). Your **CROCK-POT**® slow cooker is an ideal way to keep food hot enough without overcooking or burning it.

Replenish food as often as necessary, but avoid adding cold food to a dish that has been on the buffet table for a while. This could bring the overall temperature of the food below the 140°F safe zone. Instead, warm additional servings in a microwave, oven, or on the stove before adding them to your **CROCK-POT**® slow cooker.

Do not let cooked food stand at room temperature for longer than 2 hours. Any food that has remained unrefrigerated for more than 2 hours should be discarded.

holiday entertaining

Beef Roast with Dark Rum Sauce

- 1 teaspoon ground allspice
- ½ teaspoon salt
- ½ teaspoon black pepper
- ¼ teaspoon ground cloves
- 1 beef rump roast (about 3 pounds)
- 2 tablespoons extra-virgin olive oil
- 1 cup dark rum, divided
- ½ cup beef broth
- 2 cloves garlic, minced
- 2 whole bay leaves, broken in half
- ½ cup packed dark brown sugar
- ¼ cup lime juice

1. In a small bowl, combine allspice, salt, pepper and cloves. Rub spices onto all sides of roast.

2. Heat oil in skillet over medium heat until hot. Sear beef on all sides, turning as it browns. Transfer to **CROCK-POT**® slow cooker. Add ½ cup rum, broth, garlic and bay leaves. Cover; cook on LOW 1 hour.

3. In a small bowl, combine remaining ½ cup rum, brown sugar and lime juice, stirring well. Pour over roast. Continue cooking on LOW 4 to 6 hours, or until beef is fork-tender. Baste beef occasionally with sauce.

4. Remove and slice roast. Spoon sauce over beef to serve.

Makes 6 servings

Chicken Meatballs with Chipotle-Honey Sauce

2 pounds ground chicken

2 eggs, lightly beaten

⅓ cup plain dry bread crumbs

⅓ cup chopped fresh cilantro

2 tablespoons fresh lime juice

4 cloves garlic, minced

1 can (4 ounces) chipotle peppers in adobo sauce, divided

1½ teaspoons salt, divided

¾ cup honey

⅓ cup chicken broth

⅓ cup tomato paste

1 tablespoon lime juice

2 teaspoons Dijon mustard

2 tablespoons vegetable oil, divided

1. Line 2 baking sheets with parchment paper. Combine chicken, eggs, bread crumbs, cilantro, lime juice, garlic, 1 tablespoon adobo sauce and 1 teaspoon salt in medium bowl; mix well. Form mixture into 48 meatballs. Place meatballs in single layers on prepared baking sheets. Cover with plastic wrap; chill 1 hour.

2. Combine remaining ½ teaspoon salt, 2 to 3 chipotle peppers, honey, chicken broth, tomato paste, lime juice and Dijon mustard in blender or food processor. Process until smooth. Pour sauce into **CROCK-POT**® slow cooker. Set aside.

3. Heat 1 tablespoon oil in large skillet over medium-high heat. Working in batches, cook meatballs, turning to brown on all sides, transferring batches to **CROCK-POT**® slow cooker as they are finished. Add additional tablespoon of oil to skillet as needed for second and subsequent batches.

4. When all meatballs have been added to **CROCK-POT**® slow cooker, stir gently to coat all meatballs. Cover; cook on HIGH 3 to 4 hours or until meatballs are no longer pink in centers.

Makes 12 servings (4 meatballs each)

Corn Bread Stuffing with Sausage and Green Apples

1 package (16 ounces) honey corn bread mix, plus ingredients to prepare mix

2 cups cubed French bread

1½ pounds mild Italian sausage, casings removed

1 onion, finely chopped

1 green apple, peeled, cored and diced

2 stalks celery, finely chopped

¼ teaspoon dried sage

¼ teaspoon dried rosemary

¼ teaspoon dried thyme

½ teaspoon salt

¼ teaspoon black pepper

3 cups chicken broth

2 tablespoons fresh chopped parsley (optional)

1. Mix and bake corn bread according to package directions. When cool, cover with plastic wrap and set aside overnight.*

2. Coat **CROCK-POT®** slow cooker with nonstick cooking spray. Preheat oven to 350°F. Cut corn bread into 1-inch cubes. Spread corn bread and French bread on baking sheet. Toast in oven about 20 minutes or until dry.

3. Meanwhile, heat medium skillet over medium heat until hot. Add sausage. Cook and stir until browned. Transfer sausage to **CROCK-POT®** slow cooker with slotted spoon.

4. Add onion, apple and celery to skillet. Cook and stir 5 minutes or until softened. Stir in sage, rosemary, thyme, salt and pepper. Transfer mixture to **CROCK-POT®** slow cooker.

5. Add bread cubes and stir gently to combine. Pour broth over mixture. Cover; cook on HIGH 3 to 3½ hours or until liquid is absorbed. Garnish with parsley, if desired.

Makes 8 to 12 servings

Or purchase prepared 8-inch square pan of corn bread. Proceed as directed.

Tip

Consider using your **CROCK-POT®** slow cooker as an extra "oven" or "burner" for holiday entertaining. For example, the **CROCK-POT®** slow cooker can cook the stuffing while the holiday turkey is in the oven.

Steamed Pumpkin Cake

1½ cups all-purpose flour

1½ teaspoons baking powder

1½ teaspoons baking soda

1 teaspoon ground cinnamon

½ teaspoon salt

¼ teaspoon ground cloves

½ cup (1 stick) unsalted butter

2 cups packed light brown sugar

3 eggs, beaten

1 can (15 ounces) solid-pack pumpkin*

Whipped cream (optional)

Not pumpkin pie filling.

1. Place three 18×2-inch strips of heavy-duty foil (or regular foil folded to double thickness) in **CROCK-POT®** slow cooker, crisscrossing to form spokes across bottom and up sides. Grease 2½-quart casserole or soufflé dish.

2. Combine flour, baking powder, baking soda, cinnamon, salt and cloves in medium bowl; set aside.

3. Beat butter, brown sugar and eggs in large bowl with electric mixer on medium speed until creamy. Beat in pumpkin. Stir in flour mixture. Spoon batter into prepared casserole.

4. Place casserole into **CROCK-POT®** slow cooker. Fill **CROCK-POT®** slow cooker with 1 inch of hot water. Cover; cook on HIGH 3 to 3½ hours or until wooden toothpick inserted into center comes out clean.

5. Use foil handles to lift casserole from **CROCK-POT®** slow cooker. Cool on wire rack 15 minutes. Invert onto serving platter. Cut into wedges; serve with whipped cream, if desired.

Makes 12 servings

Molasses Maple Glazed Beef Brisket

1 teaspoon ground red pepper

1 tablespoon salt

½ teaspoon black pepper

1 beef brisket (1½ to 2 pounds), scored with a knife on both sides

2 tablespoons olive oil

½ cup maple syrup

¼ cup molasses

2 tablespoons light brown sugar

1 tablespoon tomato paste

Juice of 1 orange

2 cloves garlic, mashed

4 slices (¹⁄₁₆ inch thick each) fresh ginger

4 slices (½ inch × 1½ inches each) orange peel, avoiding bitter white pith

1. Combine red pepper, salt and black pepper in small bowl. Rub mixture over brisket. Place brisket in resealable plastic food storage bag.

2. Combine olive oil, maple syrup, molasses, brown sugar, tomato paste, orange juice, garlic, ginger and orange peel in small bowl. Pour mixture over brisket in resealable bag.

3. Refrigerate marinated brisket for at least 2 hours or overnight, turning bag several times.

4. Transfer brisket to **CROCK-POT®** slow cooker. Cover; cook on LOW 7 to 9 hours or on HIGH 3½ to 4 hours, turning once or twice. Adjust seasonings to taste. Slice thinly across grain to serve.

Makes 4 to 6 servings

Chicken and Asiago Stuffed Mushrooms

20 **large white mushrooms, stems removed and reserved**

3 **tablespoons extra-virgin olive oil, divided**

¼ **cup finely chopped onion**

2 **cloves garlic, minced**

¼ **cup Madeira wine**

½ **pound uncooked chicken sausage, removed from casings or ground chicken**

1 **cup grated Asiago cheese**

¼ **cup seasoned Italian bread crumbs**

3 **tablespoons chopped fresh parsley**

½ **teaspoon salt**

¼ **teaspoon black pepper**

1. Lightly brush mushroom caps with 1 tablespoon oil and set aside. Finely chop mushroom stems.

2. Heat remaining 2 tablespoons oil in large nonstick skillet over medium-high heat. Add onion and cook until just beginning to soften, about 1 minute. Add mushroom stems and cook until beginning to brown, 5 to 6 minutes. Stir in garlic and continue cooking 1 minute.

3. Pour in Madeira and cook until it evaporates, about 1 minute. Add sausage and cook, stirring to break into small pieces, until no longer pink, 3 to 4 minutes. Remove from heat and cool 5 minutes. Stir in cheese, bread crumbs, parsley, salt and pepper.

4. Divide mushroom-sausage mixture among mushroom caps, pressing slightly to compress. Place stuffed mushroom caps in single layer in **CROCK-POT®** slow cooker; cover and cook on LOW 4 hours or on HIGH 2 hours or until mushrooms are tender and filling is cooked through.

Makes 4 to 5 servings

 **Tip**

Stuffed mushrooms are a great way to impress guests with your gourmet home-cooking skills. These appetizers appear fancy and time-intensive, but they are actually simple with the help of a CROCK-POT® slow cooker.

English Bread Pudding

16 slices day-old, firm-textured white bread (1 small loaf)

1¾ cups milk

1 package (8 ounces) mixed dried fruit, cut into small pieces

½ cup chopped nuts

1 medium apple, chopped

⅓ cup packed brown sugar

¼ cup (½ stick) butter, melted

1 egg, lightly beaten

1 teaspoon ground cinnamon

¼ teaspoon ground nutmeg

¼ teaspoon ground cloves

1. Tear bread, with crusts, into 1- to 2-inch pieces; place in **CROCK-POT**® slow cooker. Pour milk over bread; let soak 30 minutes. Stir in dried fruit, nuts and apple.

2. Combine remaining ingredients in small bowl; pour over bread mixture. Stir well to blend. Cover; cook on LOW 3½ to 4 hours or until skewer inserted into center of pudding comes out clean.

Makes 6 to 8 servings

 **Note**

Chopping dried fruits can be difficult. To make the job easier, cut fruit with kitchen scissors. Spray scissors (or your chef's knife) with nonstick cooking spray before chopping, to prevent sticking.

Hearty Beef Short Ribs

2½ pounds flanken-style beef short ribs, bone-in

1 to 2 tablespoons coarse salt

1 to 2 tablespoons black pepper

2 tablespoons olive oil, divided

2 carrots, cut into ¼-inch dice

2 celery stalks, cut into ¼-inch dice

1 large yellow onion, cut into ¼-inch dice

3 cloves garlic, minced

3 bay leaves

⅓ cup red wine

⅓ cup crushed tomatoes

⅓ cup balsamic vinegar

1. Season ribs with salt and black pepper. Drizzle with 1 tablespoon olive oil. Heat 1 tablespoon olive oil in large skillet. Cook ribs until just browned, about 2 to 3 minutes per side. Transfer ribs to **CROCK-POT®** slow cooker. Add carrots, celery, onion, garlic and bay leaves.

2. Combine wine, tomatoes and vinegar in small bowl. Season with salt and black pepper, if desired. Pour mixture into **CROCK-POT®** slow cooker. Cover; cook on LOW 8 to 9 hours or on HIGH 5½ to 6 hours, turning once or twice, until meat is tender and falling off the bone.

3. Remove ribs from **CROCK-POT®** slow cooker. Process sauce in blender to desired consistency. To serve, pour sauce over ribs.

Makes 6 to 8 servings

Tip

For a change of pace from ordinary short rib recipes, ask your butcher for flanken-style beef short ribs. Flanken-style ribs are cut across the bones into wide, flat portions. They provide all the meaty flavor of the more common English-style short ribs with smaller, more manageable bones.

Lemon-Mint Red Potatoes

2 pounds new red potatoes

3 tablespoons extra-virgin olive oil

¾ teaspoon dried Greek seasoning or dried oregano leaves

¼ teaspoon garlic powder

1 teaspoon salt

¼ teaspoon black pepper

2 tablespoons lemon juice

1 teaspoon grated lemon peel

2 tablespoons butter

¼ cup chopped fresh mint leaves, divided

1. Coat inside of **CROCK-POT®** slow cooker with nonstick cooking spray. Add potatoes and oil, stirring gently to coat. Sprinkle with Greek seasoning, garlic powder, salt and pepper. Cover and cook on LOW 7 hours or on HIGH 4 hours.

2. Stir in lemon juice, lemon peel, butter and 2 tablespoons mint. Stir until butter is completely melted. Cover and cook 15 minutes to allow flavors to blend. Sprinkle with remaining mint.

Makes 4 servings

 Tip

It's easy to prepare these potatoes ahead of time. Simply follow the recipe and then turn off the heat. Let it stand at room temperature for up to 2 hours. You may reheat or serve the potatoes at room temperature.

Gingerbread

½ cup (1 stick) butter, softened

½ cup sugar

1 egg, lightly beaten

1 cup light molasses

2½ cups all-purpose flour

1½ teaspoons baking soda

1 teaspoon ground cinnamon

2 teaspoons ground ginger

½ teaspoon ground cloves

½ teaspoon salt

1 cup hot water

Whipped cream (optional)

1. Coat 4½-quart **CROCK-POT®** slow cooker with butter or nonstick cooking spray. Beat together butter and sugar in large bowl. Add egg, molasses, flour, baking soda, cinnamon, ginger, cloves and salt. Stir in hot water and mix well. Pour batter into **CROCK-POT®** slow cooker.

2. Cover; cook on HIGH 1½ to 1¾ hours or until toothpick inserted into center of cake comes out clean. Serve warm; top with whipped cream, if desired.

Makes 6 to 8 servings

Turkey with Chunky Cherry Relish

1   bag (16 ounces) frozen dark cherries, coarsely chopped

1   can (about 14 ounces) diced tomatoes with jalapeños

1   package (6 ounces) dried cherry-flavored cranberries or dried cherries, coarsely chopped

2   small onions, thinly sliced

1   small green bell pepper, chopped

½   cup packed brown sugar

2   tablespoons tapioca

1½ tablespoons salt

½   teaspoon ground cinnamon

½   teaspoon black pepper

1   bone-in turkey breast (about 2½ to 3 pounds)

2   tablespoons water

1   tablespoon cornstarch

1. Place cherries, tomatoes, cranberries, onions, bell pepper, brown sugar, tapioca, salt, cinnamon and black pepper in **CROCK-POT®** slow cooker; mix well.

2. Place turkey on top of mixture. Cover; cook on LOW 7 to 8 hours or until temperature registers over 170°F on meat thermometer inserted into thickest part of breast, not touching bone. Remove turkey from **CROCK-POT®** slow cooker; keep warm.

3. Increase temperature to HIGH. Combine water and cornstarch in small bowl to form smooth paste. Stir into cherry mixture. Cook, uncovered, on HIGH 15 minutes or until sauce is thickened. Adjust seasonings, if desired. Slice turkey and top with relish.

Makes 4 to 6 servings

Osso Bucco

1 large onion, cut into thin wedges

2 large carrots, sliced

4 cloves garlic, sliced

4 meaty veal shanks (3 to 4 pounds)

2 teaspoons herbes de Provence or ½ teaspoon *each* dried thyme, rosemary, oregano and basil

1 teaspoon salt

½ teaspoon black pepper

¾ cup beef broth

¼ cup dry vermouth (optional)

3 tablespoons all-purpose flour

3 tablespoons water

¼ cup minced parsley

1 clove garlic, minced

1 teaspoon grated lemon peel

1. Coat **CROCK-POT®** slow cooker with nonstick cooking spray. Place onion, carrots and sliced garlic in bottom. Arrange veal shanks over vegetables, overlapping slightly, and sprinkle herbes, salt and pepper over all. Add broth and vermouth, if desired. Cover; cook on LOW 8 to 9 hours or on HIGH 5 to 6 hours or until shanks and vegetables are tender.

2. Transfer shanks and vegetables to serving platter; cover with foil to keep warm. Turn **CROCK-POT®** slow cooker to HIGH. Combine flour with 3 tablespoons water, mixing until smooth. Stir into cooking liquid. Cover; cook on HIGH 15 minutes or until sauce thickens.

3. Serve sauce over shanks and vegetables. Combine parsley, minced garlic and lemon peel; sprinkle over shanks and vegetables.

Makes 4 servings

The Claus's Christmas Pudding

Pudding

- ⅔ cup sweetened dried cranberries
- ⅔ cup golden raisins
- ½ cup whole candied red cherries, halved
- ¾ cup plus 2 tablespoons cream sherry, divided
- 18 slices cranberry or other fruited bread
- 3 large egg yolks, beaten
- 1½ cups light cream
- ⅓ cup granulated sugar
- ¼ teaspoon kosher salt
- 1½ teaspoons cherry extract
- 1 cup white chocolate chips
- 1 cup hot water

Sauce

- 2 large egg yolks, beaten
- ¼ cup powdered sugar, sifted
- ¼ teaspoon vanilla
- ½ cup whipping cream

Prepare Pudding:

1. Preheat oven to 250°F. Generously butter 6½-cup ceramic or glass bowl. Place cranberries and raisins in small bowl; set aside. Place cherries in another bowl. Heat ¾ cup sherry until warm, and pour over cherries; set aside.

2. Place bread slices on baking sheet and bake 5 minutes. Turn over and bake 5 minutes or until bread is dry. Cool, then cut into ½-inch cubes.

3. Combine 3 egg yolks, light cream, granulated sugar and salt in heavy saucepan. Cook and stir over medium heat until mixture coats metal spoon. Remove from heat. Set saucepan in sink of ice water to cool quickly; stir 1 to 2 minutes. Stir in cherry extract. Transfer cooled mixture to large bowl. Fold bread cubes into custard until coated.

4. Drain cherries, reserving sherry. Arrange one fourth of cherries, plus ⅓ cup raisin mixture and ¼ cup white chocolate chips in prepared ceramic bowl. Add one fourth of bread cube mixture. Sprinkle with reserved sherry. Repeat layers 3 times, arranging fruit near edges of bowl. Pour remaining reserved sherry over all.

5. Cover bowl tightly with foil. Place in **CROCK-POT®** slow cooker. Pour hot water around bowl. Cover; cook on LOW 5½ hours. Remove bowl and let stand on wire rack 10 to 15 minutes before unmolding.

Prepare Sauce:

6. Combine 2 egg yolks, powdered sugar, 2 tablespoons sherry and vanilla. Beat whipping cream in small bowl until small peaks form. Fold whipped cream into egg yolk mixture. Cover; chill until serving time. Serve with warm pudding.

Makes 12 servings

Italian Braised Short Ribs in Red Wine

3 pounds beef short ribs, trimmed of excess fat

Salt and black pepper

1 tablespoon vegetable oil, plus more if needed

2 large onions, sliced

2 cloves garlic, minced

2 packages (8 ounces each) baby bella or cremini mushrooms, cleaned and quartered

2 cups red wine

2 cups beef broth

2 teaspoons Italian seasoning

Salt and black pepper

Mashed potatoes or polenta

1. Coat **CROCK-POT®** slow cooker with nonstick cooking spray. Season short ribs with salt and pepper. Heat oil in large skillet over medium-high heat. Brown ribs on all sides, working in batches and adding additional oil as needed. Transfer to prepared **CROCK-POT®** slow cooker as batches are finished.

2. Return skillet to heat. Add onions and cook, stirring frequently, until translucent (3 to 5 minutes). Stir in remaining ingredients except potatoes and bring mixture to simmer. Cook 3 minutes then pour over short ribs. Cover and cook on LOW 10 to 12 hours or on HIGH 6 to 8 hours or until beef is tender. Season to taste with salt and pepper. Transfer ribs and mushrooms to serving plate. Strain cooking liquid; serve with mashed potatoes or polenta and sauce with cooking liquid.

Makes 4 to 6 servings

Pepperoni Pizza Dip with Breadstick Dippers

1 jar or can (14 ounces) pizza sauce

¾ cup chopped turkey pepperoni

4 green onions, chopped

1 can (2¼ ounces) sliced black olives, drained

½ teaspoon dried oregano

1 cup (4 ounces) shredded mozzarella cheese

1 package (3 ounces) cream cheese, softened

Breadstick Dippers (recipe follows)

1. Combine pizza sauce, pepperoni, green onions, olives and oregano in 2-quart **CROCK-POT®** slow cooker. Cover; cook on LOW 2 hours or on HIGH 1 to 1½ hours or until mixture is hot.

2. Stir in mozzarella and cream cheese until melted and well blended. Serve with warm Breadstick Dippers.

Makes 8 servings

Breadstick Dippers

1 package (8 ounces) refrigerated breadstick dough

2 teaspoons melted butter

2 teaspoons minced fresh Italian parsley

Bake breadsticks according to package directions. Brush with melted butter and sprinkle with parsley. Serve with warm dip.

Steamed Southern Sweet Potato Custard

1 can (16 ounces) cut sweet potatoes, drained

1 can (12 ounces) evaporated milk, divided

½ cup packed light brown sugar

2 eggs, lightly beaten

1 teaspoon ground cinnamon

½ teaspoon ground ginger

¼ teaspoon salt

Whipped cream

Ground nutmeg

1. Process sweet potatoes with ¼ cup evaporated milk in food processor or blender until smooth. Add remaining milk, brown sugar, eggs, cinnamon, ginger and salt; process until well blended. Pour into ungreased 1-quart soufflé dish. Cover tightly with foil. Crumple large sheet (about 15×12 inches) of foil; place in bottom of **CROCK-POT®** slow cooker. Pour 2 cups water over foil. Make foil handles.*

2. Transfer dish to **CROCK-POT®** slow cooker using foil handles. Cover; cook on HIGH 2½ to 3 hours or until skewer inserted into center comes out clean.

3. Use foil strips to lift dish; transfer to wire rack. Uncover; let stand 30 minutes. Garnish with whipped cream and nutmeg.

Makes 4 servings

To make foil handles, tear off three 18×3-inch strips of heavy-duty foil. Crisscross the strips so they resemble the spokes of a wheel. Place the dish in the center of the strips. Pull the foil strips up and over dish. Place in the CROCK-POT® slow cooker. Leave them in while you cook so you can easily lift the dish out again when ready.

Pumpkin Soup with Crumbled Bacon and Toasted Pumpkin Seeds

2 teaspoons olive oil

½ cup raw pumpkin seeds*

3 slices thick-cut bacon

1 medium onion, chopped

1 teaspoon kosher salt

½ teaspoon chipotle chili powder, or more to taste

½ teaspoon black pepper

2 cans (29 ounces each) 100% pumpkin purée

4 cups chicken broth

¾ cup apple cider

½ cup whipping cream or half-and-half

Sour cream (optional)

*Raw pumpkin seeds may be found in the produce or ethnic food section of your local supermarket. They may be labeled "pepitas."

1. Spray inside of **CROCK-POT**® slow cooker with cooking spray.

2. In small skillet, heat olive oil over medium-high heat. Add pumpkin seeds to olive oil and stir until seeds begin to pop, about 1 minute. Spoon into small bowl and set aside.

3. Add bacon to skillet and cook until crisp. Remove bacon to paper towels and set aside to cool (do not drain drippings from pan). Reduce heat to medium and add onion to pan. Cook, stirring occasionally, until translucent, about 3 minutes. Stir in salt, chipotle chili powder and black pepper. Transfer to **CROCK-POT**® slow cooker.

4. Whisk pumpkin, chicken broth and apple cider into **CROCK-POT**® slow cooker, whisking until smooth.

5. Cover and cook on HIGH 4 hours. Turn off **CROCK-POT**® slow cooker and remove lid. Whisk in cream and adjust seasoning as necessary. Strain soup into bowls and garnish with pumpkin seeds, cooled bacon (crumbled) and sour cream, if desired.

Makes 4 servings

Pork Meatballs in Garlicky Almond Sauce

½ cup blanched whole almonds

1 cup chicken broth

⅓ cup roasted red pepper

4 teaspoons minced garlic, divided

1 teaspoon salt, divided

½ teaspoon saffron threads (optional)

1 cup fresh bread crumbs, divided

¼ cup dry white wine or chicken broth

1 pound ground pork

¼ cup finely chopped onion

1 egg, lightly beaten

3 tablespoons minced fresh parsley

1. Place almonds in food processor; process until finely ground. Add broth, red pepper, 2 teaspoons garlic, ½ teaspoon salt and saffron, if desired; process until smooth. Stir in ¼ cup bread crumbs. Transfer to **CROCK-POT®** slow cooker.

2. Place ¾ cup bread crumbs in large bowl; sprinkle with wine and stir gently. Add pork, onion, egg, parsley, remaining 2 teaspoons garlic and ½ teaspoon salt; mix well. Form pork mixture into 24 (1-inch) balls.

3. Coat a large skillet with nonstick cooking spray and place over medium-high heat. Working in batches, cook meatballs, turning to brown on all sides. Transfer to **CROCK-POT®** slow cooker with sauce as batches are done. Cover; cook on HIGH 3 to 4 hours or until meatballs are cooked through.

Makes 6 servings (4 meatballs each)

Pumpkin Custard

1 cup solid-pack pumpkin

½ cup packed brown sugar

2 eggs, beaten

½ teaspoon ground ginger

½ teaspoon grated lemon peel

½ teaspoon ground cinnamon

1 can (12 ounces) evaporated milk

Additional ground cinnamon

1. Combine pumpkin, brown sugar, eggs, ginger, lemon peel and ½ teaspoon cinnamon in large bowl. Stir in evaporated milk. Pour mixture into 1½-quart soufflé dish. Cover tightly with foil.

2. Make foil handles.* Place soufflé dish in **CROCK-POT®** slow cooker. Pour water into **CROCK-POT®** slow cooker to come about 1½ inches from top of soufflé dish. Cover; cook on LOW 4 hours.

3. Use foil handles to lift soufflé dish from **CROCK-POT®** slow cooker. Sprinkle with additional ground cinnamon. Serve warm.

Makes 6 servings

*To make foil handles, tear off three 18×3-inch strips of heavy-duty foil. Crisscross the strips so they resemble the spokes of a wheel. Place the dish in the center of the strips. Pull the foil strips up and over dish. Place in the **CROCK-POT®** slow cooker. Leave them in while you cook so you can easily lift the dish out again when ready.

Slow Cooker Turkey Breast

½ to 1 teaspoon garlic powder, or to taste

½ to 1 teaspoon paprika, or to taste

1 turkey breast (4 to 6 pounds)

1 tablespoon dried parsley flakes, or to taste

1. Blend garlic powder and paprika. Rub into turkey skin. Place turkey in **CROCK-POT®** slow cooker. Sprinkle on parsley. Cover; cook on LOW 6 to 8 hours or on HIGH 2½ to 3 hours or until internal temperature reaches 165°F when meat thermometer is inserted into thickest part of breast, not touching bone.

2. Transfer turkey to cutting board; cover with foil and let stand 10 to 15 minutes before carving. (Internal temperature will rise 5° to 10°F during stand time.)

Makes 4 to 6 servings

Chablis-Infused Swiss Fondue

- 3 cups Chablis or other white wine
- 2 teaspoons lemon juice
- ½ teaspoon grated lemon peel
- 1½ pounds Swiss cheese, shredded
- 3 tablespoons all-purpose flour
- 3 tablespoons kirsch or cherry brandy
- 1 teaspoon mace, freshly ground
- 1 teaspoon black pepper
- ½ teaspoon paprika
- 1 loaf crusty Italian peasant bread, cut into 1½-inch cubes
  Fresh vegetables, cut up for dipping

1. Place wine, lemon juice and lemon peel in saucepan over medium-high heat. Bring to a simmer.

2. Combine cheese and flour in medium mixing bowl. Gradually add cheese to saucepan, stirring constantly, until cheese is completely melted. Add kirsch and stir well to combine. Add mace, pepper and paprika, and stir again thoroughly.

3. Pour cheese mixture into **CROCK-POT®** slow cooker. Cover; cook on HIGH 30 minutes. Reduce heat to LOW, and cook 2 to 5 hours longer, stirring occasionally. Serve with Italian bread and vegetables.

Makes 6 to 8 servings

Spiced Sweet Potatoes

- 2 pounds sweet potatoes, peeled and cut into ½-inch pieces
- ¼ cup packed dark brown sugar
- 1 teaspoon ground cinnamon
- ½ teaspoon ground nutmeg
- ⅛ teaspoon salt
- 2 tablespoons butter, cut into small pieces
- 1 teaspoon vanilla

1. Combine potatoes, brown sugar, cinnamon, nutmeg and salt in **CROCK-POT®** slow cooker; mix well. Cover; cook on LOW 7 hours or on HIGH 4 hours.

2. Add butter and vanilla; gently stir to blend.

Makes 4 servings

Creamy Artichoke-Parmesan Dip

- 2 cans (14 ounces each) artichoke hearts, drained and chopped
- 2 cups (8 ounces) shredded mozzarella cheese
- 1½ cups grated Parmesan cheese
- 1½ cups mayonnaise
- ½ cup finely chopped onion
- ½ teaspoon dried oregano
- ¼ teaspoon garlic powder
- 4 pita breads, cut into wedges
  Assorted cut-up vegetables

Place artichokes, mozzarella cheese, Parmesan cheese, mayonnaise, onion, oregano and garlic powder in 1½-quart or other small-sized **CROCK-POT**® slow cooker; mix well. Cover; cook on LOW 2 hours. Arrange pita bread wedges and vegetables on platter; serve with warm dip.

Makes 16 servings (about 4 cups)

Pumpkin Bread Pudding

- 2 cups whole milk
- ½ cup plus 2 tablespoons butter, divided
- 1 cup solid-pack pumpkin
- 3 eggs
- 1 cup packed dark brown sugar, divided
- 1 tablespoon ground cinnamon
- 2 teaspoons vanilla
- ½ teaspoon ground nutmeg
- ¼ teaspoon salt
- 16 slices cinnamon raisin bread, torn into small pieces (8 cups total)
- ½ cup whipping cream
- 2 tablespoons bourbon (optional)

1. Lightly coat inside of **CROCK-POT**® slow cooker with nonstick cooking spray.

2. Combine milk and 2 tablespoons butter in medium microwavable bowl. Microwave on HIGH 2½ to 3 minutes or until very hot.

3. Whisk pumpkin, eggs, ½ cup brown sugar, cinnamon, vanilla, nutmeg and salt in large bowl until well blended. Whisk in milk mixture until blended. Add bread cubes; toss to coat.

4. Transfer to **CROCK-POT**® slow cooker. Cover; cook on HIGH 2 hours or until knife inserted in center comes out clean. Turn off heat. Uncover; let stand 15 minutes.

5. Combine remaining ½ cup butter, ½ cup brown sugar and cream in a small saucepan. Bring to a boil over high heat, stirring frequently. Remove from heat. Stir in bourbon, if desired. Spoon bread pudding into individual bowls and top with sauce.

Makes 8 servings

Turkey with Pecan-Cherry Stuffing

- 1 fresh or frozen boneless turkey breast (about 3 to 4 pounds)
- 2 cups cooked rice
- ⅓ cup chopped pecans
- ⅓ cup dried cherries or cranberries
- 1 teaspoon poultry seasoning
- ¼ cup peach, apricot or plum preserves
- 1 teaspoon Worcestershire sauce

1. Thaw turkey breast, if frozen. Remove skin and discard. Cut slices three-fourths of the way through turkey at 1-inch intervals.

2. Stir together rice, pecans, cherries and poultry seasoning in large bowl. Stuff rice mixture between slices. If necessary, skewer turkey lengthwise to hold it together.

3. Place turkey in **CROCK-POT**® slow cooker. Cover; cook on LOW 5 to 6 hours or until turkey registers 170°F on meat thermometer inserted into thickest part of breast, not touching stuffing.

4. Stir together preserves and Worcestershire sauce. Spoon over turkey. Cover; let stand for 5 minutes. Remove skewer before serving.

Makes 8 servings

Bagna Cauda

- ¾ cup olive oil
- 6 tablespoons butter, softened
- 12 anchovy fillets, drained
- 6 cloves garlic, peeled
- ⅛ teaspoon red pepper flakes

   Assorted foods for dipping such as endive spears, cauliflower florettes, cucumber spears, carrot sticks, zucchini spears, red bell pepper pieces, sugar snap peas or crusty Italian or French bread slices

Place olive oil, butter, anchovies, garlic and red pepper flakes in food processor and process until quite smooth, about 30 seconds. Scrape mixture into 2½-quart **CROCK-POT**® slow cooker. Cover and cook on LOW 2 hours or on HIGH 1 hour or until mixture is hot. Turn to LOW and serve with assorted dippers.

Makes 10 to 12 servings

Tip

Bagna cauda is a warm Italian dip similar to the more famous fondue. The name is derived from "bagno caldo," meaning "warm bath" in Italian. This dip should be kept warm while serving, just like you would fondue.

Roast Ham with Tangy Mustard Glaze

1 fully cooked boneless ham (about 3 pounds), visible fat removed

¼ cup packed dark brown sugar

2 tablespoons lemon juice, divided

1 tablespoon Dijon mustard

½ teaspoon ground allspice

¼ cup granulated sugar

2 tablespoons cornstarch

1. Place ham in **CROCK-POT®** slow cooker. Combine brown sugar, 2 teaspoons lemon juice, mustard and allspice. Spoon evenly over ham. Cover; cook on LOW 6 to 7 hours, or until ham is warm throughout and sauce is well absorbed. Transfer ham to warm serving platter.

2. Pour cooking liquid from **CROCK-POT®** slow cooker into small heavy saucepan. Add remaining lemon juice, granulated sugar and cornstarch. Cook over medium-high heat until mixture boils. Reduce to medium heat. Cook and stir until sauce is thickened and glossy.

3. Carve ham into slices and spoon sauce over individual servings.

Makes 12 to 15 servings

Rustic Cheddar Mashed Potatoes

2 pounds russet potatoes, peeled and diced

1 cup water

⅓ cup butter, cut into small pieces

½ to ¾ cup milk

1¼ teaspoons salt

½ teaspoon black pepper

½ cup finely chopped green onions

½ to ¾ cup (2 to 3 ounces) shredded Cheddar cheese

1. Combine potatoes and water in **CROCK-POT®** slow cooker; dot with butter. Cover; cook on LOW 6 hours or on HIGH 3 hours, or until potatoes are tender. Transfer potatoes to large mixing bowl.

2. Using electric mixer at medium speed, whip potatoes until well blended. Add milk, salt and pepper; whip until well blended.

3. Stir in green onions and cheese; cover. Let stand 15 minutes to allow flavors to blend and cheese to melt.

Makes 8 servings

Bean Dip for a Crowd

1½ cups dried black beans

1½ cups dried pinto beans

5 cups water

1 package (about 1¼ ounces) hot taco seasoning mix

2 tablespoons dried minced onion

3 chicken bouillon cubes

1 tablespoon dried parsley flakes

2 bay leaves

1 jar (16 ounces) thick and chunky salsa (medium or hot)

2 tablespoons lime juice

1. Place beans in large bowl; cover with water. Soak 6 to 8 hours or overnight. (To quick-soak beans, place beans in large saucepan; cover with water. Bring to a boil over high heat. Boil 2 minutes. Remove from heat; let soak, covered, 1 hour.) Drain beans; discard water.

2. Combine soaked beans, 5 cups water, taco seasoning, onion, bouillon cubes, parsley and bay leaves in **CROCK-POT**® slow cooker. Cover; cook on LOW 9 to 10 hours or until beans are tender. Add additional water, ½ cup at a time, as needed.

3. Remove and discard bay leaves. Ladle half of hot bean mixture into food processor. Add salsa and lime juice. Cover and process until smooth. Return puréed dip to **CROCK-POT**® slow cooker; stir to combine.

Makes 24 servings (about 6 cups)

Hot Mulled Cider

½ gallon apple cider

½ cup packed light brown sugar

1½ teaspoons balsamic or cider vinegar (optional)

1 teaspoon vanilla

1 cinnamon stick

6 whole cloves

½ cup applejack or bourbon (optional)

Combine all ingredients except applejack in **CROCK-POT**® slow cooker. Cover; cook on LOW 5 to 6 hours. Remove and discard cinnamon stick and cloves. Stir in applejack just before serving, if desired. Serve hot in mugs.

Makes 16 servings

Hoisin Barbecue Chicken Sliders

⅔ cup hoisin sauce

⅓ cup barbecue sauce

3 tablespoons quick-cooking tapioca

1 tablespoon sugar

1 tablespoon reduced-sodium soy sauce

¼ teaspoon red pepper flakes

12 skinless, boneless chicken thighs (3 to 3½ pounds total)

16 dinner rolls or Hawaiian sweet rolls, split

½ medium red onion, finely chopped

Sliced pickles (optional)

1. Combine hoisin sauce, barbecue sauce, tapioca, sugar, soy sauce and red pepper flakes in **CROCK-POT®** slow cooker until blended. Add chicken. Cover; cook on LOW 8 to 9 hours.

2. Remove cooked chicken thighs from sauce 1 or 2 at a time and chop or shred with 2 forks on clean cutting board. Return chopped chicken (and any sauce that may accumulate on cutting board) to **CROCK-POT®** slow cooker to keep warm until serving. Serve generous ¼ cup chicken and sauce on each bun, topped with about 1 teaspoon chopped red onion and pickles, if desired.

Makes 16 sliders

Figs Poached in Red Wine

2 cups dry red wine

1 cup packed brown sugar

2 (3-inch) cinnamon sticks

1 teaspoon finely grated orange peel

12 dried Calimyrna or Mediterranean figs (about 6 ounces)

4 tablespoons heavy cream (optional)

1. Stir together wine, brown sugar, cinnamon sticks, orange peel and figs in **CROCK-POT®** slow cooker. Cover and cook on LOW 5 to 6 hours or on HIGH 4 to 5 hours.

2. To serve, spoon some figs and syrup into serving dish. Top with spoonful of cream. May be served warm or cold.

Makes 4 servings

Orange-Spice Glazed Carrots

- 1 package (32 ounces) baby carrots
- ½ cup packed light brown sugar
- ½ cup orange juice
- 3 tablespoons butter or margarine
- ¾ teaspoon ground cinnamon
- ¼ teaspoon ground nutmeg
- ¼ cup cold water
- 2 tablespoons cornstarch

1. Combine carrots, brown sugar, orange juice, butter, cinnamon and nutmeg in **CROCK-POT®** slow cooker. Cover; cook on LOW 3½ to 4 hours or until carrots are crisp-tender.

2. Spoon carrots into serving bowl. Transfer cooking liquid to small saucepan. Bring to a boil.

3. Mix water and cornstarch until smooth; stir into saucepan. Boil 1 minute or until thickened, stirring constantly. Spoon over carrots.

Makes 6 servings

Rolled Veal Roast with Tarragon Cream Gravy

- 1 tablespoon unsalted butter
- 1 tablespoon olive oil
- 1 veal shoulder roast, boned, rolled and tied (about 4 pounds)
- 8 cremini mushrooms, cleaned and quartered
- 6 medium carrots, peeled, cut in half and cut lengthwise
- 2 tablespoons minced fresh tarragon, divided
- ⅛ teaspoon white pepper
- ¾ cup dry white wine
- ¼ cup lemon juice
- ⅓ cup whipping cream
- 3 tablespoons cornstarch
  Salt and white pepper, to taste
  Lemon peel twists (optional)

1. Heat butter and oil in large skillet over medium-high heat until hot. Sear veal roast on all sides, turning as it browns. Transfer to **CROCK-POT®** slow cooker.

2. Place mushrooms and carrots around roast. Sprinkle with 1 tablespoon tarragon and white pepper. Pour wine and lemon juice over all. Cover; cook on LOW 8 to 10 hours, or until veal is fork-tender when pierced.

3. Transfer roast to cutting board and let stand 5 minutes. Carve into thick slices and set aside on warm platter. Remove carrots and mushrooms from **CROCK-POT®** slow cooker with slotted spoon. Arrange vegetables around veal slices. Cover with aluminum foil and keep warm.

4. Turn **CROCK-POT®** slow cooker to HIGH. Whisk together cream, cornstarch and remaining tarragon. Add salt and pepper, to taste. Pour into cooking liquid. Stir well to combine. Cook and stir, uncovered, about 6 to 8 minutes or until thickened.

5. To serve, pass warm sauce to pour over veal and vegetables. Garnish with lemon twists, if desired.

Makes 6 servings

Stewed Fig and Blue Cheese Dip

- 1 tablespoon olive oil
- 1 medium onion, chopped
- ½ cup port wine
- 1 package (6 ounces) dried Calimyrna figs, finely chopped
- ½ cup orange juice
- ½ cup crumbled blue cheese, divided
- 1 tablespoon unsalted butter

1. Heat oil in small nonstick skillet over medium-high heat. Add onion and cook, stirring occasionally, until light golden, 7 to 8 minutes. Stir in port and bring to a boil; cook 1 minute. Transfer to 1½-quart **CROCK-POT®** slow cooker; stir in figs and orange juice.

2. Cover and cook on HIGH until figs are plump and tender, 1 to 1½ hours. Stir in ¼ cup blue cheese and butter. Sprinkle with remaining blue cheese and serve.

Makes 6 to 8 servings

> ## Tip
> For a party, use a small-sized **CROCK-POT®** slow cooker (1 quart or 1½ quarts) on LOW or WARM to keep hot dips warm.

Hearty Calico Bean Dip

- ¾ pound 95% lean ground beef
- ½ pound sliced bacon, crisp-cooked and crumbled
- 1 can (16 ounces) baked beans
- 1 can (15 ounces) Great Northern beans, rinsed and drained
- 1 can (15 ounces) kidney beans, rinsed and drained
- 1 small onion, chopped
- ½ cup packed dark brown sugar
- ½ cup ketchup
- 1 tablespoon cider vinegar
- 1 teaspoon prepared mustard
  Tortilla chips

1. Brown ground beef in large nonstick skillet over medium-high heat, stirring to break up meat. Drain and discard fat. Transfer to **CROCK-POT®** slow cooker.

2. Add bacon, beans, onion, brown sugar, ketchup, vinegar and mustard; mix well.

3. Cover; cook on LOW 4 hours or on HIGH 2 hours. Serve with tortilla chips.

Makes 12 servings

Thai Chicken Wings

- 1 tablespoon peanut oil
- 5 pounds chicken wings, tips removed and split at the joint
- ½ cup coconut milk
- 1 tablespoon Thai green curry paste
- 1 tablespoon fish sauce
- 1 tablespoon sugar
- ¾ cup prepared spicy peanut sauce

1. Heat oil in large nonstick skillet over medium-high heat. Add chicken wings and brown in several batches, about 6 minutes per batch. Transfer wings to **CROCK-POT®** slow cooker as they are browned.

2. Stir in coconut milk, curry paste, fish sauce and sugar. Cover and cook on LOW 6 to 7 hours or on HIGH 3 to 3½ hours or until tender. Drain cooking liquid and carefully stir in peanut sauce before serving.

Makes 8 servings

Cran-Orange Acorn Squash

- 3 small acorn or carnival squash
- 5 tablespoons instant brown rice
- 3 tablespoons minced onion
- 3 tablespoons diced celery
- 3 tablespoons dried cranberries
  Pinch ground or dried sage
- 1 teaspoon butter, cut into bits
- 3 tablespoons orange juice
- ½ cup warm water

1. Slice off tops of squash and enough of bottoms so squash will sit upright. Scoop out seeds and discard; set squash aside.

2. Combine rice, onion, celery, cranberries and sage in small bowl. Stuff each squash with rice mixture; dot with butter. Pour 1 tablespoon orange juice into each squash over stuffing. Stand squash in **CROCK-POT®** slow cooker. Pour warm water into bottom of **CROCK-POT®** slow cooker.

3. Cover; cook on LOW 2½ hours or until squash are tender.

Makes 6 servings

hearty
stews and chilies

Vegetarian Chili

- 1 tablespoon vegetable oil
- 1 cup chopped onion
- 1 cup chopped red bell pepper
- 2 tablespoons minced jalapeño pepper*
- 1 clove garlic, minced
- 1 can (28 ounces) crushed tomatoes
- 1 can (15 ounces) black beans, rinsed and drained
- 1 can (15 ounces) chickpeas, rinsed and drained
- ½ cup corn
- ¼ cup tomato paste
- 1 teaspoon sugar
- 1 teaspoon ground cumin
- 1 teaspoon dried basil
- 1 teaspoon chili powder
- ¼ teaspoon black pepper
  Sour cream and shredded Cheddar cheese (optional)

Jalapeño peppers can sting and irritate the skin, so wear rubber gloves when handling peppers and do not touch your eyes.

1. Heat oil in large skillet over medium-high heat. Add onion, bell pepper, jalapeño pepper and garlic; cook and stir 5 minutes or until vegetables are tender. Transfer vegetables to **CROCK-POT®** slow cooker.

2. Add remaining ingredients except sour cream and cheese; mix well. Cover; cook on LOW 4 to 5 hours.

3. Garnish with sour cream and cheese.

Makes 4 servings

Beef Stew with Molasses and Raisins

⅓ cup all-purpose flour

2 teaspoons salt, divided

1½ teaspoons black pepper, divided

2 pounds beef stew meat, cut into 1½-inch pieces

5 tablespoons oil, divided

2 medium onions, sliced

1 can (28 ounces) diced tomatoes, drained

1 cup beef broth

3 tablespoons molasses

2 tablespoons cider vinegar

4 cloves garlic, minced

2 teaspoons dried thyme

1 teaspoon celery salt

1 bay leaf

8 ounces baby carrots, cut in half lengthwise

2 parsnips, diced

½ cup golden raisins

1. Combine flour, 1½ teaspoons salt and 1 teaspoon pepper in large bowl. Toss meat in flour mixture. Heat 2 tablespoons oil in large skillet or Dutch oven over medium-high heat. Add half of beef and brown on all sides. Set aside browned beef and repeat with 2 additional tablespoons oil and remaining beef.

2. Add remaining 1 tablespoon oil to skillet. Add onions and cook 5 minutes, stirring to scrape up any browned bits. Add tomatoes, broth, molasses, vinegar, garlic, thyme, celery salt, bay leaf and remaining ½ teaspoon salt and ½ teaspoon pepper. Bring to a boil. Add browned beef and boil 1 minute.

3. Transfer mixture to **CROCK-POT**® slow cooker. Cover; cook on LOW 5 hours or on HIGH 2½ hours. Add carrots, parsnips and raisins. Cook 1 to 2 hours longer or until vegetables are tender. Remove and discard bay leaf.

Makes 6 to 8 servings

Chicken Stew with Herb Dumplings

2   cups sliced carrots

1   cup chopped onion

1   large green bell pepper,
    sliced

½   cup sliced celery

2   cans (about 14 ounces
    each) chicken broth,
    divided

⅔   cup all-purpose flour

1   pound boneless, skinless
    chicken breasts, cut into
    1-inch pieces

1   large red potato,
    unpeeled and cut into
    1-inch pieces

6   ounces mushrooms,
    halved

¾   cup frozen peas

1¼ teaspoons dried basil,
    divided

1   teaspoon dried rosemary,
    divided

⅜   teaspoon dried tarragon,
    divided

¼   cup heavy cream

¾   to 1 teaspoon salt

¼   teaspoon black pepper

1   cup biscuit baking mix

⅓   cup reduced-fat (2%) milk

1. Combine carrots, onion, bell pepper, celery and all but 1 cup chicken broth in **CROCK-POT**® slow cooker. Cover; cook on LOW 2 hours.

2. Stir remaining 1 cup chicken broth into flour in small bowl until smooth. Stir into vegetable mixture. Add chicken, potato, mushrooms, peas, 1 teaspoon basil, ¾ teaspoon rosemary and ¼ teaspoon tarragon. Cover; cook on LOW 4 hours or until vegetables and chicken are tender. Stir in cream, salt and pepper.

3. Combine baking mix, remaining ¼ teaspoon basil, ¼ teaspoon rosemary and ⅛ teaspoon tarragon in small bowl. Stir in milk to form soft dough. Add dumpling mixture to top of stew in 4 large spoonfuls. Cook, uncovered, 30 minutes. Cover; cook 30 to 45 minutes or until dumplings are firm and toothpick inserted in center comes out clean. Serve in shallow bowls.

Makes 4 servings

Tuscan Beef Stew

½ cup hot beef broth

¼ cup dried porcini mushrooms

3 slices bacon, diced

1 tablespoon olive oil

2 pounds lean beef for stew, cut into ½-inch pieces

Salt

Black pepper

3 cups assorted mushrooms (such as portobello, shiitake or cremini), sliced

1 cup frozen pearl onions, thawed

1 cup baby carrots, cut into ½-inch pieces

1 cup dry red wine

1 can (15 ounces) diced tomatoes with roasted garlic, undrained

¼ cup tomato paste

1 tablespoon chopped fresh rosemary *or* 1 teaspoon dried rosemary

½ teaspoon sugar

2 tablespoons all-purpose flour

2 tablespoons butter, softened

Hot cooked pasta

1. Combine hot beef broth and dried porcini mushrooms in small bowl. Let stand until softened. Remove mushrooms and chop coarsely. Reserve broth.

2. Cook bacon in large skillet over medium-high heat until crisp. Transfer with slotted spoon to paper towels to drain. Pour off bacon drippings from skillet. Add olive oil to pan. Season beef with salt and pepper and cook over medium-high heat until browned on all sides. Place in **CROCK-POT**® slow cooker.

3. Add bacon, chopped porcini mushrooms, sliced mushrooms, onions, carrots, wine, tomatoes with juice, tomato paste, rosemary and sugar. Carefully pour reserved beef broth over other ingredients, being sure to keep sediment in bottom of bowl. Cover and cook on LOW 7 to 8 hours until beef is fork-tender.

4. Combine flour and butter in small bowl and mash into smooth paste. Stir half of paste into cooking liquid. Cover and cook 15 minutes. If thicker gravy is desired, repeat with remaining flour paste. Serve over pasta.

Makes 6 to 8 servings

Jerk Pork and Sweet Potato Stew

2 tablespoons all-purpose flour

¼ teaspoon salt, or to taste

¼ teaspoon black pepper, or to taste

1¼ pounds pork shoulder, cut into bite-size pieces

2 tablespoons vegetable oil

1 large sweet potato, peeled and diced

1 cup frozen or canned corn

¼ cup minced green onions (green parts only), divided

1 clove garlic, minced

½ medium Scotch bonnet chile or jalapeño pepper, cored, seeded and minced (about 1 teaspoon)*

⅛ teaspoon ground allspice

1 cup chicken broth

1 tablespoon lime juice

2 cups cooked rice (optional)

*Scotch bonnet chiles and jalapeño peppers can sting and irritate the skin, so wear rubber gloves when handling and do not touch your eyes.

1. Combine flour, salt and pepper in resealable plastic food storage bag. Add pork and shake well to coat. Heat oil in large skillet over medium heat until hot. Add pork in a single layer (working in 2 batches, if necessary) and brown on both sides, about 5 minutes. Transfer to **CROCK-POT®** slow cooker.

2. Add sweet potato, corn, 2 tablespoons green onions, garlic, chile and allspice. Stir in broth. Cover; cook on LOW 5 to 6 hours.

3. Stir in lime juice and remaining 2 tablespoons green onions. Adjust salt and pepper to taste. Serve stew over cooked rice, if desired.

Makes 4 servings

Greek Braised Beef Stew

¼ cup all-purpose flour

2 teaspoons Greek seasoning

¼ teaspoon salt, or to taste

¼ teaspoon black pepper, or to taste

2 pounds boneless beef stew meat or beef chuck roast, cut into 1-inch cubes

2 tablespoons olive oil

2 large onions, each cut into 8 wedges

1 container (10 ounces) grape or cherry tomatoes

1 jar (8 ounces) pitted kalamata olives, drained

8 sprigs fresh oregano, divided

1 lemon, divided

2 cups fat-free, reduced-sodium beef broth

1. Combine flour, Greek seasoning, salt and pepper in large resealable plastic food storage bag. Add beef and shake to coat. Heat olive oil in large skillet over medium-high heat until hot. Add beef in single layer (working in 2 batches, if necessary) and brown on both sides, about 5 minutes. Transfer to **CROCK-POT®** slow cooker.

2. Add onions, tomatoes, olives, 4 sprigs oregano, juice of ½ lemon and broth. Cover; cook on HIGH 6 to 7 hours or until beef is tender. Add salt and pepper, if desired. Cut remaining ½ lemon into wedges and serve with stew. Garnish with remaining oregano.

Makes 6 servings

Three-Bean Chipotle Chili

2 tablespoons olive oil

1 large onion, chopped

1 medium green bell pepper, seeded, ribbed and chopped

2 cloves garlic, minced

1 or 2 canned chipotles in adobo sauce, finely chopped

1 can (6 ounces) tomato paste

1 cup water

2 cans (about 15 ounces) pinto or pink beans, rinsed and drained

1 can (about 15 ounces) small white beans, rinsed and drained

1 can (about 15 ounces) garbanzo beans

1 cup drained canned or thawed frozen corn

Salt

Sour cream (optional)

Shredded Cheddar cheese (optional)

Chopped onion (optional)

1. Heat oil in large skillet over medium heat. Add onion, bell pepper and garlic. Cook, stirring occasionally, until onion softens. Transfer to **CROCK-POT®** slow cooker.

2. Stir in chipotle peppers, tomato paste and water. Add pinto, white and garbanzo beans and corn. Cover; cook on LOW 3½ to 4 hours. Season to taste with salt. Garnish as desired with sour cream, shredded Cheddar cheese and chopped onion.

Makes 6 servings

Golden Harvest Pork Stew

1 pound boneless pork cutlets, cut into 1-inch pieces

2 tablespoons all-purpose flour, divided

1 tablespoon vegetable oil

2 medium Yukon gold potatoes, unpeeled and cut into 1-inch cubes

1 large sweet potato, peeled and cut into 1-inch cubes

1 cup chopped carrots

1 ear corn, broken into 4 pieces or ½ cup corn

½ cup chicken broth

1 jalapeño pepper, seeded and finely chopped*

1 clove garlic, minced

1 teaspoon salt

¼ teaspoon black pepper

¼ teaspoon dried thyme

Chopped parsley

*Jalapeño peppers can sting and irritate the skin, so wear rubber gloves when handling peppers and do not touch your eyes.

1. Toss pork pieces with 1 tablespoon flour; set aside. Heat oil in large skillet over medium-high heat until hot. Add pork; cook until browned on all sides. Transfer to **CROCK-POT®** slow cooker.

2. Add remaining ingredients except parsley and 1 tablespoon flour. Cover; cook on LOW 5 to 6 hours.

3. Stir ¼ cup cooking liquid into remaining 1 tablespoon flour in small bowl. Stir flour mixture into stew. Turn **CROCK-POT®** slow cooker to HIGH. Cook 10 minutes or until thickened. Adjust seasonings, if desired. To serve, sprinkle with parsley.

Makes 4 servings

Hearty Chicken Chili

1 medium onion, finely chopped

1 small jalapeño pepper, cored, seeded and minced*

1 small clove garlic, minced

1½ teaspoons medium-hot chili powder

¾ teaspoon salt, or to taste

½ teaspoon black pepper, or to taste

½ teaspoon ground cumin

½ teaspoon crushed dried oregano

2 cans (15½ ounces each) hominy, rinsed and drained

1 can (15 ounces) pinto beans, rinsed and drained

1½ pounds boneless, skinless chicken thighs, cut into 1-inch pieces

1 cup chicken broth

1 tablespoon all-purpose flour (optional)

Chopped parsley or cilantro (optional)

Jalapeño peppers can sting and irritate the skin, so wear rubber gloves when handling peppers and do not touch your eyes. For a hotter dish, add ¼ teaspoon crushed red pepper flakes with the seasonings.

1. Combine onion, jalapeño pepper, garlic, chili powder, salt, black pepper, cumin and oregano in **CROCK-POT®** slow cooker.

2. Add hominy, beans, chicken and broth. Stir well to combine. Cover; cook on LOW 7 hours.

3. If thicker gravy is desired, combine 1 tablespoon flour and 3 tablespoons cooking liquid in small bowl. Add to **CROCK-POT®** slow cooker. Cover; cook on HIGH 10 minutes or until thickened. Serve in bowls and garnish as desired.

Makes 6 servings

Greek-Style Chicken Stew

2 cups sliced mushrooms

2 cups cubed peeled eggplant

1¼ cups reduced-sodium chicken broth

¾ cup coarsely chopped onion

2 cloves garlic, minced

1½ teaspoons all-purpose flour

1 teaspoon dried oregano

½ teaspoon dried basil

½ teaspoon dried thyme

6 skinless chicken breasts (about 2 pounds)

Additional all-purpose flour

3 tablespoons dry sherry or reduced-sodium chicken broth

¼ teaspoon salt

¼ teaspoon black pepper

1 can (14 ounces) artichoke hearts, drained

12 ounces uncooked wide egg noodles

1. Combine mushrooms, eggplant, broth, onion, garlic, 1½ teaspoons flour, oregano, basil and thyme in **CROCK-POT®** slow cooker. Cover; cook on HIGH 1 hour.

2. Coat chicken very lightly with additional flour. Generously spray large nonstick skillet with cooking spray; heat over medium heat until hot. Cook chicken 10 to 15 minutes or until browned on all sides.

3. Remove vegetables to bowl with slotted spoon. Layer chicken in **CROCK-POT®** slow cooker; return vegetables to **CROCK-POT®** slow cooker. Add sherry, salt and pepper. Reduce heat to LOW. Cover; cook 6 to 6½ hours or until chicken is no longer pink in center and vegetables are tender.

4. Stir in artichokes; cover and cook 45 minutes to 1 hour or until heated through. Cook noodles according to package directions. Serve chicken stew over noodles.

Makes 6 servings

Pork and Anaheim Stew

2 tablespoons extra-virgin olive oil, divided

1½ pounds boneless pork shoulder, fat trimmed, cut into ½-inch pieces

6 Anaheim peppers, halved lengthwise, seeded and sliced*

4 cloves garlic, minced

1 pound tomatillos, papery skins removed, rinsed and chopped

2 cups chopped onions

1 can (15½ ounces) yellow hominy, rinsed and drained

1 can (about 14 ounces) fat-free chicken broth

2 teaspoons chili powder

1 teaspoon ground cumin

1 teaspoon dried oregano

1½ teaspoons sugar

1 teaspoon liquid smoke

½ teaspoon salt plus more to taste

Anaheim peppers can sting and irritate the skin, so wear rubber gloves when handling peppers and do not touch your eyes.

1. Heat 1 teaspoon olive oil in large skillet over high heat. Add half of pork and cook, stirring frequently, until browned on all sides. Transfer pork to **CROCK-POT®** slow cooker. Drain drippings from skillet and repeat with 1 teaspoon oil and remaining pork.

2. Reduce heat to medium-high. Add 1 teaspoon oil and add Anaheim peppers. Cook and stir 5 minutes or until peppers begin to brown on edges. Add garlic to peppers and cook 15 seconds, stirring constantly. Stir into **CROCK-POT®** slow cooker. Stir in tomatillos, onions, hominy, chicken broth, chili powder, cumin, oregano and sugar. Cover and cook on LOW 10 hours or on HIGH 5 hours.

3. Stir in remaining 1 tablespoon oil, liquid smoke and salt. Serve immediately or cover and refrigerate overnight (flavors intensify with time).

Makes 4 servings

Chinese Chicken Stew

1 pound boneless, skinless chicken thighs, cut into 1-inch pieces

1 teaspoon Chinese five-spice powder*

½ to ¾ teaspoon red pepper flakes

1 tablespoon peanut or vegetable oil

1 large onion, coarsely chopped

1 package (8 ounces) fresh mushrooms, sliced

2 cloves garlic, minced

1 can (about 14 ounces) chicken broth, divided

1 tablespoon cornstarch

1 large red bell pepper, cut into ¾-inch pieces

2 tablespoons soy sauce

2 large green onions, cut into ½-inch pieces

1 tablespoon sesame oil

3 cups hot cooked white rice (optional)

¼ cup coarsely chopped fresh cilantro (optional)

*Chinese five-spice powder is a blend of cinnamon, cloves, fennel seed, anise and Szechuan peppercorns. It is available in most supermarkets and at Asian grocery stores.

1. Toss chicken with five-spice powder and red pepper flakes in small bowl. Heat peanut oil in large skillet. Add onion and chicken; cook and stir about 5 minutes or until chicken is browned. Add mushrooms and garlic; cook and stir until chicken is no longer pink.

2. Combine ¼ cup broth and cornstarch in small bowl; set aside. Place cooked chicken mixture, remaining broth, bell pepper and soy sauce in **CROCK-POT**® slow cooker. Cover; cook on LOW 3½ hours or until peppers are tender.

3. Stir in cornstarch mixture, green onions and sesame oil. Cook 30 to 45 minutes or until thickened. Ladle into soup bowls; scoop ½ cup rice into each bowl and sprinkle with cilantro, if desired.

Makes 6 servings (about 5 cups)

Hearty Meatball Stew

3 pounds ground beef or ground turkey

1 cup Italian bread crumbs

4 eggs

½ cup milk

¼ cup grated Romano cheese

2 teaspoons salt

2 teaspoons garlic salt

2 teaspoons black pepper

2 tablespoons olive oil

2 cups water

2 cups beef broth

1 can (14½ ounces) stewed tomatoes, undrained

1 can (12 ounces) tomato paste

1 cup chopped carrots

1 cup chopped onions

¼ cup chopped celery

1 tablespoon Italian seasoning

1. Combine beef, bread crumbs, eggs, milk, cheese, salt, garlic salt and pepper in large bowl. Form into 2-inch-round balls. Heat oil in skillet over medium-high heat until hot. Brown meatballs on all sides. Transfer to **CROCK-POT®** slow cooker.

2. Add remaining ingredients. Stir well to combine. Cover; cook on LOW 4 to 6 hours or on HIGH 2 to 4 hours.

Makes 6 to 8 servings

Mushroom-Beef Stew

1 pound beef stew meat

1 can (10¾ ounces) condensed cream of mushroom soup, undiluted

2 cans (4 ounces each) sliced mushrooms, drained

1 package (1 ounce) dry onion soup mix

Hot cooked noodles

Combine all ingredients except noodles in **CROCK-POT®** slow cooker. Cover; cook on LOW 8 to 10 hours. Serve over noodles.

Makes 4 servings

Note

Button mushrooms are the most common mushrooms grown and sold. They are plump and dome-shaped with a smooth texture and mild flavor. The color of button mushrooms varies from white to pale tan.

Chicken and Sweet Potato Stew

4 boneless, skinless chicken breasts, cut into bite-size pieces

2 medium sweet potatoes, peeled and cubed

2 medium Yukon gold potatoes, peeled and cubed

2 medium carrots, peeled and cut into ½-inch slices

1 can (28 ounces) whole stewed tomatoes

1 teaspoon salt

1 teaspoon paprika

1 teaspoon celery seeds

½ teaspoon freshly ground black pepper

⅛ teaspoon ground cinnamon

⅛ teaspoon ground nutmeg

1 cup nonfat, low-sodium chicken broth

¼ cup fresh basil, chopped

Combine all ingredients except basil in **CROCK-POT®** slow cooker. Cover; cook on LOW 6 to 8 hours or on HIGH 3 to 4 hours. Sprinkle with basil just before serving.

Makes 6 servings

Mexican Chili Chicken

2 medium green bell peppers, cut into thin strips

1 large onion, quartered and thinly sliced

4 chicken thighs

4 chicken drumsticks

1 tablespoon chili powder

2 teaspoons dried oregano

1 jar (16 ounces) chipotle salsa

½ cup ketchup

2 teaspoons ground cumin

½ teaspoon salt

Hot cooked noodles

1. Place bell peppers and onion in **CROCK-POT®** slow cooker; top with chicken. Sprinkle chili powder and oregano evenly over chicken. Add salsa. Cover; cook on LOW 7 to 8 hours or on HIGH 2 to 3 hours or until chicken is tender.

2. Transfer chicken to serving bowl; cover with foil to keep warm. Stir ketchup, cumin and salt into cooking liquid. Cook, uncovered, on HIGH 15 minutes or until hot.

3. Pour mixture over chicken. Serve chicken and sauce over noodles.

Makes 4 servings

Tip

If you prefer a thicker sauce, whisk 1 tablespoon cornstarch into 2 tablespoons water in small bowl. Stir into cooking liquid with ketchup, cumin and salt.

Chipotle Chicken Stew

- 1 pound boneless, skinless chicken thighs, cut into cubes
- 1 can (15 ounces) navy beans, rinsed and drained
- 1 can (15 ounces) black beans, rinsed and drained
- 1 can (14½ ounces) crushed tomatoes, undrained
- 1½ cups chicken broth
- ½ cup orange juice
- 1 medium onion, diced
- 1 chipotle pepper in adobo sauce, minced
- 1 teaspoon salt
- 1 teaspoon ground cumin
- 1 bay leaf
  Cilantro sprigs (optional)

1. Combine chicken, beans, tomatoes with juice, broth, orange juice, onion, chipotle pepper, salt, cumin and bay leaf in **CROCK-POT**® slow cooker.

2. Cover; cook on LOW 7 to 8 hours or on HIGH 3½ to 4 hours. Remove bay leaf before serving. Garnish with cilantro sprigs.

Makes 6 servings

Beef and Black Bean Chili

- 1 tablespoon vegetable oil
- 1 pound boneless beef round steak, cut into 1-inch cubes
- 1 package (14 ounces) frozen green and red bell pepper strips with onions
- 1 can (15 ounces) black beans, rinsed and drained
- 1 can (about 14 ounces) fire-roasted diced tomatoes, undrained
- 2 tablespoons chili powder
- 1 tablespoon minced garlic
- 2 teaspoons ground cumin
- ½ ounce semisweet chocolate, chopped
- 2 cups hot cooked white rice
  Shredded Cheddar cheese (optional)
  Sour cream (optional)

1. Heat oil in large skillet over medium-high heat. Add beef and cook, turning occasionally, until browned on all sides, about 5 minutes. Transfer to **CROCK-POT**® slow cooker.

2. Stir in pepper strips, beans, tomatoes with juice, chili powder, garlic and cumin. Cover and cook on LOW 8 to 9 hours. Turn off heat and stir in chocolate until melted. Serve over rice and garnish with Cheddar cheese and sour cream.

Makes 4 servings

Sweet and Sour Brisket Stew

- 1   jar (12 ounces) chili sauce
- 1½   to 2 tablespoons packed dark brown sugar
- 1½   tablespoons fresh lemon juice
- ¼   cup beef broth
- 1   tablespoon Dijon mustard
- ¼   teaspoon paprika
- ½   teaspoon salt, or to taste
- ¼   teaspoon black pepper, or to taste
- 1   clove garlic, minced
- 1   small onion, chopped
- 1   well-trimmed beef brisket, cut into 1-inch pieces*
- 2   large carrots, cut into ½-inch slices
- 1   tablespoon all-purpose flour (optional)

Beef brisket has a thick layer of fat, which some supermarkets trim off. If the meat is well trimmed, buy 2½ pounds; if not, purchase 4 pounds, then trim and discard excess fat.

1. Combine chili sauce, 1½ tablespoons brown sugar, lemon juice, broth, mustard, paprika, salt and pepper in **CROCK-POT®** slow cooker. (Add remaining sugar, if desired, after tasting.)

2. Add garlic, onion, beef and carrots. Stir well to coat. Cover; cook on LOW 8 hours.

3. If thicker gravy is desired, combine 1 tablespoon flour and 3 tablespoons cooking liquid in small bowl. Add to **CROCK-POT®** slow cooker. Cover; cook on HIGH 10 minutes or until thickened.

Makes 6 to 8 servings

Chili with Chocolate

- 1   pound (16 ounces) lean ground beef
- 1   medium onion, chopped
- 3   cloves garlic, minced and divided
- 1   can (28 ounces) diced tomatoes, undrained
- 1   can (15½ ounces) chili beans in mild or spicy sauce, undrained
- 2   tablespoons chili powder
- 1   tablespoon grated semisweet baking chocolate
- 1½   teaspoons ground cumin
- ½   teaspoon salt
- ½   teaspoon black pepper
- ½   teaspoon hot pepper sauce

1. Cook and stir beef, onion and 1 clove garlic in large nonstick skillet over medium-high heat until beef is browned, stirring to break up meat. Drain fat.

2. Place beef mixture in **CROCK-POT®** slow cooker. Add tomatoes with juice, beans with sauce, chili powder, remaining 2 cloves garlic and chocolate; mix well.

3. Cover; cook on LOW 5 to 6 hours. Add cumin, salt, pepper and hot pepper sauce during last hour of cooking.

Makes 4 servings

Beef Chuck Chili

- 5 pounds beef chuck roast
- ½ cup plus 2 tablespoons olive oil, divided
- 3 cups minced onions
- 4 poblano peppers, seeded and diced*
- 2 serrano peppers, seeded and diced*
- 2 green bell peppers, seeded and diced
- 3 jalapeño peppers, seeded and diced**
- 2 tablespoons minced garlic
- 1 can (28 ounces) crushed tomatoes
- ¼ cup hot pepper sauce
- 1 tablespoon ground cumin
  Black pepper, to taste
- 4 ounces Mexican lager beer (optional)
  Corn bread or hot cooked rice

Handle fresh chile peppers as directed for jalapeño peppers. If fresh chile peppers are unavailable, use 2 cans (4 ounces each) diced green chiles and add dried ground chili powder for more heat.

**Jalapeño peppers can sting and irritate the skin. Wear rubber gloves when handling peppers and do not touch your eyes.*

1. Trim excess fat from roast and discard. Heat ½ cup olive oil in large skillet over medium-high heat until hot. Add chuck roast; sear on both sides. Transfer beef to **CROCK-POT®** slow cooker.

2. Heat remaining 2 tablespoons oil in same skillet over low heat. Add onions, peppers and garlic; cook and stir about 7 minutes or until onions are tender. Transfer to **CROCK-POT®** slow cooker. Add crushed tomatoes. Cover; cook on LOW 4 to 5 hours or until beef is fork-tender.

3. Remove beef from **CROCK-POT®** slow cooker. Shred beef with two forks. Add hot sauce, cumin, black pepper and beer, if desired, to cooking liquid. Return beef to cooking liquid and mix well. Serve over corn bread or rice.

Makes 8 to 10 servings

Chili Verde

- ¾ pound boneless lean pork, cut into 1-inch cubes
- 1 pound fresh tomatillos, husks removed, rinsed and coarsely chopped
- 1 can (15 ounces) Great Northern beans, rinsed and drained
- 1 can (14½ ounces) chicken broth
- 1 large onion, halved and thinly sliced
- 1 can (4 ounces) diced mild green chiles
- 6 cloves garlic, chopped or sliced
- 1 teaspoon ground cumin
  Salt and black pepper, to taste
- ½ cup lightly packed fresh cilantro, chopped

1. Coat large skillet with nonstick cooking spray. Heat over medium-high heat. Add pork; cook until browned on all sides.

2. Combine pork and all remaining ingredients except cilantro in **CROCK-POT®** slow cooker. Cover; cook on HIGH 3 to 4 hours.

3. Season to taste with additional salt and pepper. Turn **CROCK-POT®** slow cooker to LOW. Stir in cilantro and cook 10 minutes.

Makes 4 servings

Chili with Beans and Corn

- 1 can (about 15 ounces) black-eyed peas or cannellini beans, rinsed and drained
- 1 can (about 15 ounces) kidney or navy beans, rinsed and drained
- 1 can (about 14 ounces) whole tomatoes, drained and chopped
- 1 onion, chopped
- 1 cup frozen corn
- 1 cup water
- ½ cup chopped green onions
- ½ cup tomato paste
- ¼ cup diced jalapeño peppers*
- 1 tablespoon chili powder
- 1 teaspoon ground cumin
- 1 teaspoon prepared mustard
- ½ teaspoon dried oregano

*Jalapeño peppers can sting and irritate the skin, so wear rubber gloves when handling peppers and do not touch your eyes.

Combine all ingredients in **CROCK-POT®** slow cooker. Cover; cook on LOW 8 to 10 hours or on HIGH 4 to 5 hours.

Makes 6 to 8 servings

Mushroom Barley Stew

- 1 tablespoon olive oil
- 1 medium onion, finely chopped
- 1 cup chopped carrots (about 2 carrots)
- 1 clove garlic, minced
- 1 cup uncooked pearl barley
- 1 cup dried wild mushrooms, broken into pieces
- 1 teaspoon salt
- ½ teaspoon black pepper
- ½ teaspoon dried thyme
- 5 cups vegetable broth

1. Heat oil in medium skillet over medium-high heat. Add onion, carrots and garlic; cook and stir 5 minutes or until tender. Place in **CROCK-POT®** slow cooker.

2. Add barley, mushrooms, salt, pepper and thyme. Stir in broth. Cover; cook on LOW 6 to 7 hours. Adjust seasonings.

Makes 4 to 6 servings

Chicken and Chile Pepper Stew

- 1 pound boneless, skinless chicken thighs, cut into ½-inch pieces
- 1 pound small potatoes, cut lengthwise into halves, then crosswise into slices
- 1 cup chopped onion
- 2 poblano peppers, seeded and cut into ½-inch pieces*
- 1 jalapeño pepper, seeded and finely chopped*
- 3 cloves garlic, minced
- 3 cups fat-free reduced-sodium chicken broth
- 1 can (14 ounces) no-salt-added diced tomatoes, undrained
- 2 tablespoons chili powder
- 1 teaspoon dried oregano

Hot peppers can sting and irritate the skin, so wear rubber gloves when handling peppers and do not touch your eyes.

1. Place chicken, potatoes, onion, poblano peppers, jalapeño pepper and garlic in **CROCK-POT®** slow cooker.

2. Stir together broth, tomatoes with juice, chili powder and oregano in large bowl. Pour into **CROCK-POT®** slow cooker. Stir well to blend. Cover; cook on LOW 8 to 9 hours.

Makes 6 servings

Classic Chili

- 1½ pounds ground beef
- 1½ cups chopped onion
- 1 cup chopped green bell pepper
- 2 cloves garlic, minced
- 3 cans (15 ounces each) dark red kidney beans, rinsed and drained
- 2 cans (15 ounces each) tomato sauce
- 1 can (about 14 ounces) diced tomatoes, undrained
- 2 to 3 teaspoons chili powder
- 1 to 2 teaspoons ground mustard
- ¾ teaspoon dried basil
- ½ teaspoon black pepper
- 1 to 2 dried hot chilies (optional)

1. Cook and stir ground beef, onion, bell pepper and garlic in large skillet until meat is browned and onion is tender. Drain fat and discard. Transfer mixture to **CROCK-POT®** slow cooker.

2. Add beans, tomato sauce, tomatoes with juice, chili powder, mustard, basil, black pepper and chilies, if desired; mix well. Cover; cook on LOW 8 to 10 hours or on HIGH 4 to 5 hours.

3. If used, remove chilies before serving.

Makes 6 servings

Mediterranean Stew

- 1 medium butternut squash, peeled and cut into 1-inch cubes
- 2 cups unpeeled eggplant, cut into 1-inch cubes
- 2 cups sliced zucchini
- 1 can (15 ounces) chickpeas, rinsed and drained
- 1 package (10 ounces) frozen cut okra
- 1 can (8 ounces) tomato sauce
- 1 cup chopped onion
- 1 medium tomato, chopped
- 1 medium carrot, sliced
- ½ cup vegetable broth
- ⅓ cup raisins
- 1 clove garlic, minced
- ½ teaspoon ground cumin
- ½ teaspoon ground turmeric
- ¼ teaspoon ground red pepper
- ¼ teaspoon ground cinnamon
- ¼ teaspoon paprika
- 6 to 8 cups hot cooked couscous or rice

1. Combine all ingredients except couscous in **CROCK-POT®** slow cooker; mix well.

2. Cover; cook on LOW 8 to 10 hours or until vegetables are crisp-tender.

3. Serve over couscous. Garnish with parsley.

Makes 6 servings

Chili Mac

- 1 pound ground beef or turkey
- ½ cup chopped onion
- 1 can (about 14 ounces) diced tomatoes, drained
- 1 can (8 ounces) tomato sauce
- 2 tablespoons chili powder
- 1 teaspoon garlic salt
- ½ teaspoon ground cumin
- ¼ teaspoon red pepper flakes
- ¼ teaspoon black pepper
- 8 ounces uncooked elbow macaroni
  Shredded Cheddar cheese (optional)

1. Brown beef and onion 6 to 8 minutes in large skillet over medium heat, stirring to break up meat. Drain drippings from pan. Transfer beef to **CROCK-POT®** slow cooker.

2. Add tomatoes, tomato sauce, chili powder, garlic salt, cumin, red pepper flakes and black pepper; mix well. Cover; cook on LOW 4 hours.

3. Cook macaroni according to package directions until al dente; drain. Add macaroni to **CROCK-POT®** slow cooker; mix well. Cover; cook on LOW 1 hour. Garnish with cheese.

Makes 4 to 6 servings

Swiss Steak Stew

2 to 3 boneless beef top sirloin steaks (about 4 pounds)

2 cans (about 14 ounces each) diced tomatoes, undrained

2 medium green bell peppers, cut into ½-inch strips

2 medium onions, chopped

1 tablespoon seasoned salt

1 teaspoon black pepper

Cut each steak into 3 to 4 pieces; place in **CROCK-POT®** slow cooker. Add tomatoes with juice, bell peppers and onions. Season with salt and pepper. Cover; cook on LOW 8 hours or until meat is tender.

Makes 10 servings

Bean and Corn Chili

2 medium onions, finely chopped

5 cloves garlic, minced

½ teaspoon olive oil

2 tablespoons red wine

1 green bell pepper, seeded and finely chopped

1 red bell pepper, seeded and finely chopped

1 stalk celery, finely sliced

6 Roma tomatoes, chopped

2 cans (15 ounces each) kidney beans, rinsed and drained

1 can (6 ounces) tomato paste

1 cup frozen corn kernels

1 teaspoon salt

1 teaspoon chili powder

¼ teaspoon black pepper

¼ teaspoon cumin

¼ teaspoon ground red pepper

¼ teaspoon dried oregano

¼ teaspoon ground coriander

1½ cups nonfat chicken or vegetable broth

1. Cook onions and garlic in olive oil and red wine in medium skillet until onions are tender. Add onion mixture, bell peppers, celery, tomatoes, beans, tomato paste, corn, salt, chili powder, black pepper, cumin, ground red pepper, oregano, coriander and broth to **CROCK-POT®** slow cooker. Mix thoroughly.

2. Cover; cook on LOW 6 to 8 hours or on HIGH 3 to 4 hours.

Makes 6 servings

Ranch Stew

2 pounds beef for stew

6 medium potatoes, diced

2 cups sliced carrots

2 medium onions, chopped

1 medium green bell pepper, chopped (optional)

1 cup diced celery (optional)

1 can (10¾ ounces) condensed tomato soup, undiluted

1 soup can water

2 tablespoons tapioca

1 tablespoon Worcestershire sauce

2 teaspoons salt

1 teaspoon soy sauce

¼ teaspoon black pepper

1 bay leaf

Combine all ingredients in **CROCK-POT**® slow cooker. Cover and cook on LOW 10 to 12 hours or until meat and vegetables are tender. Remove and discard bay leaf before serving.

Makes 6 servings

Tip

Tapping or spinning the cover until the condensation falls off will allow you to see inside the **CROCK-POT**® slow cooker without removing the lid.

Chunky Chili

1 pound 90% lean ground beef

1 medium onion, chopped

2 cans (14½ ounces each) diced tomatoes, undrained

1 can (15 ounces) pinto beans, rinsed and drained

½ cup prepared salsa

1 tablespoon chili powder

1½ teaspoons ground cumin

Salt and black pepper, to taste

½ cup (2 ounces) shredded Cheddar cheese

¼ cup diced onions

4 teaspoons sliced black olives

1. Cook and stir beef and onion in large skillet over medium-high heat until beef is browned and onion is tender. Drain and discard fat.

2. Place beef mixture, tomatoes with juice, beans, salsa, chili powder and cumin in **CROCK-POT**® slow cooker; stir. Cover; cook on LOW 5 to 6 hours or until flavors are blended. Season with salt and pepper. Serve with cheese, onions and olives.

Makes 4 servings

Cajun Beef Stew

1 tablespoon Cajun or blackened seasoning mix

1½ pounds beef for stew, cut into 1½-inch pieces

2 medium red potatoes, cut into 1½-inch pieces

3 carrots, cut into 1-inch pieces

1 medium onion, cut into 1½-inch pieces

1 stalk celery, sliced

1 can (14½ ounces) beef broth

3 tablespoons cornstarch

3 tablespoons water

Salt

1 cup frozen peas, thawed

¼ teaspoon dried thyme

1. Coat **CROCK-POT®** slow cooker with nonstick cooking spray. Sprinkle seasoning mix over meat in medium bowl; toss to coat. Place potatoes, carrots, onion and celery in **CROCK-POT®** slow cooker. Place beef on top of vegetables. Add broth. Cover; cook on LOW 7 to 8 hours or on HIGH 4 to 5 hours or until beef and vegetables are tender.

2. Transfer beef and vegetables to bowl with slotted spoon. Cover and keep warm. Turn **CROCK-POT®** slow cooker to HIGH. Combine cornstarch and water until smooth; stir into juices. Cover; cook 10 to 15 minutes or until thickened. Season with salt.

3. Return beef and vegetables to **CROCK-POT®** slow cooker. Stir in peas and thyme. Cook on HIGH 15 minutes or until heated through.

Makes 4 servings

Weeknight Chili

1 pound ground beef or ground turkey

1 package (1¼ ounces) chili seasoning mix

1 can (about 14 ounces) diced tomatoes with green chiles, undrained

1 can (about 15 ounces) red kidney beans, rinsed and drained

1 can (8 ounces) tomato sauce

1 cup (4 ounces) shredded Cheddar cheese

1. Brown ground beef in large skillet, stirring to break up meat; drain fat. Stir in seasoning mix.

2. Place beef, tomatoes with juice, beans and tomato sauce in **CROCK-POT®** slow cooker. Cover and cook on LOW 4 to 6 hours or on HIGH 2 to 3 hours. Top each serving with cheese.

Makes 4 servings

Wild Mushroom Beef Stew

1½ to 2 pounds beef stew meat, cut into 1-inch cubes

  2 tablespoons all-purpose flour

  ½ teaspoon salt

  ½ teaspoon black pepper

1½ cups beef broth

  1 teaspoon Worcestershire sauce

  1 clove garlic, minced

  1 bay leaf

  1 teaspoon paprika

  4 shiitake mushrooms, sliced

  2 medium carrots, sliced

  2 medium potatoes, diced

  1 small white onion, chopped

  1 stalk celery, sliced

1. Put beef in **CROCK-POT®** slow cooker. Mix together flour, salt and pepper and sprinkle over meat; stir to coat each piece of meat with flour. Add remaining ingredients and stir to mix well.

2. Cover; cook on LOW 10 to 12 hours or on HIGH 4 to 6 hours. Remove and discard bay leaf. Stir stew before serving.

Makes 5 servings

Savory Chicken and Oregano Chili

  3 cans (15 ounces each) Great Northern or cannellini beans, drained

3½ cups chicken broth

  2 cups chopped cooked chicken

  2 medium red bell peppers, cored, seeded and chopped

  1 medium onion, peeled and chopped

  1 can (4 ounces) diced green chiles

  3 cloves garlic, minced

  2 teaspoons ground cumin

  1 teaspoon salt

  1 tablespoon minced fresh oregano

1. Place beans, broth, chicken, bell peppers, onion, chiles, garlic, cumin and salt in **CROCK-POT®** slow cooker. Mix well to combine. Cover; cook on LOW 8 to 10 hours or on HIGH 4 to 5 hours.

2. Stir in oregano before serving.

Makes 8 servings

New Mexican Green Chile Pork Stew

1½ pounds boneless pork shoulder, cut into 1-inch cubes

2 medium baking potatoes or sweet potatoes, peeled and cut into large chunks

1 cup chopped onion

1 can (4 ounces) diced green chiles

1 cup frozen corn

2 teaspoons sugar

2 teaspoons cumin or chili powder

1 teaspoon dried oregano

1 jar (16 ounces) salsa verde (green salsa)

Hot cooked rice

¼ cup chopped fresh cilantro

1. Place pork, potatoes, onion, chiles and corn into **CROCK-POT**® slow cooker. Stir sugar, cumin and oregano into salsa and pour over pork and vegetables. Stir gently to mix.

2. Cover and cook on LOW 6 to 8 hours or on HIGH 4 to 5 hours, or until pork is tender. Serve stew over hot rice and garnish with cilantro.

Makes 6 servings

White Bean Chili

Nonstick cooking spray

1 pound ground chicken

3 cups coarsely chopped celery

1 can (28 ounces) whole tomatoes, undrained and coarsely chopped

1 can (15½ ounces) Great Northern beans, rinsed and drained

1½ cups coarsely chopped onions

1 cup chicken broth

3 cloves garlic, minced

4 teaspoons chili powder

1½ teaspoons ground cumin

¾ teaspoon ground allspice

¾ teaspoon ground cinnamon

½ teaspoon black pepper

1. Spray large nonstick skillet with nonstick cooking spray; brown chicken over medium-high heat, stirring to break up chicken.

2. Combine chicken, celery, tomatoes with juice, beans, onions, broth, garlic, chili powder, cumin, allspice, cinnamon and pepper in **CROCK-POT**® slow cooker. Cover; cook on LOW 5½ to 6 hours.

Makes 6 servings

meaty
main dishes

Middle Eastern-Spiced Beef, Tomatoes and Beans

2 tablespoons extra-virgin olive oil, divided

1½ pounds lean boneless beef chuck roast, cut into 1-inch pieces, divided

1 can (14½ ounces) diced tomatoes with peppers and onions, undrained

6 ounces fresh green beans, trimmed and broken into 1-inch pieces

1 cup chopped onion

½ teaspoon ground cinnamon

¼ teaspoon ground allspice

1½ teaspoons sugar

¼ teaspoon garlic powder

½ teaspoon salt, or to taste

¼ teaspoon black pepper

Hot cooked couscous or rice (optional)

1. Heat 2 teaspoons oil in large skillet over medium-high heat. Add half of beef cubes and cook, stirring frequently, until browned on all sides. Transfer to **CROCK-POT®** slow cooker. Add additional 2 teaspoons oil and repeat with remaining beef.

2. Stir in tomatoes with juice, beans, onion, cinnamon, allspice, sugar and garlic powder. Cover and cook on LOW 8 hours or on HIGH 4 hours.

3. Stir in salt, pepper and remaining 2 teaspoons oil and let stand uncovered 15 minutes to allow flavors to absorb and thicken slightly. Serve as is or over cooked couscous or rice.

Makes about 4 servings

Bacon, Onion & Stout Braised Short Ribs

4   pounds bone-in beef
    short ribs, well trimmed

1   teaspoon salt, plus
    additional for seasoning

½   teaspoon ground black
    pepper, plus additional
    for seasoning

1   tablespoon vegetable oil

6   ounces thick-cut bacon,
    cut into ¼-inch dice

1   large onion, halved and
    cut into ¼-inch slices

1   tablespoon tomato paste

2   tablespoons all-purpose
    flour

2   tablespoons spicy brown
    mustard

1   bottle (12 ounces) Irish
    stout

1   bay leaf

1   cup beef broth

2   tablespoons finely
    chopped parsley leaves

    Hot mashed potatoes
    or cooked egg noodles
    (optional)

1. Season beef with salt and pepper. Heat oil in large skillet over medium-high heat until almost smoking. Working in batches, cook short ribs in skillet, turning to brown all sides. Transfer each batch to **CROCK-POT®** slow cooker as it is finished. Wipe out pan with paper towels and return to heat.

2. Cook bacon, stirring occasionally, until crisp, about 4 minutes. Transfer with slotted spoon to paper towel-lined plate to drain. Remove and discard all but 1 tablespoon drippings from pan. Reduce heat to medium and add onion. Cook until softened and translucent, stirring occasionally. Add tomato paste, flour, mustard, 1 teaspoon salt and ½ teaspoon pepper. Cook, stirring constantly, 1 minute. Remove skillet from heat and pour in stout, stirring to scrape browned bits from bottom of pan. Pour over short ribs. Add drained bacon, bay leaf and beef broth. Cover and cook on LOW 8 hours or until meat is tender and falls off the bone.

3. Remove beef and skim fat from cooking liquid. Remove bay leaf and stir in parsley. Serve with mashed potatoes or egg noodles.

Makes 4 to 6 servings

Tip

This recipe only gets better if made ahead and refrigerated overnight. This makes skimming any fat from the surface easier, too.

Stuffed Chicken Breasts

6 boneless, skinless chicken breasts

8 ounces feta cheese, crumbled

3 cups chopped fresh spinach leaves

⅓ cup oil-packed sun-dried tomatoes, drained and chopped

1 teaspoon minced lemon peel

1 teaspoon dried basil, oregano or mint

½ teaspoon garlic powder

Freshly ground black pepper, to taste

1 can (15 ounces) diced tomatoes, undrained

½ cup oil-cured olives*

Hot cooked polenta

*If using pitted olives, add to CROCK-POT® slow cooker in the final hour of cooking.

1. Place chicken breast between 2 pieces of plastic wrap. Using tenderizer mallet or back of skillet, pound breast until about ¼-inch thick. Repeat with remaining chicken.

2. Combine feta, spinach, sun-dried tomatoes, lemon peel, basil, garlic powder and pepper in medium bowl.

3. Lay pounded chicken, smooth side down, on work surface. Place about 2 tablespoons feta mixture on wide end of breast. Roll tightly. Repeat with remaining chicken.

4. Place rolled chicken, seam side down, in **CROCK-POT®** slow cooker. Top with diced tomatoes with juice and olives. Cover; cook on LOW 5½ to 6 hours or on HIGH 4 hours. Serve with polenta.

Makes 6 servings

Tip

For easier cleanup of the **CROCK-POT®** slow cooker stoneware, spray the inside with nonstick cooking spray before adding ingredients.

Turkey Piccata

2½ tablespoons all-purpose flour

¼ teaspoon salt, or to taste

¼ teaspoon black pepper

1 pound turkey breast meat, cut into short strips*

1 tablespoon butter

1 tablespoon olive oil

½ cup chicken broth

2 teaspoons freshly squeezed lemon juice

Grated peel of 1 lemon

2 tablespoons finely chopped parsley

2 cups cooked rice (optional)

*You may substitute turkey tenderloins; cut as directed.

1. Combine flour, salt and pepper in resealable plastic food storage bag. Add turkey strips and shake well to coat. Heat butter and oil in large skillet over medium-high heat until hot. Add turkey strips in single layer. Brown on all sides, about 2 minutes per side. Transfer to **CROCK-POT®** slow cooker, arranging on bottom in single layer.

2. Pour broth into skillet. Cook and stir to scrape up any browned bits. Pour into **CROCK-POT®** slow cooker. Add lemon juice and peel. Cover; cook on LOW 1 hour. Sprinkle with parsley before serving. Serve over rice, if desired.

Makes 4 servings

Tip

This recipe will also work with chicken strips. Start with boneless, skinless chicken breasts, then follow the recipe as directed.

Slow-Cooked Beef Brisket Dinner

1 beef brisket (4 pounds), cut in half

4 to 6 medium potatoes, cut into large chunks

6 carrots, cut into 1-inch pieces

8 ounces mushrooms, sliced

½ large onion, sliced

1 stalk celery, cut into 1-inch pieces

3 cubes beef bouillon

5 cloves garlic, crushed

1 teaspoon black peppercorns

2 bay leaves

Water, as needed

Salt and black pepper, to taste

Chopped parsley (optional)

1. Place brisket, potatoes, carrots, mushrooms, onion, celery, bouillon cubes, garlic, peppercorns and bay leaves in **CROCK-POT®** slow cooker. Add enough water to cover ingredients. Cover; cook on LOW 6 to 8 hours.

2. Remove and discard bay leaves. Transfer brisket to cutting board. Season with salt and pepper, to taste. Slice meat across grain. Serve with vegetables. Garnish with parsley.

Makes 8 to 10 servings

Ham with Fruited Bourbon Sauce

1 **bone-in ham, butt portion (about 6 pounds)**

½ **cup apple juice**

¾ **cup packed dark brown sugar**

½ **cup raisins**

1 **teaspoon ground cinnamon**

¼ **teaspoon red pepper flakes**

⅓ **cup dried cherries**

¼ **cup cornstarch**

¼ **cup bourbon, rum or apple juice**

1. Coat **CROCK-POT®** slow cooker with nonstick cooking spray. Add ham, cut side up. Combine apple juice, brown sugar, raisins, cinnamon and red pepper flakes in small bowl; stir well. Pour mixture evenly over ham. Cover; cook on LOW 9 to 10 hours or on HIGH 4½ to 5 hours. Add cherries 30 minutes before end of cooking time.

2. Transfer ham to cutting board. Let stand 15 minutes before slicing.

3. Pour cooking liquid into large measuring cup and let stand 5 minutes. Skim and discard excess fat. Return cooking liquid to **CROCK-POT®** slow cooker.

4. Turn **CROCK-POT®** slow cooker to HIGH. Whisk cornstarch and bourbon in small bowl until cornstarch is dissolved. Stir into cooking liquid. Cover; cook on HIGH 15 to 20 minutes longer or until thickened. Serve sauce over sliced ham.

Makes 10 to 12 servings

Shepherd's Pie

1 pound lean ground beef

1 pound ground lamb

1 package (12 ounces) frozen chopped onions

2 teaspoons minced garlic

1 can (about 14 ounces) diced tomatoes, drained

1 package (16 ounces) frozen peas and carrots

3 tablespoons quick-cooking tapioca

2 teaspoons dried oregano

1 teaspoon salt

½ teaspoon black pepper

2 packages (24 ounces each) prepared mashed potatoes

1. Cook beef and lamb in large nonstick skillet over medium-high heat, stirring occasionally, until no longer pink. Transfer to **CROCK-POT®** slow cooker. Return skillet to heat and add onions and garlic. Cook, stirring frequently, until onions begin to soften. Transfer to **CROCK-POT®** slow cooker with beef and lamb.

2. Stir in tomatoes, peas and carrots, tapioca, oregano, salt and pepper. Cover and cook on LOW 7 to 8 hours.

3. Top with prepared mashed potatoes. Cover and cook on LOW until potatoes are heated through, about 30 minutes.

Makes 6 servings

East Indian Curried Chicken with Capers and Brown Rice

2 cups ripe plum tomatoes, diced

1 cup artichoke hearts, drained and chopped

1 cup chicken broth

1 medium red onion, chopped

⅓ cup dry white wine

¼ cup capers, drained

2 tablespoons quick-cooking tapioca

2 teaspoons curry powder

½ teaspoon ground thyme

¼ teaspoon salt

¼ teaspoon black pepper

1½ pounds boneless, skinless chicken breasts

4 cups cooked brown rice

1. Combine tomatoes, artichokes, broth, onion, wine and capers in **CROCK-POT®** slow cooker.

2. Combine tapioca, curry, thyme, salt and pepper in small bowl. Add to **CROCK-POT®** slow cooker. Stir well to combine. Add chicken. Spoon sauce over chicken to coat. Cover; cook on LOW 7 to 9 hours or on HIGH 3 to 4 hours.

3. Serve chicken and vegetables over rice. Spoon sauce over chicken.

Makes 6 servings

Chicken Saltimbocca-Style

6 boneless, skinless chicken breasts

12 slices prosciutto

12 slices provolone cheese

½ cup all-purpose flour

½ cup grated Parmesan cheese

2 teaspoons salt

2 teaspoons black pepper

Olive oil

2 cans (10¾ ounces each) condensed cream of mushroom soup, undiluted

¾ cup white wine (optional)

1 teaspoon ground sage

1. Split each chicken breast into two thin pieces. Place between 2 pieces of waxed paper or plastic wrap. Pound until ⅓-inch thick. Place one slice of prosciutto and one slice of provolone on each chicken piece and roll up. Secure with toothpicks.

2. Combine flour, Parmesan cheese, salt and pepper on rimmed plate. Dredge chicken in flour mixture, shaking off excess. Reserve excess flour mixture.

3. Heat oil in skillet over medium heat until hot. Brown chicken on both sides, turning as it browns. Transfer to **CROCK-POT®** slow cooker. Add soup, wine, if desired, and sage. Cover; cook on LOW 5 to 7 hours or on HIGH 2 to 3 hours.

4. To thicken sauce, stir in 2 to 3 tablespoons leftover flour mixture and cook 15 minutes longer before serving.

Makes 6 servings

Herbed Turkey Breast with Orange Sauce

1 large onion, chopped

3 cloves garlic, minced

1 teaspoon dried rosemary

½ teaspoon black pepper

1 boneless, skinless turkey breast (3 pounds)

1½ cups orange juice

1. Place onion in **CROCK-POT®** slow cooker. Combine garlic, rosemary and pepper in small bowl; set aside.

2. Cut slices about three-fourths of the way through turkey at 2-inch intervals. Rub garlic mixture between slices. Place turkey, cut side up, in **CROCK-POT®** slow cooker. Pour orange juice over turkey. Cover; cook on LOW 7 to 8 hours.

3. Serve sliced turkey with orange sauce.

Makes 4 to 6 servings

 **Tip**

Don't peek! The **CROCK-POT®** slow cooker can take as long as 30 minutes to regain heat lost when the cover is removed. Only remove the cover when instructed to do so by the recipe.

Boneless Chicken Cacciatore

Olive oil

6 boneless, skinless chicken breasts, sliced in half horizontally

4 cups tomato-basil sauce or marinara sauce

1 cup coarsely chopped yellow onion

1 cup coarsely chopped green bell pepper

1 can (6 ounces) sliced mushrooms

¼ cup dry red wine (optional)

2 teaspoons minced garlic

2 teaspoons dried oregano, crushed

2 teaspoons dried thyme, crushed

2 teaspoons salt

2 teaspoons black pepper

1. Heat oil in skillet over medium heat until hot. Brown chicken on both sides, turning as it browns. Drain and transfer to **CROCK-POT®** slow cooker.

2. Add remaining ingredients, and stir well to combine. Cover; cook on LOW 5 to 7 hours or on HIGH 2 to 3 hours.

Makes 6 servings

Heidi's Chicken Supreme

1 can (10¾ ounces) condensed cream of chicken soup, undiluted

1 package (1 ounce) dry onion soup mix

6 boneless, skinless chicken breasts (about 1½ pounds)

½ cup imitation bacon bits or ½ pound bacon, crisp-cooked and crumbled

1 container (16 ounces) reduced-fat sour cream

1. Spray **CROCK-POT®** slow cooker with nonstick cooking spray. Combine soup and soup mix in medium bowl; mix well. Layer chicken breasts and soup mixture in **CROCK-POT®** slow cooker. Sprinkle with bacon. Cover; cook on LOW 8 hours or on HIGH 4 hours.

2. During last hour of cooking, stir in sour cream.

Makes 6 servings

Tip

Condensed cream of mushroom soup or condensed cream of celery soup can be substituted for cream of chicken soup.

Bacon and Onion Brisket

6 slices bacon, cut crosswise into ½-inch strips

1 flat-cut boneless brisket, seasoned with salt and black pepper (about 2½ pounds)

3 medium onions, sliced

2 cans (10½ ounces each) condensed beef consommé, undiluted

1. Cook bacon strips in large skillet over medium-high heat about 3 minutes. Do not overcook. Transfer bacon with slotted spoon to **CROCK-POT**® slow cooker.

2. Sear brisket in hot bacon fat on all sides, turning as it browns. Transfer to **CROCK-POT**® slow cooker.

3. Lower skillet heat to medium. Add sliced onions to skillet. Cook and stir 3 to 5 minutes or until softened. Add to **CROCK-POT**® slow cooker. Pour in consommé. Cover; cook on HIGH 6 to 8 hours or until meat is tender.

4. Transfer brisket to cutting board and let rest 10 minutes. Slice brisket against the grain into thin slices and arrange on platter. Add salt and pepper, if desired. Spoon bacon, onions and cooking liquid over brisket to serve.

Makes 6 servings

Asian Beef with Broccoli

1½ **pounds boneless beef chuck roast, about 1½ inches thick, sliced into thin strips***

1 **can (10½ ounces) condensed beef consommé, undiluted**

½ **cup oyster sauce**

2 **tablespoons cornstarch**

1 **bag (16 ounces) fresh broccoli florets**

Hot cooked rice

Sesame seeds (optional)

*To make slicing steak easier, place in freezer for 30 minutes to firm up.

1. Place beef in **CROCK-POT**® slow cooker. Pour consommé and oyster sauce over beef. Cover; cook on HIGH 3 hours.

2. Combine cornstarch and 2 tablespoons cooking liquid in small bowl. Add to **CROCK-POT**® slow cooker. Stir well to combine. Cover; cook on HIGH 15 minutes longer or until thickened.

3. Poke holes in broccoli bag with fork. Microwave on HIGH (100 %) 3 minutes. Empty bag into **CROCK-POT**® slow cooker. Gently toss beef and broccoli together. Serve over cooked rice. Garnish with sesame seeds.

Makes 4 to 6 servings

Easy Family Burritos

1 boneless beef chuck shoulder roast (2 to 3 pounds)

1 jar (24 ounces) or 2 jars (16 ounces each) salsa

Flour tortillas, warmed

Optional toppings: shredded cheese, sour cream, salsa, shredded lettuce, diced tomato, diced onion or guacamole

1. Place roast in **CROCK-POT®** slow cooker; top with salsa. Cover; cook on LOW 8 to 10 hours.

2. Remove beef from **CROCK-POT®** slow cooker. Shred beef with 2 forks. Return to cooking liquid and mix well. Cover; cook 1 to 2 hours longer or until heated through.

3. Serve shredded beef wrapped in warm tortillas. Top as desired.

Makes 8 servings

Braised Fruited Lamb

6 tablespoons extra-virgin olive oil

4 pounds lamb shanks

2 tablespoons salt

2 tablespoons black pepper

1 cup dried apricots

1 cup dried figs

1½ cups water

½ cup white vinegar or white wine

¼ cup raspberry jam

½ teaspoon ground allspice

½ teaspoon ground cinnamon

1. Preheat broiler. Brush oil on lamb shanks and season with salt and pepper. Place shanks in broiler-safe pan and broil in oven to brown, about 5 minutes per side. Remove from oven and transfer to **CROCK-POT®** slow cooker. Add dried fruits.

2. Combine water, vinegar, jam, allspice and cinnamon in small bowl. Pour over lamb shanks. Cover; cook on LOW 8 to 9 hours or on HIGH 4 to 5 hours.

Makes 6 to 8 servings

Herbed Artichoke Chicken

- 1½ pounds boneless, skinless chicken breasts
- 1 can (14 ounces) tomatoes, drained and diced
- 1 can (14 ounces) artichoke hearts in water, drained
- 1 small onion, chopped
- ½ cup kalamata olives, pitted and sliced
- 1 cup fat-free chicken broth
- ¼ cup dry white wine
- 3 tablespoons quick-cooking tapioca
- 2 teaspoons curry powder
- 1 tablespoon chopped fresh Italian parsley
- 1 teaspoon dried sweet basil
- 1 teaspoon dried thyme leaves
- ½ teaspoon salt
- ½ teaspoon freshly ground black pepper

1. Combine all ingredients in **CROCK-POT®** slow cooker. Mix thoroughly.

2. Cover; cook on LOW 6 to 8 hours or on HIGH 3½ to 4 hours or until chicken is no longer pink in center.

Makes 6 servings

Fantastic Pot Roast

- 1 can (12 ounces) cola
- 1 bottle (10 ounces) chili sauce
- 2 cloves garlic (optional)
- 2½ pounds boneless beef chuck roast

Combine cola, chili sauce and garlic, if desired, in **CROCK-POT®** slow cooker. Add beef, and turn to coat. Cover; cook on LOW 6 to 8 hours. Serve with sauce.

Makes 6 servings

Easy Beef Stroganoff

3   cans (10¾ ounces each) condensed cream of mushroom soup, undiluted

1   cup sour cream

½   cup water

1   package (1 ounce) dry onion soup mix

2   pounds beef stew meat, cut into 1-inch pieces

Combine soup, sour cream, water and soup mix in **CROCK-POT**® slow cooker. Add beef; stir until well coated. Cover; cook on LOW 6 hours or on HIGH 3 hours.

Makes 4 to 6 servings

Fresh Herbed Turkey Breast

2   tablespoons butter, softened

¼   cup fresh sage leaves, minced

¼   cup fresh tarragon leaves, minced

1   clove garlic, minced

1   teaspoon black pepper

½   teaspoon salt

1   (4-pound) split turkey breast

1   tablespoon plus 1½ teaspoons cornstarch

1. Mix together butter, sage, tarragon, garlic, pepper and salt. Rub butter mixture all over turkey breast.

2. Place turkey breast in **CROCK-POT**® slow cooker. Cover; cook on LOW 8 to 10 hours or on HIGH 4 to 5 hours or until turkey is no longer pink in the center.

3. Transfer turkey breast to serving platter; cover with foil to keep warm. Turn **CROCK-POT**® slow cooker to HIGH. Slowly whisk cornstarch into cooking juices; cook until thickened and smooth. Slice turkey breast. Serve sauce on the side.

Makes 8 servings

Turkey Scalloppini in Alfredo Sauce

2 tablespoons all-purpose flour

¼ teaspoon salt, or to taste

¼ teaspoon black pepper

1 pound turkey tenderloins, cut lengthwise in half

1 tablespoon butter

1 tablespoon olive oil

1 cup refrigerated Alfredo pasta sauce

12 ounces spinach noodles

¼ cup shredded Asiago or Parmesan cheese

1. Place flour, salt and pepper in resealable plastic food storage bag. Add turkey and shake well to coat. Heat butter and oil in large skillet over medium-high heat until hot. Add turkey in single layer. Brown on all sides, about 3 minutes per side. Arrange turkey in single layer in **CROCK-POT®** slow cooker.

2. Add Alfredo sauce. Cover; cook on LOW 1 to 1½ hours or until turkey is tender.

3. Meanwhile, cook noodles until tender. Drain and place in large shallow bowl. Spoon turkey and sauce over noodles. Garnish with cheese.

Makes 4 servings

Corned Beef and Cabbage

1 head cabbage (about 1½ pounds), cut into 6 wedges

4 ounces baby carrots

1 corned beef (about 3 pounds) with seasoning packet (perforate packet with knife tip)

4 cups water

⅓ cup prepared mustard

⅓ cup honey

1. Place cabbage and carrots in **CROCK-POT®** slow cooker. Place seasoning packet on top. Add corned beef, fat side up. Pour in water. Cover; cook on LOW 10 hours.

2. Remove and discard seasoning packet. Combine mustard and honey in small bowl. Slice beef; serve with vegetables and mustard sauce.

Makes 6 servings

Big Al's Hot and Sweet Sausage Sandwich

4 to 5 pounds hot Italian sausage links

1 jar (26 ounces) spaghetti sauce

1 large Vidalia onion (or other sweet onion), sliced

1 green bell pepper, cored, seeded and sliced

1 red bell pepper, cored, seeded and sliced

¼ cup packed dark brown sugar

Italian rolls, cut in half

Provolone cheese, sliced (optional)

1. Combine sausages, spaghetti sauce, onion, bell peppers and brown sugar in **CROCK-POT®** slow cooker. Cover; cook on LOW 8 to 10 hours or on HIGH 4 to 6 hours.

2. Place sausages in rolls. Top with vegetable mixture. Add provolone cheese, if desired.

Makes 8 to 10 servings

Chipotle Chicken Casserole

1 pound boneless, skinless chicken thighs, cut into cubes

1 teaspoon salt

1 teaspoon ground cumin

1 bay leaf

1 chipotle pepper in adobo sauce, minced

1 medium onion, diced

1 can (15 ounces) navy beans, rinsed and drained

1 can (15 ounces) black beans, rinsed and drained

1 can (14½ ounces) crushed tomatoes, undrained

1½ cups chicken broth

½ cup orange juice

¼ cup chopped fresh cilantro (optional)

Combine chicken, salt, cumin, bay leaf, chipotle pepper, onion, beans, tomatoes with juice, broth and orange juice in **CROCK-POT®** slow cooker. Cover; cook on LOW 7 to 8 hours or on HIGH 3½ to 4 hours. Remove bay leaf before serving. Garnish with cilantro.

Makes 6 servings

Slow Cooker Chicken Dinner

  4 boneless, skinless chicken breasts
  1 can (10¾ ounces) condensed cream of chicken soup, undiluted
  ⅓ cup milk
  1 package (6 ounces) stuffing mix
1⅔ cups water

1. Place chicken in **CROCK-POT®** slow cooker. Combine soup and milk in small bowl; mix well. Pour soup mixture over chicken.

2. Combine stuffing mix and water. Spoon stuffing over chicken. Cover; cook on LOW 6 to 8 hours.

Makes 4 servings

Hungarian Lamb Goulash

  1 package (16 ounces) frozen cut green beans, thawed
  1 cup chopped onion
1¼ pounds lean lamb for stew, cut into 1-inch cubes
  1 can (15 ounces) chunky tomato sauce
1¾ cups fat-free reduced-sodium chicken broth
  1 can (6 ounces) tomato paste
  4 teaspoons paprika
  3 cups hot cooked egg noodles

1. Place green beans and onion in **CROCK-POT®** slow cooker. Top with lamb.

2. Combine tomato sauce, broth, tomato paste and paprika in large bowl; mix well. Pour over lamb mixture. Cover; cook on LOW 6 to 8 hours. Stir goulash before serving over noodles.

Makes 6 servings

Lemon and Herb Turkey Breast

1 split turkey breast (about 3 pounds)

½ cup lemon juice

6 cloves garlic, minced

¼ teaspoon dried parsley

¼ teaspoon dried tarragon

¼ teaspoon dried rosemary

¼ teaspoon dried sage

¼ teaspoon salt

¼ teaspoon black pepper

½ cup dry white wine

1. Place turkey breast in **CROCK-POT®** slow cooker, adjusting turkey to fit as needed.

2. Combine remaining ingredients in small bowl. Pour over turkey breast. Cover; cook on LOW 8 to 10 hours or on HIGH 4 to 5 hours.

Makes 6 servings

Barley Beef Stroganoff

⅔ cup uncooked pearl barley (not quick-cooking)

2½ cups fat-free low-sodium vegetable broth or water

1 package (6 ounces) sliced mushrooms

½ teaspoon dried marjoram

½ pound 95% lean ground beef

½ cup chopped celery

½ cup minced green onions

½ teaspoon black pepper

¼ cup fat-free half-and-half

Minced fresh parsley (optional)

1. Place barley, broth, mushrooms and marjoram in **CROCK-POT®** slow cooker. Cover; cook on LOW 6 to 7 hours.

2. Cook and stir ground beef in large nonstick skillet over medium heat until browned and crumbly, about 7 minutes. Drain and discard fat. Add celery, green onions and pepper; cook and stir 3 minutes. Transfer to **CROCK-POT®** slow cooker.

3. Mix in half-and-half. Cover; cook on HIGH 10 to 15 minutes, until beef is hot and vegetables are tender. Garnish with parsley.

Makes 4 servings

German-Style Bratwurst

4 pounds bratwurst

2 pounds sauerkraut, drained

6 apples, peeled, cored and thinly sliced

1 white onion, thinly sliced

1 teaspoon caraway seed

   Black pepper

5 bottles (12 ounces each) any German-style beer

Combine all ingredients in **CROCK-POT®** slow cooker. Cover; cook on LOW 6 to 8 hours or on HIGH 3 to 4 hours or until done.

Makes 6 to 8 servings

Tip

This hearty, homestyle main dish can also be served as a great appetizer. Just cut the bratwurst into 1-inch pieces before adding them to your **CROCK-POT®** slow cooker. Serve on split-top dinner rolls for delicious mini-brat sandwiches!

Scalloped Potatoes and Ham

6 large russet potatoes, sliced into ¼-inch rounds

1 ham steak (about 1½ pounds), cut into cubes

1 can (10¾ ounces) condensed cream of mushroom soup, undiluted

1 soup can water

1 cup (about 4 ounces) shredded Cheddar cheese

   Grill seasoning, to taste

1. Coat **CROCK-POT®** slow cooker with nonstick cooking spray. Arrange potatoes and ham in layers in **CROCK-POT®** slow cooker.

2. Combine soup, water, cheese and grill seasoning in medium bowl; pour over potatoes and ham. Cover; cook on HIGH about 3½ hours or until potatoes are fork-tender. Turn heat to LOW and cook 1 hour.

Makes 5 to 6 servings

Beef with Green Chiles

¼ cup plus **1** tablespoon all-purpose flour, divided

½ teaspoon salt

¼ teaspoon black pepper

1 pound beef stew meat

1 tablespoon vegetable oil

2 cloves garlic, minced

1 cup beef broth

1 can (7 ounces) diced mild green chiles, drained

½ teaspoon dried oregano

2 tablespoons water

Hot cooked rice (optional)

Diced tomato (optional)

1. Combine ¼ cup flour, salt and pepper in resealable food storage bag. Add beef; shake to coat beef. Heat oil in large skillet over medium-high heat. Add beef and garlic. Brown beef on all sides. Place beef mixture into **CROCK-POT®** slow cooker. Add broth to skillet, scraping up any browned bits. Pour broth mixture into **CROCK-POT®** slow cooker. Add green chiles and oregano.

2. Cover; cook on LOW 7 to 8 hours. For thicker sauce, combine remaining 1 tablespoon flour and water in small bowl, stirring until mixture is smooth. Stir mixture into **CROCK-POT®** slow cooker; mix well. Cover and cook until thickened.

3. Serve with rice and garnish with diced tomato.

Makes 4 servings

Meatballs in Burgundy Sauce

60 frozen fully cooked meatballs, partially thawed and separated

3 cups chopped onions

1½ cups water

1 cup Burgundy or other red wine

2 packages (about 1 ounce each) beef gravy mix

¼ cup ketchup

1 tablespoon dried oregano

1 package (8 ounces) egg noodles

1. Combine meatballs, onions, water, wine, gravy mix, ketchup and oregano in **CROCK-POT®** slow cooker; stir to blend.

2. Cover; cook on LOW 8 to 10 hours or on HIGH 4 to 5 hours.

3. Meanwhile, cook noodles according to package directions. Serve meatballs with noodles.

Makes 6 to 8 servings

Serving Suggestion
Meatballs may also be served as an appetizer with remaining sauce as a dip.

Slow-Cooked Pot Roast

- 1 tablespoon vegetable oil
- 1 beef brisket (3 to 4 pounds)
- 3 teaspoons garlic powder, divided
- 3 teaspoons salt, divided
- 3 teaspoons black pepper, divided
- 1 teaspoon paprika, divided
- 5 to 6 new potatoes, cut into quarters
- 4 to 5 medium onions, sliced
- 1 pound baby carrots
- 1 can (about 14½ ounces) beef broth

1. Heat oil in large skillet over high heat. Brown brisket on all sides. Add to **CROCK-POT®** slow cooker. Season with 1½ teaspoons garlic powder, 1½ teaspoons salt, 1½ teaspoons pepper and ½ teaspoon paprika; set aside.

2. Season potatoes and onions with remaining 1½ teaspoons garlic powder, 1½ teaspoons salt, 1½ teaspoons pepper and ½ teaspoon paprika. Add potatoes and onions to **CROCK-POT®** slow cooker.

3. Add carrots and broth to **CROCK-POT®** slow cooker. Cover; cook on LOW 8 to 10 hours or on HIGH 4 to 5 hours or until beef is tender.

Makes 6 to 8 servings

Tip

Because **CROCK-POT®** slow cookers cook at a low heat for a long time, they're a great way to cook dishes calling for less-tender cuts of meat, since long, slow cooking helps tenderize these cuts.

Cashew Chicken

- 6 boneless, skinless chicken breasts
- 1½ cups cashews
- 1 cup sliced mushrooms
- 1 cup sliced celery
- 1 can (10¾ ounces) condensed cream of mushroom soup, undiluted
- ¼ cup chopped green onion
- 2 tablespoons butter
- 1½ tablespoons soy sauce
  Hot cooked rice

Combine chicken, cashews, mushrooms, celery, soup, onion, butter and soy sauce in **CROCK-POT®** slow cooker. Cover; cook on LOW 6 to 8 hours or on HIGH 4 to 6 hours or until done. Serve over rice.

Makes 6 servings

Brisket with Bacon, Bleu Cheese & Onions

2   large sweet onions, sliced into ½-inch rounds*

6   slices bacon

1   flat-cut boneless beef brisket (about 3½ pounds)

Salt and black pepper, to taste

2   cans (10½ ounces each) condensed beef consommé, undiluted

1   teaspoon cracked black peppercorns

¾   cup crumbled bleu cheese

Maui, Vidalia or Walla Walla onions are preferred.

1. Coat **CROCK-POT®** slow cooker with nonstick cooking spray. Line bottom with onion slices.

2. Heat large skillet over medium-high heat until hot. Add bacon and cook only until chewy, not crisp. Remove from skillet using slotted spoon. Drain on paper towels and chop.

3. Season brisket with salt and pepper. Place in skillet. Sear brisket in bacon fat on all sides, turning as it browns. Transfer to **CROCK-POT®** slow cooker.

4. Pour in consommé. Sprinkle brisket with peppercorns and half of reserved bacon. Cover; cook on HIGH 5 to 7 hours or until meat is tender.

5. Transfer brisket to cutting board and let stand 10 minutes. Slice against the grain into ¾-inch slices. To serve, arrange onions on serving platter and spread slices of brisket on top. Sprinkle on bleu cheese and remaining bacon. Add salt and pepper to cooking liquid, if desired, and serve with brisket.

Makes 6 to 8 servings

Smothered Beef Patties

Worcestershire sauce, to taste

Garlic powder, to taste

Salt and black pepper, to taste

1   can (about 14 ounces) Mexican-style diced tomatoes with green chiles, undrained, divided

8   frozen beef patties, unthawed

1   onion, cut into 8 slices

Sprinkle bottom of **CROCK-POT®** slow cooker with small amount of Worcestershire sauce, garlic powder, salt, pepper and 2 tablespoons tomatoes with juice. Add 1 frozen beef patty. Top with small amount of Worcestershire sauce, garlic powder, salt, pepper, 2 tablespoons tomatoes with juice and 1 onion slice. Repeat layers 7 times. Cover; cook on LOW 8 hours.

Makes 8 servings

lighter bites

Chicken Enchilada Roll-Ups

6 boneless, skinless chicken breasts (about 1½ pounds)

½ cup plus 2 tablespoons all-purpose flour, divided

½ teaspoon salt

2 tablespoons butter

1 cup chicken broth

1 small onion, diced

¼ to ½ cup canned jalapeño peppers, sliced

½ teaspoon dried oregano

2 tablespoons heavy cream or milk

6 (7- to 8-inch) flour tortillas

6 thin slices American cheese or American cheese with jalapeño peppers

1. Cut each chicken breast lengthwise into 2 or 3 strips. Combine ½ cup flour and salt in resealable plastic food storage bag. Add chicken strips and shake to coat with flour mixture. Melt butter in large skillet over medium heat. Brown chicken strips in batches, cooking 2 to 3 minutes per side. Transfer to **CROCK-POT**® slow cooker.

2. Add chicken broth to skillet and scrape up any browned bits. Pour broth mixture into **CROCK-POT**® slow cooker. Add onion, jalapeño peppers and oregano. Cover; cook on LOW 7 to 8 hours or on HIGH 3 to 4 hours.

3. Blend remaining 2 tablespoons flour and cream in small bowl until smooth. Stir into chicken mixture. Cook, uncovered, on HIGH 15 minutes or until thickened. Spoon chicken mixture onto center of flour tortillas. Top each with cheese slice. Fold up tortillas and serve.

Makes 6 servings

Suzie's Sloppy Joes

3 pounds 95% lean ground beef

1 cup chopped onion

3 cloves garlic, minced

1¼ cups ketchup

1 cup chopped red bell pepper

¼ cup plus 1 tablespoon Worcestershire sauce

¼ cup packed dark brown sugar

3 tablespoons prepared mustard

3 tablespoons vinegar

2 teaspoons chili powder

Toasted hamburger buns

1. Cook and stir ground beef, onion and garlic in large nonstick skillet over medium-high heat until beef is browned and onion is tender. Drain and discard fat.

2. Combine ketchup, bell pepper, Worcestershire sauce, brown sugar, mustard, vinegar and chili powder in **CROCK-POT®** slow cooker. Stir in beef mixture. Cover; cook on LOW 6 to 8 hours. To serve, spoon mixture onto hamburger buns.

Makes 8 servings

Tip

Recipes often provide a range of cooking times to account for variables, such as the temperature of the ingredients before cooking, the quantity of food in your **CROCK-POT®** slow cooker and the altitude; cooking times will be longer at higher altitudes.

Chicken Parisienne

6 boneless, skinless chicken breasts (about 1½ pounds), cubed

½ teaspoon salt

½ teaspoon black pepper

½ teaspoon paprika

1 can (10¾ ounces) condensed cream of mushroom or cream of chicken soup, undiluted

2 cans (4 ounces each) sliced mushrooms, drained

½ cup dry white wine

1 container (8 ounces) sour cream

Hot cooked egg noodles

1. Place chicken in **CROCK-POT®** slow cooker. Sprinkle with salt, pepper and paprika. Add soup, mushrooms and wine; mix well. Cover; cook on HIGH 2 to 3 hours.

2. Add sour cream during last 30 minutes of cooking. Serve over noodles.

Makes 6 servings

Tip
Opening the lid and checking on food in the **CROCK-POT®** slow cooker can affect both cooking time and results. Due to the nature of slow cooking, there's no need to stir the food unless the recipe method says to do so.

Thai Steak Salad

Steak

¼ cup soy sauce

3 cloves garlic, minced

3 tablespoons honey

1 pound boneless beef chuck steak, about ¾ inch thick

Dressing

¼ cup hoisin sauce

2 tablespoons creamy peanut butter

½ cup water

1 tablespoon minced fresh ginger

1 tablespoon ketchup or tomato paste

2 teaspoons lime juice

1 teaspoon sugar

2 cloves garlic, minced

¼ teaspoon hot chili sauce or sriracha*

Salad

½ head savoy cabbage, shredded

1 bag (10 ounces) romaine lettuce with carrots and red cabbage

1 cup fresh cilantro leaves

½ cup chopped peanuts

¾ cup chopped mango

Fresh lime wedges

Sriracha is a Thai hot sauce, sometimes called "rooster sauce" because of the label on the bottle, and is available in Asian specialty markets.

1. Prepare steak: Coat **CROCK-POT®** slow cooker with nonstick cooking spray. Combine soy sauce, garlic and honey in small bowl. Pour into **CROCK-POT®** slow cooker. Add steak, turning to coat. Cover; cook on HIGH 3 hours or until tender.

2. Transfer steak to cutting board and let stand 10 minutes. Slice against the grain into ¼-inch strips. Cover with plastic wrap and refrigerate until needed.

3. Prepare dressing: Blend hoisin sauce and peanut butter until smooth. Add remaining dressing ingredients and mix until well blended.

4. Assemble salad: Toss cabbage and romaine salad mixture with dressing in large salad bowl. Top with reserved steak. Sprinkle with cilantro, peanuts and mango. Serve with lime wedges.

Makes 4 to 6 servings

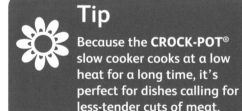

Tip

Because the **CROCK-POT®** slow cooker cooks at a low heat for a long time, it's perfect for dishes calling for less-tender cuts of meat.

Chicken Sausage with Peppers & Basil

1 tablespoon olive oil

½ yellow onion, minced (about ½ cup)

1 clove garlic, minced

1 pound sweet or hot Italian chicken sausage

1 can (28 ounces) whole tomatoes, drained and seeded

½ red bell pepper, cut into ½-inch slices

½ yellow bell pepper, cut into ½-inch slices

½ orange bell pepper, cut into ½-inch slices

¾ cup chopped fresh basil

Crushed red pepper flakes, to taste

Salt and black pepper, to taste

Hot cooked pasta

1. Heat oil in large skillet over medium heat. Add onion and garlic and cook until translucent.

2. Remove sausage from casings and cut into 1-inch chunks. Add to skillet and cook 3 to 4 minutes or until just beginning to brown. Transfer to **CROCK-POT**® slow cooker with slotted spoon, skimming off some fat.

3. Add tomatoes, bell peppers, basil, red pepper flakes, salt and black pepper to **CROCK-POT**® slow cooker and stir to blend. Cook on HIGH 2½ to 3 hours or until bell peppers have softened. Adjust seasonings to taste. Serve over pasta.

Makes 4 servings

Greek Chicken Pitas with Creamy Mustard Sauce

Filling

1 medium green bell pepper, cored, seeded and sliced into ½-inch strips

1 medium onion, cut into 8 wedges

1 pound boneless, skinless chicken breasts, rinsed and patted dry

1 tablespoon extra-virgin olive oil

2 teaspoons dried Greek seasoning blend

¼ teaspoon salt

Sauce

¼ cup plain fat-free yogurt

¼ cup mayonnaise

1 tablespoon prepared mustard

¼ teaspoon salt

4 whole pita rounds

½ cup crumbled feta cheese

Optional toppings: sliced cucumbers, sliced tomatoes, kalamata olives

1. Coat **CROCK-POT®** slow cooker with nonstick cooking spray. Place bell pepper and onion in bottom. Add chicken, and drizzle with oil. Sprinkle evenly with Greek seasoning and ¼ teaspoon salt. Cover; cook on HIGH 1¾ hours or until chicken is no longer pink in center (vegetables will be slightly tender-crisp).

2. Remove chicken and slice. Remove vegetables using slotted spoon.

3. Prepare sauce: Combine yogurt, mayonnaise, mustard and ¼ teaspoon salt in small bowl. Whisk until smooth.

4. Warm pitas according to package directions. Cut in half, and layer with chicken, sauce, vegetables and feta cheese. Top as desired.

Makes 4 servings

Spinach Risotto

- 2 teaspoons butter
- 2 teaspoons olive oil
- 3 tablespoons finely chopped shallot
- 1¼ cups arborio rice
- ½ cup dry white wine
- 3 cups chicken broth
- ½ teaspoon salt
- 2 cups baby spinach
- ¼ cup grated Parmesan cheese
- 2 tablespoons pine nuts, toasted

1. Melt butter in medium skillet over medium heat; add olive oil. Add shallot and cook, stirring frequently, until softened but not browned.

2. Stir in rice and cook 2 to 3 minutes or until chalky and well coated. Stir in wine and cook until reduced by half. Transfer to **CROCK-POT®** slow cooker. Stir in broth and salt.

3. Cover and cook on HIGH 2 to 2½ hours or until rice is almost cooked but still contains a little liquid. Stir in spinach. Cover and cook 15 to 20 minutes or until spinach is cooked and rice is tender and creamy. Gently stir in Parmesan cheese and pine nuts just before serving.

Makes 4 servings

Turkey Vegetable Chili Mac

¾ **pound ground turkey breast**

1 **can (about 15 ounces) black beans, rinsed and drained**

1 **can (about 14 ounces) Mexican-style diced tomatoes**

1 **can (about 14 ounces) no-salt-added diced tomatoes**

1 **cup frozen corn**

½ **cup chopped onion**

2 **cloves garlic, minced**

1 **teaspoon Mexican seasoning**

½ **cup (about 2 ounces) uncooked elbow macaroni**

⅓ **cup sour cream**

1. Lightly coat large nonstick skillet with nonstick cooking spray. Add turkey; cook until browned. Transfer to **CROCK-POT®** slow cooker. Add beans, tomatoes, corn, onion, garlic and seasoning. Cover; cook on LOW 4 to 5 hours.

2. Stir in macaroni. Cover; cook 10 minutes. Stir. Cover; cook 20 to 30 minutes or until pasta is tender. Serve with sour cream.

Makes 6 servings

 **Tip**

Substitute 2 ounces of any other pasta. Short pasta shapes like cavatappi, penne or rigatoni can be added straight out of the packages. Longer shapes such as linguine, fettuccine or spaghetti should be broken in halves or thirds so they can be fully immersed in the sauce.

Tarragon Turkey and Pasta

1½ to 2 pounds turkey tenderloins

½ cup thinly sliced celery

¼ cup thinly sliced green onions

4 tablespoons fresh tarragon, minced, divided

¼ cup dry white wine

1 teaspoon salt

1 teaspoon freshly ground black pepper

½ cup plain yogurt

1 tablespoon fresh minced Italian parsley

1 tablespoon lemon juice

1½ tablespoons cornstarch

2 tablespoons water

4 cups pasta of your choice, cooked al dente

1. Combine turkey, celery, green onions, 2 tablespoons fresh tarragon, wine, salt and pepper in **CROCK-POT®** slow cooker. Mix thoroughly. Cover; cook on LOW 6 to 8 hours or on HIGH 3½ to 4 hours or until turkey is no longer pink.

2. Remove turkey; cut into ½-inch-thick medallions. Turn **CROCK-POT®** slow cooker to HIGH. Stir yogurt, remaining 2 tablespoons fresh tarragon, parsley and lemon juice into cooking liquid.

3. Combine cornstarch and water in small bowl. Stir into cooking liquid and cook until thickened. Serve turkey medallions over pasta. Drizzle with tarragon sauce.

Makes 4 servings

 Note

This easy dish is elegant enough to serve at a dinner party.

Ginger Beef with Peppers and Mushrooms

1½ **pounds beef top round steak for London broil, cut into ¾-inch cubes**

24 **baby carrots**

1 **red bell pepper, seeded and chopped**

1 **green bell pepper, seeded and chopped**

1 **onion, chopped**

1 **package (8 ounces) fresh mushrooms, cut in halves**

2 **tablespoons grated fresh ginger**

1 **cup reduced-sodium beef broth**

½ **cup hoisin sauce**

¼ **cup quick-cooking tapioca**

Hot cooked white rice (optional)

Combine all ingredients except cooked rice in **CROCK-POT®** slow cooker. Cover and cook on LOW 8 to 9 hours. Serve over white rice, if desired.

Makes 6 servings

Cream Cheese Chicken with Broccoli

4 pounds boneless, skinless chicken breasts, cut into ½-inch pieces

1 tablespoon olive oil

1 package (1 ounce) Italian salad dressing mix

2 cups sliced mushrooms

1 cup chopped onion

1 can (10¾ ounces) condensed low-fat cream of chicken soup, undiluted

1 bag (10 ounces) frozen broccoli florets, thawed

1 package (8 ounces) low-fat cream cheese, cubed

¼ cup dry sherry

Hot cooked pasta

1. Toss chicken with olive oil. Sprinkle with Italian salad dressing mix. Place in **CROCK-POT®** slow cooker. Cover; cook on LOW 3 hours.

2. Coat large skillet with nonstick cooking spray. Add mushrooms and onion; cook 5 minutes over medium heat or until onion is tender, stirring occasionally.

3. Add soup, broccoli, cream cheese and sherry to skillet; cook and stir until hot. Transfer to **CROCK-POT®** slow cooker. Cover; cook on LOW 1 hour. Serve chicken and sauce over pasta.

Makes 10 to 12 servings

Tip

For easier preparation, cut up the chicken and vegetables for this recipe the night before. Do not place the **CROCK-POT®** stoneware in the refrigerator. Instead, wrap the chicken and vegetables separately, and store in the refrigerator.

Grandma Ruth's Minestrone

1 pound ground beef

1 cup dried red beans

1 package (16 ounces) frozen mixed vegetables

2 cans (8 ounces each) tomato sauce

1 can (14 ounces) diced tomatoes, drained

¼ head shredded cabbage

1 cup chopped onions

1 cup chopped celery

½ cup chopped fresh parsley

1 tablespoon dried basil

1 tablespoon Italian seasoning

1 teaspoon salt

1 teaspoon black pepper

1 cup cooked elbow macaroni

1. Combine ground beef and beans in **CROCK-POT®** slow cooker. Cover; cook on HIGH 2 hours.

2. Add all remaining ingredients except macaroni and stir to blend. Cover; cook on LOW 6 to 8 hours or until beans are tender.

3. Stir in macaroni. Cover; cook on HIGH 1 hour.

Makes 4 servings

Thai Chili Chicken and Noodles

2 teaspoons olive oil

1½ pounds boneless, skinless chicken breasts, cut into thin strips

1 bottle (about 10 ounces) Asian-style sweet chili sauce*

3 tablespoons creamy peanut butter

3 cloves garlic, minced

1 can (about 14 ounces) chicken broth

1 package (8 ounces) vermicelli noodles

1 cup shredded cabbage and carrot mix

Bean sprouts (optional)

Chopped fresh cilantro (optional)

Chopped roasted peanuts (optional)

Asian-style sweet chili sauce can be found in the ethnic foods aisle of many supermarkets.

1. Heat oil in large nonstick skillet over medium-high heat. Add chicken (in batches, if necessary) and cook, stirring frequently, until lightly browned on all sides. Transfer to **CROCK-POT®** slow cooker.

2. Stir together sweet chili sauce, peanut butter and garlic in a small bowl. Pour over chicken. Stir until chicken is well coated with sauce. Add chicken broth and stir well. Cover and cook on LOW 2 hours.

3. Add noodles and cabbage and carrot mix. Cover and cook 30 minutes more or until noodles and vegetables are tender. Garnish with bean sprouts, cilantro and peanuts, if desired.

Makes 4 to 6 servings

Easy Cheesy Aruban-Inspired Chicken

1 can (14½ ounces) diced tomatoes in sauce

½ cup chicken broth

¼ cup ketchup

2 teaspoons yellow mustard

1 teaspoon Worcestershire sauce

¾ teaspoon hot sauce

3 cloves garlic, crushed

½ teaspoon salt

¼ teaspoon black pepper

1 large onion, thinly sliced

1 large green bell pepper, seeded, cored and thinly sliced

¼ cup sliced black olives

¼ cup raisins

1 tablespoon capers

4 to 6 chicken thighs or 4 boneless, skinless breasts

1½ cups (6 ounces) shredded Edam or Gouda cheese

2 tablespoons chopped flat-leaf parsley

Hot cooked rice (optional)

1. Coat **CROCK-POT®** slow cooker with nonstick cooking spray. Add tomatoes in sauce, broth, ketchup, mustard, Worcestershire sauce, hot sauce, garlic, salt and black pepper. Stir well to combine.

2. Add onion, bell pepper, olives, raisins and capers. Stir well to combine.

3. Add chicken. Spoon sauce mixture over chicken until well coated. Cover; cook on HIGH 3 to 4 hours or until chicken is fork-tender.

4. Turn off **CROCK-POT®** slow cooker and uncover. Sprinkle cheese and parsley over chicken. Cover and let stand 3 to 5 minutes or until cheese is melted. Serve over rice, if desired.

Makes 4 servings

Kale, Olive Oil and Parmesan Soup

- 2 tablespoons olive oil
- 1 small Spanish onion, sliced
- 3 cloves garlic, minced

  Kosher salt and black pepper
- 2 pounds kale, washed and chopped
- 8 cups chicken stock

  Parmesan cheese, grated

  Extra-virgin olive oil to garnish

1. Heat olive oil in large, heavy skillet over medium-high heat. Add onion and garlic; season with salt and pepper. Cook 4 to 5 minutes, stirring often, or until onion begins to soften. Stir in kale and cook, stirring, 2 to 4 minutes or until kale becomes bright green and tender. Remove from heat and reserve in refrigerator until needed.

2. Add chicken stock to **CROCK-POT**® slow cooker. Cover and cook on LOW 6 hours or on HIGH 3½ hours.

3. Add kale mixture and cook until heated through, 15 to 20 minutes.

4. Spoon soup into individual serving bowls, sprinkle with Parmesan and drizzle with extra-virgin olive oil immediately before serving.

Makes 4 to 6 servings

Chicken in Honey Sauce

- 6 boneless, skinless chicken breasts (about 1½ pounds)

  Salt and black pepper
- 2 cups honey
- 1 cup soy sauce
- ½ cup ketchup
- ¼ cup vegetable oil
- 2 cloves garlic, minced

  Sesame seeds (optional)

1. Place chicken in **CROCK-POT**® slow cooker; season with salt and pepper.

2. Combine honey, soy sauce, ketchup, oil and garlic in medium bowl. Pour over chicken. Cover; cook on LOW 6 to 8 hours or on HIGH 3 to 4 hours.

3. Garnish with sesame seeds before serving. Serve extra sauce on side, if desired.

Makes 6 servings

Chicken Teriyaki

1	pound boneless, skinless chicken tenders
1	can (6 ounces) pineapple juice
¼	cup soy sauce
1	tablespoon sugar
1	tablespoon minced fresh ginger
1	tablespoon minced garlic
1	tablespoon vegetable oil
1	tablespoon molasses
24	cherry tomatoes (optional)
2	cups hot cooked rice

Combine all ingredients except rice in **CROCK-POT**® slow cooker. Cover; cook on LOW 2 hours or until chicken is tender. Serve chicken and sauce over rice.

Makes 4 servings

Lemon Pork Chops

1	tablespoon vegetable oil
4	boneless pork chops
3	cans (8 ounces each) tomato sauce
1	large onion, quartered and sliced
1	large green bell pepper, cut into strips
1	tablespoon lemon-pepper seasoning
1	tablespoon Worcestershire sauce
1	large lemon, quartered
	Lemon wedges (optional)

1. Heat oil in large skillet over medium-low heat. Brown pork chops on both sides. Drain excess fat and discard. Transfer to **CROCK-POT**® slow cooker.

2. Combine tomato sauce, onion, bell pepper, lemon-pepper seasoning and Worcestershire sauce. Add to **CROCK-POT**® slow cooker.

3. Squeeze juice from lemon quarters over mixture; drop squeezed lemons into **CROCK-POT**® slow cooker. Cover; cook on LOW 6 to 8 hours or until pork is tender. Remove squeezed lemons before serving. Serve with additional lemon wedges, if desired.

Makes 4 servings

Penne Pasta Zuppa

- 1 can (15 ounces) white beans
- 2 medium yellow squash, diced
- 2 ripe tomatoes, diced
- 2 small red potatoes, cubed
- 2 leeks, sliced lengthwise into quarters then chopped
- 1 carrot, peeled and diced
- ¼ pound fresh green beans, washed, stemmed and diced
- 2 fresh sage leaves, minced
- 1 teaspoon salt
- ½ teaspoon black pepper
- 8 cups water
- ¼ pound uncooked penne pasta
  Grated Romano cheese (optional)

1. Combine beans, squash, tomatoes, potatoes, leeks, carrot, green beans, sage, salt and pepper in **CROCK-POT**® slow cooker. Add water. Stir well to combine. Cover; cook on HIGH 2 hours, stirring occasionally. Turn **CROCK-POT**® slow cooker to LOW. Cook, covered, 8 hours longer. Stir occasionally.

2. Turn **CROCK-POT**® slow cooker to HIGH. Add pasta. Cover; cook 30 minutes longer or until pasta is done.

3. To serve, garnish with Romano cheese.

Makes 6 servings

Chicken Sausage Pilaf

- 1 pound uncooked chicken or turkey sausage, casings removed
- 1 package (about 7 ounces) uncooked chicken-flavored rice and vermicelli pasta mix
- 4 cups chicken broth
- 2 stalks celery, diced
- ¼ cup slivered almonds
  Salt and black pepper

1. Brown sausage in large skillet over medium-high heat, stirring to break up meat. Drain fat. Add rice and pasta mix to skillet. Cook and stir 1 minute.

2. Place mixture in **CROCK-POT**® slow cooker. Add broth, celery, almonds, salt and pepper to **CROCK-POT**® slow cooker; mix well.

3. Cover; cook on LOW 7 to 10 hours or on HIGH 3 to 4 hours or until rice is tender.

Makes 4 servings

Corned Beef and Cabbage

12 new red potatoes, quartered

4 carrots, sliced

1 corned beef brisket (about 4 pounds)

2 onions, sliced

3 whole bay leaves

8 whole black peppercorns

1 head cabbage, cut into wedges

1. Place potatoes and carrots in bottom of **CROCK-POT®** slow cooker. Add brisket, onions, bay leaves and peppercorns. Add enough water to cover brisket. Cover; cook on LOW 4 to 5 hours or on HIGH 2 to 2½ hours.

2. Add cabbage. Continue cooking on LOW 4 to 5 hours longer or on HIGH 2 to 2½ hours longer. Slice brisket against the grain, and serve with vegetables.

Makes 6 to 8 servings

Thai Chicken

2½ pounds chicken pieces

1 cup hot salsa

¼ cup peanut butter

2 tablespoons lime juice

1 tablespoon soy sauce

1 teaspoon minced fresh ginger

Hot cooked rice (optional)

½ cup peanuts, chopped

2 tablespoons chopped fresh cilantro

1. Place chicken in **CROCK-POT®** slow cooker. Mix together salsa, peanut butter, lime juice, soy sauce and ginger in small bowl; pour over chicken.

2. Cover; cook on LOW 8 to 9 hours or on HIGH 3 to 4 hours or until done.

3. Serve over rice, if desired, topped with sauce, peanuts and cilantro.

Makes 6 servings

Chicken Provençal

2 pounds boneless, skinless chicken thighs, each cut into quarters

2 medium red peppers, cut into ¼-inch-thick slices

1 medium yellow pepper, cut into ¼-inch-thick slices

1 onion, thinly sliced

1 can (28 ounces) plum tomatoes, drained

3 cloves garlic, minced

¼ teaspoon salt

¼ teaspoon thyme

¼ teaspoon fennel seeds, crushed

3 strips orange peel

½ cup fresh basil leaves, chopped

1. Place thighs, bell peppers, onion, tomatoes, garlic, salt, thyme, fennel seeds and orange peel in **CROCK-POT**® slow cooker. Mix thoroughly.

2. Cover; cook on LOW 7 to 9 hours or on HIGH 3 to 4 hours. Sprinkle with basil to serve.

Makes 8 servings

Curry Beef

1 pound lean ground beef

1 medium onion, thinly sliced

½ cup beef broth

1 tablespoon curry powder

1 teaspoon ground cumin

2 cloves garlic, minced

1 cup sour cream

½ cup raisins, divided

¼ cup reduced-fat (2%) milk

1 teaspoon sugar

12 ounces wide egg noodles

¼ cup chopped walnuts, almonds or pecans

1. Brown beef in large skillet over medium-high heat, stirring to break up meat. Drain and discard fat. Add onion, broth, curry powder, cumin, garlic and beef to **CROCK-POT**® slow cooker. Cover; cook on LOW 4 hours.

2. Stir in sour cream, ¼ cup raisins, milk and sugar. Cover; cook on LOW 30 minutes or until thickened and heated through.

3. Cook noodles according to package directions; drain. Serve curry beef over noodles. Sprinkle with remaining ¼ cup raisins and walnuts.

Makes 4 servings

Spanish-Style Couscous

 1 pound lean ground beef

 1 can (about 14 ounces) beef broth

 1 small green bell pepper, cut into ½-inch pieces

 ½ cup pimiento-stuffed green olives, sliced

 ½ medium onion, chopped

 2 cloves garlic, minced

 1 teaspoon ground cumin

 ½ teaspoon dried thyme

 1⅓ cups water

 1 cup uncooked couscous

1. Brown beef in large skillet over medium-high heat, stirring to break up meat. Drain fat and discard.

2. Place broth, bell pepper, olives, onion, garlic, cumin, thyme and beef in **CROCK-POT**® slow cooker. Cover; cook on LOW 4 hours or until bell pepper is tender.

3. Bring water to a boil over high heat in small saucepan. Stir in couscous. Cover; remove from heat. Let stand 5 minutes; fluff with fork. Spoon couscous onto plates; top with beef mixture.

Makes 4 servings

Mediterranean Chicken

 1 tablespoon olive oil

 2 pounds boneless, skinless chicken breasts

 1 can (28 ounces) diced tomatoes, undrained

 2 onions, chopped

 ½ cup dry sherry

 6 teaspoons minced garlic

   Juice of 2 lemons

 2 cinnamon sticks

 1 bay leaf

 ½ teaspoon black pepper

 1 pound cooked egg noodles

 ½ cup feta cheese

1. Heat oil in large skillet. Add the chicken and lightly brown.

2. Combine tomatoes with juice, onions, sherry, garlic, lemon juice, cinnamon sticks, bay leaf and pepper in **CROCK-POT**® slow cooker. Add chicken. Cover; cook on LOW 8 to 10 hours or on HIGH 4 to 5 hours or until done.

3. Discard cinnamon sticks and bay leaf. Serve chicken and sauce over cooked noodles. Sprinkle with cheese just before serving.

Makes 6 servings

Greek-Style Chicken

6 boneless, skinless chicken thighs

½ teaspoon salt

½ teaspoon black pepper

1 tablespoon olive oil

½ cup chicken broth

1 lemon, thinly sliced

¼ cup pitted kalamata olives

1 clove garlic, minced

½ teaspoon dried oregano

Hot cooked orzo or rice

1. Remove and discard visible fat from chicken. Season chicken with salt and pepper. Heat oil in large skillet over medium-high heat until hot. Brown chicken on all sides. Transfer to **CROCK-POT®** slow cooker.

2. Add broth, lemon, olives, garlic and oregano. Cover; cook on LOW 5 to 6 hours or until chicken is tender. Serve with orzo.

Makes 4 to 6 servings

Hoppin' John

1 package (1 pound) andouille or smoked sausage, sliced

2½ cups chicken broth, divided

2 cans (15 ounces each) black-eyed peas, rinsed and drained

1 box (about 8 ounces) dirty rice mix

½ cup salsa

½ to ¾ cup lump crabmeat (optional)

Chopped green onions (optional)

1. Cook sausage in large skillet over medium heat, stirring frequently, 5 minutes or until browned all over. Transfer to **CROCK-POT®** slow cooker with slotted spoon; discard any drippings from pan. Return skillet to heat and pour in ½ cup chicken broth. Cook and stir, scraping up any browned bits from skillet. Pour over sausage.

2. Stir peas, rice mix, remaining broth and salsa into **CROCK-POT®** slow cooker with sausage. Cover and cook on LOW 3 to 4 hours or until rice is tender. Stir in crabmeat, if desired. Cover; cook until heated through. Garnish with green onions.

Makes 6 servings

Ham and Cheese Pasta Bake

- 6 cups water
- 2 teaspoons salt
- 12 ounces uncooked rigatoni
- 1 ham steak, cubed
- 1 container (10 ounces) refrigerated light Alfredo sauce
- 2 cups mozzarella cheese, divided
- 2 cups hot half-and-half
- 1 tablespoon cornstarch

1. Bring water to a boil in medium saucepan. Stir in salt. Add rigatoni and boil 7 minutes. Drain well and transfer to **CROCK-POT®** slow cooker.

2. Stir in ham, Alfredo sauce and 1 cup mozzarella cheese. Whisk together half-and-half and cornstarch in small bowl. Pour half-and-half mixture over pasta to cover. Sprinkle with remaining cheese. Cover; cook on LOW 3½ to 4 hours. (Dish is done when rigatoni is tender and excess liquid is absorbed.)

Makes 6 servings

Citrus Mangoretto Chicken

- 4 boneless, skinless chicken breasts (about 1 pound)
- 1 large ripe mango, peeled and diced
- 3 tablespoons freshly squeezed lime juice
- 1 tablespoon grated lime peel
- ¼ cup Amaretto liqueur
- 1 tablespoon chopped fresh rosemary or 1 teaspoon crushed dried rosemary
- 1 cup chicken broth
- 1 tablespoon water
- 2 teaspoons cornstarch

1. Place 2 chicken breasts side by side on bottom of **CROCK-POT®** slow cooker.

2. Combine mango, lime juice, lime peel, Amaretto and rosemary in medium bowl. Spread half of mango mixture over chicken in **CROCK-POT®** slow cooker. Lay remaining 2 chicken breasts on top crosswise, and spread with remaining mango mixture. Carefully pour broth around edges of chicken. Cover; cook on LOW 3 to 4 hours.

3. Combine water and cornstarch. Stir into cooking liquid. Cook 15 minutes longer or until sauce has thickened. Serve mango and sauce over chicken.

Makes 4 servings

Southwestern Mac and Cheese

1 package (8 ounces) elbow macaroni, uncooked

1 can (about 14 ounces) diced tomatoes with green peppers and onions, undrained

1 can (10 ounces) diced tomatoes with green chiles, undrained

1½ cups salsa

3 cups (about 12 ounces) shredded Mexican cheese blend, divided

1. Lightly coat inside of **CROCK-POT**® slow cooker with nonstick cooking spray. Stir together macaroni, tomatoes and their juices, salsa and 2 cups cheese in prepared **CROCK-POT**® slow cooker. Cover and cook on LOW 3¾ hours or until macaroni is tender.

2. Sprinkle remaining 1 cup cheese over contents of **CROCK-POT**® slow cooker. Cover and cook 15 minutes more or until cheese on top melts.

Makes 6 servings

Mediterranean Chicken Breasts and Wild Rice

1 pound boneless, skinless chicken breasts, lightly pounded

　Kosher salt, to taste

　Black pepper, to taste

1 cup wild rice blend

10 cloves garlic, crushed

½ cup sun-dried tomatoes, packed in oil or dried*

½ cup capers, drained

2 cups water

½ cup fresh-squeezed lemon juice

¼ cup extra-virgin olive oil

If using dry sun-dried tomatoes, soak in boiling water to soften before chopping.

1. Season chicken with salt and pepper. Place chicken in **CROCK-POT**® slow cooker. Add rice, garlic, tomatoes and capers; stir well.

2. Mix water, lemon juice and oil in small mixing bowl. Pour mixture over rice and chicken. Stir once to coat chicken. Cover; cook on LOW 8 hours.

Makes 4 servings

Jamaica-Me-Crazy Chicken Tropicale

2 medium sweet potatoes, peeled and cut into 2-inch pieces

1 can (8 ounces) water chestnuts, drained and sliced

1 cup golden raisins

1 can (20 ounces) pineapple tidbits in pineapple juice, drained and juice reserved

4 boneless, skinless chicken breasts

4 teaspoons Jamaican jerk seasoning, or to taste

¼ cup dried onion flakes

3 tablespoons grated fresh ginger

2 tablespoons Worcestershire sauce

1 tablespoon grated lime peel

1 teaspoon cumin seed, slightly crushed

   Hot cooked rice (optional)

1. Place sweet potatoes in **CROCK-POT**® slow cooker. Add water chestnuts, raisins and pineapple tidbits; mix well.

2. Sprinkle chicken with jerk seasoning. Place chicken over potato mixture.

3. Combine reserved pineapple juice, onion flakes, ginger, Worcestershire sauce, lime peel and cumin in small bowl. Pour mixture over chicken. Cover; cook on LOW 7 to 9 hours or on HIGH 3 to 4 hours, or until chicken and potatoes are fork-tender. Serve with rice, if desired.

Makes 4 servings

Chinese Cashew Chicken

1 can (16 ounces) bean sprouts, drained

2 cups sliced cooked chicken

1 can (10¾ ounces) condensed cream of mushroom soup, undiluted

1 cup sliced celery

½ cup chopped green onions with tops

1 can (4 ounces) sliced mushrooms, drained

3 tablespoons butter

1 tablespoon soy sauce

1 cup whole cashews

   Hot cooked rice

1. Combine bean sprouts, chicken, soup, celery, onions, mushrooms, butter and soy sauce in **CROCK-POT**® slow cooker; mix well. Cover; cook on LOW 4 to 6 hours or on HIGH 2 to 3 hours.

2. Stir in cashews just before serving. Serve over rice.

Makes 4 servings

Slow-Simmered Curried Chicken

1½ cups chopped onions

1 medium green bell pepper, chopped

1 pound boneless, skinless chicken breasts or thighs, cut into bite-size pieces

1 cup medium salsa

2 teaspoons grated fresh ginger

½ teaspoon garlic powder

½ teaspoon red pepper flakes

¼ cup chopped fresh cilantro

1 teaspoon sugar

1 teaspoon curry powder

¾ teaspoon salt

Hot cooked rice (optional)

1. Place onions and bell pepper in **CROCK-POT®** slow cooker. Place chicken on top.

2. Combine salsa, ginger, garlic powder and red pepper flakes in small bowl; spoon over chicken. Cover; cook on LOW 5 to 6 hours or until chicken is tender.

3. Combine cilantro, sugar, curry powder and salt in small bowl; stir into **CROCK-POT®** slow cooker. Cover; cook 15 minutes or until hot. Serve over rice.

Makes 4 servings

Smoky Chipotle Cassoulet

1 pound boneless, skinless chicken thighs, cubed

1 teaspoon salt

1 teaspoon ground cumin

1 bay leaf

1 chipotle pepper in adobo sauce, minced

1 medium onion, diced

1 can (15 ounces) navy beans, rinsed and drained

1 can (15 ounces) black beans, rinsed and drained

1 can (14½ ounces) crushed tomatoes, undrained

1½ cups chicken stock

½ cup fresh-squeezed orange juice

¼ cup chopped fresh cilantro (optional)

1. Combine all ingredients except cilantro in **CROCK-POT®** slow cooker. Cover; cook on LOW 7 to 8 hours or on HIGH 4 to 5 hours.

2. Remove bay leaf before serving. Garnish with cilantro.

Makes 6 servings

Super Easy Chicken Noodle Soup

- 1 can (about 48 ounces) chicken broth
- 2 boneless, skinless chicken breasts, cut into bite-size pieces
- 4 cups water
- ⅔ cup diced onion
- ⅔ cup diced celery
- ⅔ cup diced carrots
- ⅔ cup sliced mushrooms
- ½ cup frozen peas
- 4 chicken bouillon cubes
- 2 tablespoons butter or margarine
- 1 tablespoon dried parsley flakes
- 1 teaspoon salt
- 1 teaspoon ground cumin
- 1 teaspoon dried marjoram
- 1 teaspoon black pepper
- 2 cups cooked egg noodles

Combine all ingredients except noodles in **CROCK-POT®** slow cooker. Cover; cook on LOW 5 to 7 hours or on HIGH 3 to 4 hours. Stir in noodles 30 minutes before serving.

Makes 4 servings

Three-Bean Mole Chili

- 1 can (15½ ounces) chili beans in spicy sauce, undrained
- 1 can (15 ounces) pinto beans, rinsed and drained
- 1 can (15 ounces) black beans, rinsed and drained
- 1 can (14½ ounces) Mexican or chili-style diced tomatoes, undrained
- 1 large green bell pepper, diced
- 1 small onion, diced
- ½ cup beef, chicken or vegetable broth
- ¼ cup prepared mole paste*
- 2 teaspoons minced garlic
- 2 teaspoons ground cumin
- 2 teaspoons chili powder
- 2 teaspoons ground coriander (optional)

    Optional toppings: crushed tortilla chips, chopped cilantro, shredded cheese

Mole paste is available in the supermarket's Mexican section or in specialty markets.

Combine all ingredients in **CROCK-POT®** slow cooker; mix well. Cover; cook on LOW 5 to 6 hours or until vegetables are tender. Serve with desired toppings.

Makes 4 to 6 servings

brunch and breakfast

Wake-Up Potato and Sausage Breakfast Casserole

1 pound kielbasa or smoked sausage, diced

1 cup chopped onion

1 cup chopped red bell pepper

1 package (20 ounces) refrigerated Southwestern-style hash browns*

10 large eggs

1 cup milk

1 cup shredded Monterey Jack or sharp Cheddar cheese

If unavailable, you may substitute O'Brien potatoes and add ½ teaspoon chili pepper.

1. Coat **CROCK-POT®** slow cooker with nonstick cooking spray. Heat large skillet over medium-high heat until hot. Add sausage and onion. Cook and stir until sausage is browned. Drain and discard excess fat. Stir in bell pepper.

2. Place ⅓ of potatoes in **CROCK-POT®** slow cooker. Top with ½ of sausage mixture. Repeat layers. Spread remaining ⅓ of potatoes evenly on top.

3. Whisk eggs and milk in medium bowl. Pour evenly over potatoes. Cover; cook on LOW 6 to 7 hours.

4. Turn off **CROCK-POT®** slow cooker. Sprinkle on cheese, and let stand 10 minutes or until cheese is melted. To serve, spoon onto plates.

Makes 8 servings

Tip

For an attractive presentation on a buffet table, display this casserole on a serving plate. To serve this way, omit step 4. Instead, loosen the casserole in the **CROCK-POT®** slow cooker by running a rubber spatula around the outer edges, lifting the bottom slightly. Invert onto a plate. Place a serving plate on top and invert again. Sprinkle with the cheese and let stand until cheese is melted. To serve, cut in wedges.

Bran Muffin Bread

2 cups all-bran cereal

2 cups whole wheat flour*

2 teaspoons baking powder

1 teaspoon baking soda

¼ teaspoon ground cinnamon

½ teaspoon salt

1 egg

1½ cups buttermilk

¼ cup molasses

¼ cup (½ stick) unsalted butter, melted

1 cup chopped walnuts

½ cup raisins

Honey butter or cream cheese (optional)

For proper texture of finished bread, spoon flour into measuring cup and level off. Do not dip into bag, pack down flour or tap on counter to level when measuring.

1. Generously butter and flour 8-cup mold that fits into 6-quart **CROCK-POT®** slow cooker; set aside. Combine cereal, flour, baking powder, baking soda, cinnamon and salt in large bowl. Stir to blend well.

2. Beat egg in medium bowl. Add buttermilk, molasses and melted butter. Mix well to blend. Add to flour mixture. Stir only until ingredients are combined. Stir in walnuts and raisins. Spoon batter into prepared mold. Cover with buttered foil, butter side down.

3. Place rack in **CROCK-POT®** slow cooker or prop up mold with a few equal-size potatoes. Pour 1 inch hot water into **CROCK-POT®** slow cooker (water should not come to top of rack). Place mold on rack. Cover; cook on LOW 3½ to 4 hours.

4. To check for doneness, lift foil. Bread should just start to pull away from sides of mold, and toothpick inserted into center of bread should come out clean. If necessary, replace foil and continue cooking 45 minutes longer.

5. Remove mold from **CROCK-POT®** slow cooker. Let stand 10 minutes. Remove foil and run rubber spatula around outer edges, lifting bottom slightly to loosen. Invert bread onto wire rack. Cool until lukewarm. Slice and serve with honey butter, if desired.

Makes 12 servings

French Toast Bread Pudding

2 tablespoons packed dark brown sugar

2½ teaspoons ground cinnamon

1 loaf (24 ounces) Texas toast-style bread*

2 cups whipping cream

2 cups half-and-half

2 teaspoons vanilla

¼ teaspoon salt

4 egg yolks

1¼ cups granulated sugar

¼ teaspoon ground nutmeg

Maple syrup

Whipped cream (optional)

If unavailable, cut day-old 24-ounce loaf of white sandwich bread into 1-inch-thick slices.

1. Coat **CROCK-POT**® slow cooker with nonstick cooking spray. Combine brown sugar and cinnamon in small bowl. Reserve 1 tablespoon; set aside.

2. Cut bread slices in half diagonally. Using heels on bottom, if desired, arrange bread slices in single layer in bottom of **CROCK-POT**® slow cooker, keeping as flat as possible. Evenly sprinkle on rounded tablespoon of cinnamon mixture. Repeat layering with remaining bread and cinnamon mixture, keeping layers as flat as possible. Tuck bread into vertical spaces, if necessary.

3. Cook and stir cream, half-and-half, vanilla and salt in large saucepan over medium heat, allowing mixture to come to a boil. Reduce heat to low.

4. Meanwhile, whisk egg yolks and granulated sugar in medium bowl. Continue to whisk quickly while adding ¼ cup of hot cream mixture.** Add warmed egg mixture to saucepan and increase heat to medium-high. Cook and stir about 5 minutes or until mixture thickens slightly. Do not boil.

5. Remove from heat and stir in nutmeg. Pour mixture over bread and press bread down lightly. Sprinkle reserved cinnamon mixture on top. Cover; cook on LOW 3 to 4 hours or on HIGH 1½ to 2 hours, or until tester inserted into center comes out clean.

6. Turn off **CROCK-POT**® slow cooker and uncover. Let pudding rest 10 minutes before spooning into bowls. Serve with maple syrup and whipped cream, if desired.

Makes 6 to 8 servings

**Place bowl on damp towel to prevent slipping.*

Tip

Allow breads, cakes and puddings to cool at least 5 minutes before scooping or removing them from the **CROCK-POT**® stoneware.

Glazed Cinnamon Coffee Cake

Streusel

- ¼ cup biscuit baking mix
- ¼ cup packed light brown sugar
- ½ teaspoon ground cinnamon

Batter

- 1½ cups biscuit baking mix
- ¾ cup granulated sugar
- ½ cup vanilla or plain yogurt
- 1 large egg, lightly beaten
- 1 teaspoon vanilla

Glaze

- 1 to 2 tablespoons milk
- 1 cup powdered sugar
- ½ cup sliced almonds (optional)

1. Generously coat 4-quart **CROCK-POT®** slow cooker with butter or nonstick cooking spray. Cut parchment paper to fit bottom of stoneware* and press into place. Spray paper lightly with nonstick cooking spray.

2. Prepare streusel: Blend ¼ cup baking mix, brown sugar and cinnamon in small bowl; set aside.

3. Prepare batter: Mix 1½ cups baking mix, granulated sugar, yogurt, egg and vanilla in medium bowl until well blended. Spoon half of batter into **CROCK-POT®** slow cooker. Sprinkle half of streusel over top. Repeat with remaining batter and streusel.

4. Line lid with 2 paper towels. Cover tightly; cook on HIGH 1¾ to 2 hours or until tester inserted into center comes out clean and cake springs back when gently pressed. Allow cake to rest 10 minutes. Invert onto plate and peel off paper. Invert again onto serving plate.

5. Prepare glaze: Whisk milk into powdered sugar, 1 tablespoon at a time, until desired consistency. Spoon glaze over top of cake. Garnish with sliced almonds. Cut into wedges. Serve warm or cold.

Makes 6 to 8 servings

To cut parchment paper to fit, trace around the stoneware bottom, then cut the paper slightly smaller to fit. If parchment paper is unavailable, substitute waxed paper.

Note

This recipe works best in a round **CROCK-POT®** slow cooker.

Banana Nut Bread

⅓ cup butter or margarine

⅔ cup sugar

2 eggs, well beaten

2 tablespoons dark corn syrup

3 ripe bananas, well mashed

1¾ cups all-purpose flour

2 teaspoons baking powder

½ teaspoon salt

¼ teaspoon baking soda

½ cup chopped walnuts

1. Grease and flour inside of **CROCK-POT**® slow cooker. Cream butter in large bowl with electric mixer until fluffy. Slowly add sugar, eggs, corn syrup and mashed bananas. Beat until smooth.

2. Sift together flour, baking powder, salt and baking soda in small bowl. Slowly beat flour mixture into creamed mixture. Add walnuts and mix thoroughly. Pour into **CROCK-POT**® slow cooker. Cover; cook on HIGH 2 to 3 hours.

3. Let cool, then turn bread out onto serving platter.

Makes 6 servings

Note

Banana nut bread has always been a favorite way to use up those overripe bananas. Not only is it delicious, but it also freezes well for future use.

Chocolate-Stuffed Slow Cooker French Toast

6 slices ¾-inch-thick day-old challah*

½ cup semisweet chocolate chips

6 eggs

3 cups half-and-half

⅔ cup granulated sugar

1 teaspoon vanilla

¼ teaspoon salt

Powdered sugar or warm maple syrup

Fresh fruit (optional)

Challah is usually braided. If you use brioche or another rich egg bread, slice bread to fit baking dish.

1. Generously butter 2½-quart baking dish that fits inside **CROCK-POT®** slow cooker. Arrange 2 bread slices in bottom of dish. Sprinkle on ¼ cup chocolate chips. Add 2 more bread slices. Sprinkle with remaining ¼ cup chocolate chips. Top with remaining 2 bread slices.

2. Beat eggs in large bowl. Stir in half-and-half, sugar, vanilla and salt. Pour egg mixture over bread layers. Press bread into liquid. Set aside 10 minutes or until bread has absorbed liquid. Cover dish with buttered foil, butter side down.

3. Pour 1 inch hot water into **CROCK-POT®** slow cooker. Add baking dish. Cover; cook on HIGH 3 hours or until toothpick inserted into center comes out clean. Remove dish and let stand 10 minutes to firm up. Serve with powdered sugar. Garnish with fresh fruit.

Makes 6 servings

Ham and Cheddar Brunch Strata

8 ounces French bread, torn into small pieces

2 cups shredded sharp Cheddar cheese, divided

1½ cups diced ham

½ cup finely chopped green onions (white and green parts), divided

4 large eggs

1 cup half-and-half or whole milk

1 tablespoon Worcestershire sauce

⅛ teaspoon ground red pepper

1. Coat **CROCK-POT®** slow cooker with nonstick cooking spray. Cut parchment paper to fit bottom of stoneware* and press into place. Spray paper lightly with nonstick cooking spray.

2. Layer in following order; bread, 1½ cups cheese, ham and all but 2 tablespoons green onions.

3. Whisk eggs, half-and-half, Worcestershire sauce and red pepper in small bowl. Pour evenly over layered ingredients in **CROCK-POT®** slow cooker. Cover; cook on LOW 3½ hours or until knife inserted into center comes out clean. Turn off heat. Sprinkle evenly with reserved ½ cup cheese and 2 tablespoons green onions. Let stand, covered, 10 minutes or until cheese has melted.

4. To serve, run a knife or rubber spatula around outer edges, lifting bottom slightly. Invert onto plate and peel off paper. Invert again onto serving plate.

Makes 6 to 8 servings

To cut parchment paper to fit, trace around the stoneware bottom, then cut the paper slightly smaller to fit. If parchment paper is unavailable, substitute waxed paper.

Apple-Cinnamon Breakfast Risotto

¼ cup (½ stick) butter

4 medium Granny Smith apples (about 1½ pounds), peeled, cored and diced into ½-inch cubes

1½ teaspoons ground cinnamon

¼ teaspoon ground allspice

¼ teaspoon salt

1½ cups arborio rice

½ cup packed dark brown sugar

4 cups unfiltered apple juice, at room temperature*

1 teaspoon vanilla

Optional toppings: dried cranberries, sliced almonds, milk

*If unfiltered apple juice is unavailable, use any apple juice.

1. Coat **CROCK-POT®** slow cooker with nonstick cooking spray; set aside. Melt butter in large skillet over medium-high heat. Add apples, cinnamon, allspice and salt. Cook and stir 3 to 5 minutes or until apples begin to release juices. Transfer to **CROCK-POT®** slow cooker.

2. Add rice and stir to coat. Sprinkle brown sugar evenly over top. Add apple juice and vanilla. Cover; cook on HIGH 1½ to 2 hours or until all liquid is absorbed. Ladle risotto into bowls and serve hot. Garnish as desired.

Makes 6 servings

Oatmeal Crème Brûlée

4 cups water

3 cups quick-cooking oatmeal

½ teaspoon salt

6 egg yolks

½ cup granulated sugar

2 cups whipping cream

1 teaspoon vanilla

¼ cup packed light brown sugar

Fresh berries (optional)

1. Coat **CROCK-POT®** slow cooker with nonstick cooking spray. Cover and preheat on HIGH to heat. Meanwhile, bring water to a boil. Immediately pour into preheated **CROCK-POT®** slow cooker. Stir in oatmeal and salt. Cover.

2. Combine egg yolks and granulated sugar in small bowl. Mix well; set aside. Heat cream and vanilla in medium saucepan over medium heat until mixture begins to simmer (small bubbles begin to form at edge of pan). Do not boil. Remove from heat. Whisk ½ cup hot cream into yolks, stirring rapidly so yolks don't cook.* Whisk warmed egg mixture into cream, stirring rapidly to blend well. Spoon mixture over oatmeal. Do not stir.

3. Turn **CROCK-POT®** slow cooker to LOW. Line lid with 2 paper towels. Cover tightly; cook on LOW 3 to 3½ hours or until custard has set.

4. Uncover and sprinkle brown sugar over surface of custard. Line lid with 2 dry paper towels. Cover tightly; continue cooking on LOW 10 to 15 minutes or until brown sugar has melted. Serve with fresh berries, if desired.

Makes 4 to 6 servings

Place bowl on damp towel to prevent slipping.

Tip

This rich, sweet dish is delicious for breakfast or lunch, but also can be served as an unusual dessert.

Glazed Orange Poppy Seed Cake

Batter

1½	**cups biscuit baking mix**
¾	**cup granulated sugar**
2	**tablespoons poppy seeds**
½	**cup sour cream**
1	**egg**
2	**tablespoons milk**
1	**teaspoon vanilla**
2	**teaspoons orange peel**

Glaze

¼	**cup orange juice**
2	**cups powdered sugar, sifted**
2	**teaspoons poppy seeds**

1. Coat inside of 4-quart **CROCK-POT®** slow cooker with nonstick cooking spray. Cut waxed paper circle to fit bottom of **CROCK-POT®** slow cooker (trace insert bottom and cut slightly smaller to fit). Spray lightly with nonstick cooking spray.

2. Prepare batter: Whisk together baking mix, granulated sugar and 2 tablespoons poppy seeds in medium bowl; set aside. In another bowl, blend sour cream, egg, milk, vanilla and orange peel. Whisk wet ingredients into dry mixture until thoroughly blended.

3. Spoon batter into prepared **CROCK-POT®** slow cooker and smooth top. Place paper towel under lid, then cover. Cook on HIGH 1 hour 30 minutes. (Cake is done when top is no longer shiny and a toothpick inserted into center comes out clean.)

4. Invert cake onto cooling rack, peel off waxed paper and allow to cool (right side up) on cooling rack.

5. Prepare glaze: Whisk orange juice into powdered sugar. Cut cake into 8 wedges and place on cooling rack with a tray underneath to catch drips. With a small spatula or knife, spread glaze over top and cut sides of each wedge. Sprinkle 2 teaspoons poppy seeds over wedges and allow glaze to set.

Makes 8 servings

Cheesy Shrimp on Grits

1 cup finely chopped green bell pepper

1 cup finely chopped red bell pepper

½ cup thinly sliced celery

1 bunch green onions, chopped, divided

¼ cup (½ stick) butter, cubed

1¼ teaspoons seafood seasoning

2 bay leaves

¼ teaspoon ground red pepper

1 pound uncooked shrimp, peeled, deveined and cleaned

5⅓ cups water

1⅓ cups quick-cooking grits

8 ounces shredded sharp Cheddar cheese

¼ cup whipping cream or half-and-half

1. Coat **CROCK-POT**® slow cooker with nonstick cooking spray. Add bell peppers, celery, all but ½ cup green onions, butter, seafood seasoning, bay leaves and red pepper. Cover; cook on LOW 4 hours or on HIGH 2 hours.

2. Turn **CROCK-POT**® slow cooker to HIGH. Add shrimp. Cover; cook 15 minutes longer. Meanwhile, bring water to a boil in medium saucepan. Add grits and cook according to directions on package.

3. Discard bay leaves from shrimp mixture. Stir in cheese, cream and remaining ½ cup green onions. Cook 5 minutes longer or until cheese has melted. Serve over grits.

Makes 6 servings

 **Variation**

This dish is also delicious served over polenta.

Cinnamon Latté

- 6 cups double-strength brewed coffee*
- 2 cups half-and-half
- 1 cup sugar
- 1 teaspoon vanilla
- 3 cinnamon sticks, plus additional for garnish
  Whipped cream (optional)

Double the amount of coffee grounds normally used to brew coffee. Or, substitute 8 teaspoons instant coffee dissolved in 6 cups boiling water.

1. Blend coffee, half-and-half, sugar and vanilla in 3- to 4-quart **CROCK-POT®** slow cooker. Add 3 cinnamon sticks. Cover; cook on HIGH 3 hours.

2. Remove cinnamon sticks. Serve latté in tall coffee mugs with whipped cream and additional cinnamon stick, if desired.

Makes 6 to 8 servings

Whoa Breakfast

- 1½ cups steel-cut or old-fashioned oats
- 3 cups water
- 2 cups chopped peeled apples
- ¼ cup sliced almonds
- ½ teaspoon ground cinnamon

Combine oats, water, apples, almonds and cinnamon in **CROCK-POT®** slow cooker. Cover; cook on LOW 8 hours.

Makes 6 servings

Breakfast Berry Bread Pudding

6 cups bread, preferably dense peasant-style or sourdough, cut into ¾- to 1-inch cubes

1 cup raisins

½ cup slivered almonds, toasted*

6 large eggs, beaten

1½ cups packed light brown sugar

1¾ cups milk (1% or greater)

1½ teaspoons cinnamon

1 teaspoon vanilla

3 cups sliced fresh strawberries

2 cups fresh blueberries

Fresh mint leaves (optional)

To toast almonds, spread in single layer in heavy-bottomed skillet. Cook over medium heat 1 to 2 minutes, stirring frequently, until nuts are lightly browned. Remove from skillet immediately. Cool before using.

1. Coat **CROCK-POT®** slow cooker with nonstick cooking spray or butter. Add bread, raisins and almonds and toss to combine.

2. Whisk eggs, brown sugar, milk, cinnamon and vanilla in separate bowl. Pour egg mixture over bread mixture; toss to blend. Cover; cook on LOW 4 to 4½ hours or on HIGH 3 hours.

3. Remove stoneware from **CROCK-POT®** slow cooker base and allow bread pudding to cool and set before serving. Serve with berries and garnish with mint leaves.

Makes 10 to 12 servings

Streusel Pound Cake

1 package (16 ounces) pound cake mix, plus ingredients to prepare mix

¼ cup packed light brown sugar

1 tablespoon all-purpose flour

¼ cup chopped nuts

1 teaspoon ground cinnamon

Strawberries, blueberries, raspberries and/or powdered sugar (optional)

Coat 4½-quart **CROCK-POT®** slow cooker with nonstick cooking spray. Prepare cake mix according to package directions; stir in sugar, flour, nuts and cinnamon. Pour batter into **CROCK-POT®** slow cooker. Cover; cook on HIGH 1½ to 1¾ hours or until toothpick inserted into center of cake comes out clean. Serve with berries and powdered sugar, if desired.

Makes 6 to 8 servings

Cinn-Sational Swirl Cake

1 box (21½ ounces) cinnamon swirl cake mix

1 cup sour cream

1 cup cinnamon-flavored baking chips

1 package (4-serving size) instant French vanilla pudding and pie filling mix

1 cup water

¾ cup vegetable oil

Cinnamon ice cream (optional)

1. Coat 4½-quart **CROCK-POT**® slow cooker with nonstick cooking spray. Set cinnamon swirl mix packet aside. Place remaining cake mix in **CROCK-POT**® slow cooker.

2. Add sour cream, cinnamon chips, pudding mix, water and oil; stir well to combine. Batter will be slightly lumpy. Add reserved cinnamon swirl mix, slowly swirling through batter with knife. Cover; cook on LOW 3 to 4 hours or on HIGH 1½ to 1¾ hours or until toothpick inserted into center of cake comes out clean.

3. Serve warm with cinnamon ice cream, if desired.

Makes 10 to 12 servings

Pear Crunch

1 can (8 ounces) crushed pineapple in juice, undrained

¼ cup pineapple or apple juice

3 tablespoons dried cranberries

1½ teaspoons quick-cooking tapioca

¼ teaspoon vanilla

2 pears, cored and halved

¼ cup granola with almonds

Mint leaves (optional)

1. Combine undrained pineapple, juice, cranberries, tapioca and vanilla in **CROCK-POT**® slow cooker; mix well. Place pears cut side down on pineapple mixture.

2. Cover; cook on LOW 3½ to 4½ hours. Arrange pear halves on serving plates. Spoon pineapple mixture over pear halves. Garnish with granola and mint leaves.

Makes 4 servings

Orange Cranberry-Nut Bread

- 2 cups all-purpose flour
- 1 teaspoon baking powder
- ½ teaspoon baking soda
- ¼ teaspoon salt
- ½ cup chopped pecans
- 1 cup dried cranberries
- 2 teaspoons dried orange peel
- ⅔ cup boiling water
- ¾ cup sugar
- 2 tablespoons shortening
- 1 egg, lightly beaten
- 1 teaspoon vanilla

1. Coat 3-quart **CROCK-POT®** slow cooker with nonstick cooking spray. Blend flour, baking powder, baking soda and salt in medium bowl. Mix in pecans; set aside.

2. Combine cranberries and orange peel in separate medium bowl; pour boiling water over fruit mixture and stir. Add sugar, shortening, egg and vanilla; stir just until blended. Add flour mixture; stir just until blended.

3. Pour batter into **CROCK-POT®** slow cooker. Cover; cook on HIGH 1¼ to 1½ hours or until edges begin to brown and cake tester inserted into center comes out clean. Remove insert from **CROCK-POT®** slow cooker. Cool on wire rack about 10 minutes; remove bread from insert and cool completely on rack.

Makes 8 to 10 servings

Apple and Granola Breakfast Cobbler

- 4 Granny Smith apples, peeled, cored and sliced
- ½ cup packed light brown sugar
- 1 teaspoon ground cinnamon
- 1 tablespoon lemon juice
- 2 tablespoons butter, cut into small pieces
- 2 cups granola cereal, plus additional for garnish

  Cream, half-and-half or vanilla yogurt (optional)

1. Place apples in **CROCK-POT®** slow cooker. Sprinkle brown sugar, cinnamon and lemon juice over apples. Stir in butter and 2 cups granola.

2. Cover; cook on LOW 6 hours or on HIGH 2 to 3 hours. Serve hot with additional granola sprinkled on top. Serve with cream, if desired.

Makes 4 servings

Hawaiian Fruit Compote

3 cups coarsely chopped fresh pineapple

3 grapefruits, peeled and sectioned

2 cups chopped fresh peaches

2 to 3 limes, peeled and sectioned

1 mango, peeled and chopped

2 bananas, peeled and sliced

1 tablespoon lemon juice

1 can (21 ounces) cherry pie filling

Slivered almonds (optional)

1. Place all ingredients except almonds in **CROCK-POT®** slow cooker and toss lightly. Cover; cook on LOW 4 to 5 hours or on HIGH 2 to 3 hours.

2. Serve with slivered almonds, if desired.

Makes 6 to 8 servings

Serving Suggestion

Try warm, fruity compote in place of maple syrup on your favorite pancakes or waffles for a great way to start your day. This sauce is also delicious served over roasted turkey, pork roast or baked ham.

Cheese Grits with Chiles and Bacon

6 strips bacon, divided

1 serrano or jalapeño pepper, cored, seeded and minced*

1 large shallot or small onion, finely chopped

1 cup grits**

4 cups chicken broth

¼ teaspoon black pepper

Salt, to taste

½ cup half-and-half

1 cup shredded Cheddar cheese

2 tablespoons finely chopped green onion (green parts only)

Hot peppers can sting and irritate the skin, so wear rubber gloves when handling peppers and do not touch your eyes.

**You may use coarse, instant, yellow or stone-ground grits.*

1. Fry bacon on both sides in medium skillet until crisp. Remove bacon and drain on paper towels. Cut 2 strips into bite-size pieces. Refrigerate and reserve remaining bacon. Place cut-up bacon in **CROCK-POT®** slow cooker.

2. Drain all but 1 tablespoon bacon drippings in skillet. Add serrano pepper and shallot. Cook and stir over medium-high heat 1 minute or until shallot is transparent and lightly browned. Transfer to **CROCK-POT®** slow cooker. Stir in grits, broth, black pepper and salt. Cover; cook on LOW 4 hours.

3. Stir in half-and-half and cheese. Sprinkle on green onion. Chop remaining bacon into bite-size pieces and stir into grits or sprinkle on top of each serving. Serve immediately.

Makes 4 servings

Bacon and Cheese Brunch Potatoes

- 3 medium russet potatoes (about 2 pounds), peeled and cut into 1-inch dice
- 1 cup chopped onion
- ½ teaspoon seasoned salt
- 4 slices crisply cooked bacon, crumbled
- 1 cup (4 ounces) shredded sharp Cheddar cheese
- 1 tablespoon water or chicken broth

1. Coat **CROCK-POT®** slow cooker with nonstick cooking spray. Place half of potatoes in **CROCK-POT®** slow cooker. Sprinkle half of onion and seasoned salt over potatoes; top with half of bacon and cheese. Repeat layers. Sprinkle water over top.

2. Cover; cook on LOW 6 hours or on HIGH 3½ hours, or until potatoes and onion are tender. Stir gently to mix and serve hot.

Makes 6 servings

Mucho Mocha Cocoa

- 1 cup chocolate syrup
- ⅓ cup instant coffee granules
- 2 tablespoons sugar (or more to taste)
- 2 whole cinnamon sticks
- 1 quart whole milk
- 1 quart half-and-half

Combine all ingredients in **CROCK-POT®** slow cooker. Stir until well blended. Cover and cook on LOW 3 hours. Serve hot in mugs.

Makes 9 servings

Tip

This is great for a party. If desired, add 1 ounce of rum or whiskey to each serving.

Viennese Coffee

3 cups strong freshly brewed hot coffee

3 tablespoons chocolate syrup

1 teaspoon sugar

⅓ cup whipping cream

¼ cup crème de cacao or Irish cream (optional)

Whipped cream (optional)

Chocolate shavings (optional)

1. Combine coffee, chocolate syrup and sugar in **CROCK-POT®** slow cooker. Cover and cook on LOW 2 to 2½ hours. Stir in whipping cream and crème de cacao, if desired. Cover and cook 30 minutes or until heated through.

2. Ladle coffee into coffee cups. Top with whipped cream and chocolate shavings, if desired.

Makes 4 servings

Orange Date-Nut Bread

2 cups unbleached all-purpose flour

½ cup chopped pecans

1 teaspoon baking powder

½ teaspoon baking soda

¼ teaspoon salt

1 cup chopped dates

2 teaspoons dried orange peel

⅔ cup boiling water

¾ cup sugar

2 tablespoons shortening

1 egg, lightly beaten

1 teaspoon vanilla

1. Spray 1-quart casserole, soufflé dish or other high-sided baking pan with nonstick cooking spray; dust with flour. Set aside.

2. Combine 2 cups flour, pecans, baking powder, baking soda and salt in medium bowl; set aside.

3. Combine dates and orange peel in separate medium bowl; pour boiling water over date mixture. Add sugar, shortening, egg and vanilla; stir just until blended.

4. Add flour mixture to date mixture; stir just until blended. Pour batter into prepared dish; place in 4½-quart **CROCK-POT®** slow cooker. Cover; cook on HIGH about 2½ hours or until edges begin to brown.

5. Remove dish. Cool on wire rack about 10 minutes; remove bread from dish and cool completely on rack.

Makes 8 to 10 servings

Variation

Substitute 1 cup dried cranberries for dates.

Savory Sausage Bread Pudding

- 4 eggs
- 2 cups milk or 1 cup half-and-half and 1 cup milk
- ¼ teaspoon salt
- ¼ teaspoon black pepper
- ¼ teaspoon crushed dried thyme
- ⅛ teaspoon red pepper flakes
- 1 package (10 ounces) smoky breakfast sausage links, cut into ½-inch pieces
- ¾ cup shredded Cheddar cheese
- 2 cups day-old bread cubes, cut into ½-inch pieces

1. Beat eggs in large bowl. Add milk, salt, black pepper, thyme and red pepper flakes; stir in well. Stir in sausage, cheese and bread. Press bread into egg mixture. Set aside 10 minutes or until bread has absorbed liquid.

2. Generously butter 2-quart baking dish that fits inside **CROCK-POT®** slow cooker. Pour sausage mixture into baking dish. Cover dish with buttered foil, butter side down.

3. Pour 1 inch hot water into **CROCK-POT®** slow cooker. Add baking dish. Cover; cook on LOW 4 to 5 hours or until tester inserted into center comes out clean.

Makes 4 to 6 servings

Breakfast Bake

- 3 to 4 cups diced crusty bread (¾- to 1-inch dice)
- ½ pound bacon, cut into ½-inch dice
- 2 cups sliced mushrooms
- 2 cups torn fresh spinach
- 8 eggs
- ½ cup milk
- ¾ cup roasted red peppers, drained and chopped
- 1 cup shredded cheese, such as Cheddar or Monterey Jack
- Salt and black pepper, to taste

1. Coat **CROCK-POT®** slow cooker with nonstick cooking spray. Add bread.

2. Heat skillet on medium heat until hot. Cook bacon until crispy. Remove and discard all but 1 tablespoon of drippings. Add mushrooms and spinach to skillet and toss to coat. Cook 1 to 2 minutes or until spinach wilts. Transfer to **CROCK-POT®** slow cooker with bread; toss to combine.

3. Beat eggs and milk in medium bowl. Stir in red peppers, cheese, salt and black pepper. Pour into **CROCK-POT®** slow cooker.

4. Cover; cook on LOW 3 to 3½ hours or on HIGH 2 to 2½ hours until eggs are firm but still moist. Adjust seasonings, if desired.

Makes 6 to 8 servings

fresh catch

Mom's Tuna Casserole

2 cans (12 ounces each) tuna, drained and flaked

3 cups diced celery

3 cups crushed potato chips, divided

6 hard-cooked eggs, chopped

1 can (10¾ ounces) condensed cream of mushroom soup, undiluted

1 can (10¾ ounces) condensed cream of celery soup, undiluted

1 cup mayonnaise

1 teaspoon dried tarragon

1 teaspoon black pepper

1. Combine tuna, celery, 2½ cups potato chips, eggs, soups, mayonnaise, tarragon and pepper in **CROCK-POT®** slow cooker; stir well. Cover; cook on LOW 5 to 8 hours.

2. Sprinkle with remaining ½ cup potato chips before serving.

Makes 8 servings

Tip

Don't use your **CROCK-POT®** slow cooker to reheat leftover foods. Transfer cooled leftover food to a resealable plastic food storage bag or plastic storage container with a tight-fitting lid and refrigerate. Use a microwave oven, the stove top or the oven for reheating.

Seafood and Tomato Herb Ragout

1   can (28 ounces) crushed tomatoes, undrained

1   can (8 ounces) tomato sauce

1   cup water

1   cup white wine

1   leek, chopped

1   small green bell pepper, cored, seeded and chopped

½   cup chopped celery

⅓   cup chopped flat-leaf parsley

¼   cup extra-virgin olive oil

3   cloves garlic, minced

2   tablespoons chopped fresh basil

1   tablespoon chopped fresh thyme

1   tablespoon chopped fresh oregano

1   teaspoon salt

½   teaspoon paprika

¼   teaspoon crushed red pepper

1   pound orange roughy fillets or other firm white fish such as cod or haddock, cubed

12   prawns, peeled, deveined and cleaned

12   scallops, cleaned

Fresh parsley (optional)

1. Place all ingredients, except fish, prawns and scallops, in **CROCK-POT®** slow cooker. Stir well to combine. Cover; cook on LOW 6 to 8 hours or on HIGH 3 to 4 hours.

2. Turn **CROCK-POT®** slow cooker to HIGH. Add fish, prawns and scallops. Cook 15 to 30 minutes longer or until seafood is just cooked through. Garnish with parsley.

Makes 6 to 8 servings

Tip

Seafood is delicate and should be added to the **CROCK-POT®** slow cooker during the last 15 to 30 minutes of the cooking time if you're cooking on HIGH, and during the last 30 to 45 minutes if you're cooking on LOW. This type of seafood overcooks easily, becoming tough and rubbery. So watch your cooking times and cook only as long as necessary.

Cod Tapenade

4   cod fillets, or other firm
    white fish (2 to 3 pounds
    total)

    Salt and black pepper

2   lemons, thinly sliced,
    pluss additional for
    garnish

    Tapenade (recipe follows)

1. Season fish with salt and pepper.

2. Arrange half of lemon slices in bottom of **CROCK-POT®** slow cooker.
Top with fish. Cover fish with remaining lemon slices. Cover. Cook on
HIGH 1 hour or until fish is just cooked through (actual time depends on
thickness of fish).

3. Remove fish to serving plates; discard lemon. Top with Tapenade and
additional lemon slices.

Makes 4 servings

Tapenade

½   pound pitted kalamata
    olives

2   tablespoons anchovy
    paste

2   tablespoons capers,
    drained

1   clove garlic

⅛   teaspoon ground red
    pepper

¼   teaspoon grated orange
    peel

2   tablespoons chopped
    fresh thyme or flat-leaf
    parsley

½   cup olive oil

Place all ingredients except oil in food processor. Pulse to roughly chop.
Add oil and pulse briefly to form a chunky paste.

Makes 4 servings

Tip

In a hurry? Substitute
store-brought tapenade
for homemade!

Thai Shrimp Soup Infused with Lemongrass, Ginger and Chiles

¾ pound large shrimp, peeled and deveined, shells reserved

8 cups fish stock or chicken stock

1 cup diced carrots

3 stalks lemongrass, thinly sliced

2 to 3 tablespoons fresh ginger, peeled and grated

2 tablespoons minced garlic

1½ tablespoons finely chopped fresh Thai basil or basil

1½ tablespoons finely chopped fresh mint

1½ tablespoons finely chopped cilantro

1 serrano pepper, stemmed and thinly sliced*

1 to 2 limes, juiced

1 can unsweetened coconut milk

¼ to ½ teaspoon sambal oelek chile paste**

6 thin lime slices

*Serrano peppers can sting and irritate the skin, so wear rubber gloves when handling peppers and do not touch your eyes.

**Chile pepper pastes, such as sambal oelek, are commonly used condiments in Southeast Asia. You can find them in the ethnic section of many grocery stores, in Asian markets or online.

1. Halve shrimp lengthwise. Place in refrigerator.

2. Place shrimp shells, stock, carrots, lemongrass, ginger and garlic in **CROCK-POT**® slow cooker. Cover and cook on LOW 3½ to 4½ hours or on HIGH 2 to 3 hours.

3. Strain broth and return to **CROCK-POT**® slow cooker; discard solids. Add shrimp, Thai basil, mint, cilantro, serrano pepper, lime juice, coconut milk and chile paste. Cover and cook on HIGH until shrimp are cooked through, about 15 minutes.

4. Taste and adjust seasonings. Ladle soup into serving bowls and garnish with lime slices.

Makes 6 servings

Seafood Bouillabaisse

½   bulb fennel, chopped

1   medium onion, chopped

2   cloves garlic, minced

2   bottles (12 ounces each) beer, divided

1   can (28 ounces) tomato purée

8   ounces clam juice

1   bay leaf

½   teaspoon salt

¼   teaspoon black pepper

2   cups water

½   pound red snapper, pin bones removed and cut into 1-inch pieces

8   mussels, scrubbed and debearded

8   cherry stone clams

8   large shrimp, unpeeled

4   lemon wedges

    Italian parsley sprigs (optional)

1. To prepare tomato broth, cook fennel, onion and garlic in large skillet over medium-high heat until onion is soft and translucent. Transfer mixture to **CROCK-POT®** slow cooker and top with beer, tomato purée, clam juice, bay leaf, salt and pepper. Cover, cook on LOW 6 to 8 hours or on HIGH 3 to 4 hours.

2. During last 15 minutes of cooking, place fish and shellfish into **CROCK-POT®** slow cooker. Cover and cook until fish cooks through, discarding any mussels or clams that do not open.

3. Remove bay leaf from tomato broth. Ladle broth into wide soup bowls. Place fish, mussels, clams and shrimp on top. Squeeze lemon over fish and seafood. Garnish with parsley sprigs.

Makes 4 servings

Shrimp Fondue Dip

1 pound shrimp, peeled, cleaned and deveined

½ cup water

½ teaspoon salt, divided

2 tablespoons butter

4 teaspoons Dijon mustard

6 slices thick-sliced white bread, crusts removed*

2 eggs, beaten

1 cup milk

¼ teaspoon black pepper

2 cups (8 ounces) shredded Gruyére or Swiss cheese

Crusty French bread, sliced

*Thick-sliced bread is often sold as "Texas Toast" in supermarket bread aisles.

1. Coat **CROCK-POT®** slow cooker with nonstick cooking spray. Place shrimp, water and ¼ teaspoon salt in small saucepan. Cover; cook over medium heat about 3 minutes or until shrimp are pink and cooked through. Remove shrimp with slotted spoon and reserve ½ cup broth.

2. Combine butter and mustard in small bowl. Spread mixture onto bread slices. Cut bread into 1-inch cubes; set aside.

3. Beat eggs, milk, reserved ½ cup broth, remaining ¼ teaspoon salt and pepper in small bowl; set aside.

4. Spread one third bread cubes in bottom of **CROCK-POT®** slow cooker. Top with one third shrimp. Sprinkle with one third cheese. Repeat layers 2 more times. Pour egg mixture over layers. Use rubber spatula to push bread below surface to absorb liquid. Line lid with 2 paper towels. Cover tightly; cook on LOW 2 hours or until mixture is hot and thick. Serve with French bread for dipping.

Makes 5 cups

Sweet and Sour Shrimp

1 can (16 ounces) sliced peaches in syrup, undrained

½ cup chopped green onions

½ cup chopped red bell pepper

½ cup chopped green bell pepper

½ cup chopped celery

⅓ cup vegetable broth

¼ cup light soy sauce

2 tablespoons rice wine vinegar

2 tablespoons dark sesame oil

1 teaspoon red pepper flakes

2 tablespoons cornstarch

¼ cup water

1 package (6 ounces) snow peas

1 pound cooked medium shrimp

1 cup cherry tomatoes, cut into halves

½ cup toasted walnut pieces

Hot cooked rice

1. Place peaches, green onions, bell peppers, celery, broth, soy sauce, vinegar, sesame oil and red pepper flakes in **CROCK-POT®** slow cooker. Cover; cook on LOW 3 to 4 hours or on HIGH 2 to 3 hours or until vegetables are tender. Stir well.

2. Whisk cornstarch into water in small bowl; mix into vegetable mixture. Add snow peas. Cover; cook on HIGH 15 minutes or until thickened.

3. Add shrimp, tomatoes and walnuts. Cover; cook on HIGH 4 to 5 minutes or until shrimp are hot. Serve over rice.

Makes 4 to 6 servings

Salmon with Beer

4 salmon fillets
(6 ounces each)

Salt and black pepper

1 cup Italian salad dressing

3 tablespoons olive oil

1 yellow bell pepper, sliced

1 red bell pepper, sliced

1 orange bell pepper, sliced

1 large onion, sliced

½ teaspoon dried basil

2 cloves garlic, minced

1 teaspoon lemon peel

2 cups spinach, stems
removed

¾ cup amber ale

½ lemon, cut into quarters

Additional salt and black
pepper (optional)

1. Season both sides of fillets with salt and black pepper. Place in baking dish and pour Italian dressing over fillets. Cover and refrigerate 30 minutes or up to 2 hours. Discard marinade.

2. Pour oil into **CROCK-POT®** slow cooker and lay salmon fillets on top, stacking as necessary. Top with bell peppers, onion, basil, garlic and lemon peel. Cover with spinach. Pour beer over top. Cover; cook on HIGH 1½ hours.

3. Remove fillets to platter and top with vegetables. Squeeze lemon over salmon and season with additional salt and pepper, if desired.

Makes 4 servings

Sweet and Sour Shrimp with Pineapple

3 **cans (8 ounces each) pineapple chunks**

2 **packages (6 ounces each) frozen snow peas, thawed**

⅓ **cup plus 2 teaspoons sugar**

¼ **cup cornstarch**

2 **chicken bouillon cubes**

2 **cups boiling water**

4 **teaspoons soy sauce**

1 **teaspoon ground ginger**

1 **pound medium shrimp, peeled and deveined***

¼ **cup cider vinegar**

Hot cooked rice

*Or 1 pound frozen, peeled, deveined shrimp, unthawed

1. Drain pineapple chunks, reserving 1 cup juice. Place pineapple and snow peas in **CROCK-POT®** slow cooker.

2. Combine sugar and cornstarch in medium saucepan. Dissolve bouillon cubes in water and add to saucepan. Mix in reserved pineapple juice, soy sauce and ginger. Bring to a boil and cook for 1 minute. Pour into **CROCK-POT®** slow cooker. Cover; cook on LOW 4½ to 5½ hours.

3. Add shrimp and vinegar. Cover; cook on LOW 30 minutes or until shrimp are done. Serve over rice.

Makes 4 servings

Scallop and Corn Chowder

6 tablespoons butter, divided

1 bunch leeks, cleaned well and diced

¾ pound pancetta, diced

5 small Yukon gold potatoes, diced

5¼ cups fish stock

2 cups corn

1 to 2 tablespoons minced fresh thyme, divided

¼ cup all-purpose flour

1 pound sea scallops, quartered

1 pint heavy cream

Freshly ground black pepper

1. Heat 2 tablespoons butter in skillet over medium-high heat. Add leeks and cook, stirring until softened and just beginning to brown. Transfer to **CROCK-POT®** slow cooker.

2. In same skillet over medium heat, cook pancetta until lightly browned; transfer to **CROCK-POT®** slow cooker. Add potatoes, stock, corn and ½ to 1 tablespoon thyme. Cover and cook on LOW 4 to 6 hours or on HIGH 2 to 3 hours or until potatoes are tender.

3. In large saucepan, combine remaining 4 tablespoons butter and flour and stir constantly 5 minutes over medium heat to make roux. Stir in 2 large ladles of stock from **CROCK-POT®** slow cooker. Stir until fully combined and return mixture to **CROCK-POT®** slow cooker, stirring until roux blends with stock. Add scallops and cook about 10 minutes or until scallops are just cooked through.

4. Stir in cream and garnish with pepper and remaining thyme.

Makes 6 to 8 servings

Southwestern Salmon Po' Boys

1 red bell pepper, cored, seeded and sliced

1 green bell pepper, cored, seeded and sliced

1 onion, sliced

½ teaspoon zesty Southwest chipotle seasoning

¼ teaspoon salt

¼ teaspoon black pepper

4 salmon fillets (about 6 ounces each), rinsed and patted dry

¾ cup Italian dressing

¼ cup water

4 large French sandwich rolls, split or French bread cut into 6-inch pieces and split

Chipotle mayonnaise, to taste*

Fresh cilantro (optional)

If unavailable, combine ¼ cup mayonnaise with ½ teaspoon adobo sauce. Or substitute regular mayonnaise.

1. Coat **CROCK-POT®** slow cooker with nonstick cooking spray. Arrange half of sliced bell peppers and onion in bottom.

2. Blend seasoning, salt and black pepper. Season both sides of salmon. Place salmon on top of vegetables in **CROCK-POT®** slow cooker. Pour Italian dressing over salmon. Spread remaining peppers and onion over salmon. Add water. Cover; cook on HIGH 1½ hours.

3. Toast rolls, if desired. Spread tops with chipotle mayonnaise and garnish with cilantro. Spoon 1 to 2 tablespoons cooking liquid onto roll bottoms. Place warm fillet on each roll (remove skin first, if desired). Top with vegetable mixture and roll tops.

Makes 4 servings

Saffron-Scented Shrimp Paella

3 tablespoons olive oil, divided

1½ cups chopped onions

4 cloves garlic, sliced thin

Salt, to taste

1 cup roasted red bell pepper, diced

1 cup chopped tomato

1 whole bay leaf

1 large pinch saffron

1 cup white wine

8 cups chicken broth

4 cups rice

25 large shrimp, peeled, deveined and cleaned

Salt and white pepper, to taste

1. Heat 2 tablespoons oil in large skillet over medium heat until hot. Add onions, garlic and salt. Cook and stir until translucent, about 5 minutes. Add bell pepper, tomato, bay leaf and saffron. Cook and stir until heated through. Add wine. Continue cooking until liquid is reduced by half. Add broth. Bring to a simmer. Adjust seasonings, if desired, and stir in rice. Transfer to **CROCK-POT**® slow cooker. Cover; cook on HIGH 30 minutes to 1 hour or until rice has absorbed all of liquid.

2. Toss shrimp in remaining 1 tablespoon oil and season with salt and white pepper. Place shrimp on rice in **CROCK-POT**® slow cooker. Cover; cook about 10 minutes or until shrimp are just cooked through.

Makes 4 to 6 servings

Cioppino

- 1 pound cod, halibut or any firm white fish, cubed
- 1 cup sliced mushrooms
- 2 carrots, sliced
- 1 onion, chopped
- 1 green bell pepper, chopped
- 1 teaspoon minced garlic
- 1 can (15 ounces) tomato sauce
- 1 can (14 ounces) beef broth
- 1 teaspoon salt
- ½ teaspoon black pepper
- ½ teaspoon dried oregano
- 1 can (7 ounces) cooked clams
- ½ pound cooked shrimp
- 1 package (6 ounces) cooked crabmeat
- Minced fresh parsley

1. Combine fish pieces, mushrooms, carrots, onion, green bell pepper, garlic, tomato sauce, broth, salt, black pepper and oregano in **CROCK-POT®** slow cooker. Cover; cook on LOW 10 to 12 hours.

2. Turn **CROCK-POT®** slow cooker to HIGH. Add clams, shrimp and crabmeat. Cover; cook on HIGH 30 minutes or until seafood is heated through. Garnish with parsley before serving.

Makes 6 servings

Scallops in Fresh Tomato and Herb Sauce

2 tablespoons vegetable oil

1 medium red onion, peeled and diced

1 clove garlic, minced

3½ cups fresh tomatoes, peeled*

1 can (12 ounces) tomato pureé

1 can (6 ounces) tomato paste

¼ cup dry red wine

2 tablespoons chopped flat-leaf parsley

1 tablespoon chopped fresh oregano

¼ teaspoon black pepper

1½ pounds fresh scallops, cleaned and drained

*To peel tomatoes, place one at a time in simmering water about 10 seconds. (Add 30 seconds if tomatoes are not fully ripened.) Immediately plunge into a bowl of cold water for another 10 seconds. Peel skin with a knife.

1. Heat oil in skillet over medium heat until hot. Add onion and garlic. Cook and stir 7 to 8 minutes or until onion is soft and translucent. Transfer to **CROCK-POT®** slow cooker.

2. Add tomatoes, tomato purée, tomato paste, wine, parsley, oregano and pepper. Cover; cook on LOW 6 to 8 hours.

3. Turn **CROCK-POT®** slow cooker to HIGH. Add scallops. Cook on HIGH 15 minutes longer or until scallops are just cooked through. Serve over pasta or rice.

Makes 4 servings

Cape Cod Stew

2 pounds shrimp, peeled, deveined and cleaned

2 pounds fresh cod or other firm white fish

3 lobsters (1½ to 2½ pounds each), uncooked

1 pound mussels or clams

2 cans (16 ounces each) chopped tomatoes

4 cups beef broth

½ cup chopped onions

½ cup chopped carrots

½ cup chopped cilantro

2 tablespoons sea salt

2 teaspoons crushed or minced garlic

2 teaspoons lemon juice

4 whole bay leaves

1 teaspoon dried thyme

½ teaspoon saffron

1. Cut shrimp and fish into bite-size chunks and place in large bowl; refrigerate. Remove lobster tails and claws. Chop tail into 2-inch pieces, and separate claws at joints. Place lobster and mussels in large bowl; refrigerate.

2. Combine remaining ingredients in **CROCK-POT**® slow cooker. Cover; cook on LOW 7 hours.

3. Add seafood. Cover; cook on HIGH 45 minutes to 1 hour or until seafood is just cooked through.

Makes 8 servings

Shrimp Creole

¼ cup (½ stick) butter

1 onion, chopped

¼ cup biscuit baking mix

3 cups water

2 cans (6 ounces each) tomato paste

1 cup chopped celery

1 cup chopped green bell pepper

2 teaspoons salt

½ teaspoon sugar

2 bay leaves

Black pepper, to taste

4 pounds shrimp, peeled, deveined and cleaned

Hot cooked rice

1. Cook and stir butter and onion in medium skillet over reduced heat until onion is tender. Stir in biscuit mix. Place mixture in **CROCK-POT**® slow cooker.

2. Add water, tomato paste, celery, bell pepper, salt, sugar, bay leaves and black pepper. Cover; cook on LOW 6 to 8 hours.

3. Turn **CROCK-POT**® slow cooker to HIGH and add shrimp. Cook on HIGH 45 minutes to 1 hour or until shrimp are done. Remove bay leaves. Serve over rice.

Makes 8 to 10 servings

Mediterranean Shrimp Soup

2 cans (about 14 ounces each) fat-free reduced-sodium chicken broth

1 can (about 14 ounces) diced tomatoes

1 can (8 ounces) tomato sauce

1 medium onion, chopped

½ medium green bell pepper, chopped

½ cup orange juice

½ cup dry white wine (optional)

1 jar (2½ ounces) sliced mushrooms

¼ cup sliced pitted black olives

2 cloves garlic, minced

1 teaspoon dried basil

2 bay leaves

¼ teaspoon whole fennel seeds, crushed

⅛ teaspoon black pepper

1 pound medium raw shrimp, peeled and deveined

1. Place all ingredients except shrimp in **CROCK-POT®** slow cooker. Cover; cook on LOW 4 to 4½ hours or until vegetables are crisp-tender.

2. Stir in shrimp. Cover; cook 15 to 30 minutes or until shrimp are pink and opaque. Remove and discard bay leaves.

Makes 6 servings

New England Clam Chowder

6 slices bacon, diced

2 onions, chopped

5 cans (6½ ounces each) clams, drained and liquid reserved

6 medium red potatoes, cubed

2 tablespoons minced garlic

1 teaspoon black pepper

2 cans (12 ounces each) evaporated milk

Salt (optional)

Snipped fresh chives (optional)

1. Cook and stir bacon and onions in medium skillet over medium heat until onions are tender. Place in **CROCK-POT®** slow cooker.

2. Add enough water to reserved clam liquid to make 3 cups. Pour into **CROCK-POT®** slow cooker. Add potatoes, garlic and pepper. Cover; cook on LOW 5 to 8 hours or on HIGH 1 to 3 hours.

3. Mix in reserved clams and milk. Cover; cook on LOW 30 to 45 minutes. Add salt to taste, if desired. Garnish with snipped fresh chives.

Makes 6 to 8 servings

Warm Blue Crab Bruschetta

- 4 cups peeled, seeded and diced plum tomatoes
- 1 cup diced white onion
- ⅓ cup olive oil
- 2 tablespoons sugar
- 2 tablespoons balsamic vinegar
- 2 teaspoons minced garlic
- ½ teaspoon dried oregano
- 1 pound lump blue crabmeat, picked over for shells
- 1½ teaspoons kosher salt
- ½ teaspoon cracked black pepper
- ⅓ cup minced fresh basil
- 2 baguettes, sliced and toasted

1. Combine tomatoes, onion, oil, sugar, vinegar, garlic and oregano in **CROCK-POT®** slow cooker. Cover; cook on LOW 2 hours.

2. Add crabmeat, salt and pepper. Stir gently to mix, taking care not to break up crabmeat lumps. Cook on LOW 1 hour.

3. Fold in basil. Serve on toasted baguette slices.

Makes 16 servings

Zuppa De Clams

- 4 tablespoons olive oil
- 1 red onion, peeled and diced
- 1 package (8 ounces) shiitake mushrooms
- ½ pound cooked chorizo sausage, thinly sliced
- ½ cup sweet red vermouth
- 1½ cups homemade or best quality tomato sauce
- 1 cup dry white wine
- 24 littleneck clams, scrubbed and rinsed

1. Heat oil in skillet over medium heat. Add onion, mushrooms and chorizo, and cook, stirring, until onion is softened, about 8 minutes. Transfer to **CROCK-POT®** slow cooker.

2. Add vermouth, tomato sauce and wine. Cover and cook on LOW 6 to 7 hours or on HIGH 3½ hours. Add clams and cook 10 to 15 minutes more or until clams open. Discard any clams that do not open and serve.

Makes 3 to 4 servings

Serving Suggestion

Serve with crusty Italian bread or over cooked pasta.

Shrimp Jambalaya

- 1 can (28 ounces) diced tomatoes, undrained
- 1 medium onion, chopped
- 1 medium red bell pepper, chopped
- 1 stalk celery, chopped
- 2 tablespoons minced garlic
- 2 teaspoons dried parsley flakes
- 2 teaspoons dried oregano
- 1 teaspoon hot pepper sauce
- ½ teaspoon dried thyme
- 2 pounds cooked large shrimp
- 2 cups uncooked instant rice
- 2 cups fat-free reduced-sodium chicken broth

1. Combine tomatoes with juice, onion, bell pepper, celery, garlic, parsley, oregano, hot pepper sauce and thyme in **CROCK-POT®** slow cooker. Cover; cook on LOW 8 hours or on HIGH 4 hours.

2. Stir in shrimp. Cover; cook on LOW 20 minutes.

3. Meanwhile, prepare rice according to package directions, substituting broth for water. Serve jambalaya over rice.

Makes 6 servings

Manhattan Clam Chowder

- 3 slices bacon, diced
- 2 stalks celery, chopped
- 3 onions, chopped
- 2 cups water
- 1 can (15 ounces) stewed tomatoes, undrained and chopped
- 4 small red potatoes, diced
- 2 carrots, diced
- ½ teaspoon dried thyme
- ½ teaspoon black pepper
- ½ teaspoon Louisiana-style hot sauce
- 1 pound minced clams*

*If fresh clams are unavailable, use canned clams; 6 (6½-ounce) cans yield about 1 pound of clam meat. Drain and discard liquid.

1. Cook and stir bacon in medium skillet until crisp. Remove bacon and place in **CROCK-POT®** slow cooker.

2. Add celery and onions to skillet. Cook and stir until tender. Place in **CROCK-POT®** slow cooker.

3. Mix in water, tomatoes with juice, potatoes, carrots, thyme, pepper and hot sauce. Cover; cook on LOW 6 to 8 hours or on HIGH 4 to 6 hours. Add clams during last half hour of cooking.

Makes 4 servings

Paella

4   cups boneless, skinless chicken breasts, cut into 1-inch cubes

1   cup chopped onion

1   cup chopped tomatoes

4   teaspoons chopped pimientos

1   teaspoon salt

1   teaspoon black pepper

½   teaspoon dried oregano

¼   teaspoon saffron

4   cups cooked rice

4   cups shucked whole clams or canned clams

1   pound shrimp, peeled, deveined and cleaned

1   cup or 2 cans (8 ounces each) lobster meat

8   ounces scallops

1. Place chicken, onion, tomatoes, pimientos, salt, pepper, oregano and saffron in **CROCK-POT®** slow cooker. Cover; cook on LOW 6 hours or on HIGH 2 to 4 hours.

2. Add rice, clams, shrimp, lobster and scallops. Cover; cook on HIGH 15 minutes longer, or until shrimp are pink and firm.

Makes 8 servings

Shrimp and Pepper Bisque

1   bag (12 ounces) frozen bell pepper stir-fry mix, thawed

½   pound frozen cauliflower florets, thawed

1   can (14½ ounces) 99% fat-free chicken broth

1   stalk celery, sliced

1   tablespoon seafood seasoning

½   teaspoon dried thyme

12   ounces medium raw shrimp, peeled

2   cups half-and-half

2   to 3 green onions, finely chopped

1. Combine stir-fry mix, cauliflower, broth, celery, seasoning and thyme in **CROCK-POT®** slow cooker. Cover; cook on LOW 8 hours or on HIGH 4 hours.

2. Stir in shrimp. Cover and cook 15 minutes or until shrimp are pink and opaque. Purée soup in batches in blender or food processor. Return to **CROCK-POT®** slow cooker. Stir in half-and-half. Ladle into bowls and sprinkle with green onions.

Makes 4 servings

Tip

For a creamier, smoother consistency strain through several layers of damp cheesecloth.

Caribbean Shrimp with Rice

  1 package (12 ounces) frozen shrimp, thawed
½ cup fat-free, reduced-sodium chicken broth
  1 clove garlic, minced
  1 teaspoon chili powder
½ teaspoon salt
½ teaspoon dried oregano
  1 cup frozen peas, thawed
½ cup diced tomatoes
  2 cups cooked long grain white rice

1. Combine shrimp, broth, garlic, chili powder, salt and oregano in **CROCK-POT®** slow cooker. Cover; cook on LOW 2 hours.

2. Add peas and tomatoes. Cover; cook on LOW 5 minutes. Stir in rice. Cover; cook on LOW 5 minutes longer or until rice is heated through.

Makes 4 servings

Cream of Scallop Soup

1½ pounds red potatoes, cubed
  3 cups water
1½ cups milk
  2 onions, chopped
  2 carrots, shredded
½ cup vegetable broth
  2 tablespoons white wine
½ teaspoon garlic powder
½ teaspoon dried thyme
  2 egg yolks, lightly beaten
  1 pound sea scallops
  1 cup shredded Cheddar cheese

1. Combine potatoes, water, milk, onions, carrots, broth, wine, garlic powder and thyme in **CROCK-POT®** slow cooker. Cover; cook on LOW 6 to 8 hours or on HIGH 3 to 5 hours.

2. Mix in egg yolks. Cover; cook on LOW 1 hour.

3. Add scallops and cook, uncovered, on LOW 10 minutes. Mix in cheese and cook, uncovered, on LOW 5 minutes or until cheese is melted and scallops are opaque.

Makes 4 to 6 servings

Creamy Seafood Dip

1   package (8 ounces) pepper jack cheese, shredded

1   can (6 ounces) lump crabmeat, drained

1   pound cooked shrimp, peeled, deveined and chopped

1   cup heavy whipping cream, divided

1   round sourdough bread loaf (about 1 pound)

1. Place cheese in **CROCK-POT®** slow cooker and turn to HIGH. Add crabmeat, shrimp and ¾ cup cream. Stir well to combine. Cover; cook 10 to 15 minutes or until cheese is melted.

2. Meanwhile, cut off top of bread and hollow out to create bowl. Cut extra bread into large pieces. Place bread bowl on serving plate. Place extra bread around bowl.

3. Check consistency of dip. Stir in up to ¼ cup additional cream, as needed. To serve, pour into bread bowl.

Makes 6 to 8 servings

Cajun Chicken and Shrimp Creole

1   pound skinless chicken thighs

1   red bell pepper, chopped

1   large onion, chopped

1   stalk celery, diced

1   can (15 ounces) stewed tomatoes, undrained and chopped

1   clove garlic, minced

1   tablespoon sugar

1   teaspoon paprika

1   teaspoon Cajun seasoning

1   teaspoon salt

1   teaspoon freshly ground black pepper

1   pound shelled shrimp, deveined and cleaned

1   tablespoon fresh lemon juice
    Louisiana-style hot sauce, to taste

1   cup prepared quick-cooking rice

1. Place the chicken thighs in the **CROCK-POT®** slow cooker. Add the bell pepper, onion, celery, tomatoes with juice, garlic, sugar, paprika, Cajun seasoning, salt and black pepper.

2. Cover; cook on LOW 8 to 10 hours or on HIGH 4 to 5 hours.

3. In the last hour of cooking, add the shrimp, lemon juice and hot sauce. Serve over the hot rice.

Makes 6 servings

 Note
Enjoy the full flavors of chicken, shrimp and spices in this delicious creole!

Braised Sea Bass with Aromatic Vegetables

- 2 **tablespoons butter or olive oil**
- 2 **bulbs fennel, thinly sliced**
- 3 **large carrots, julienned**
- 3 **large leeks, cleaned and thinly sliced**
  Kosher salt and black pepper
- 6 **sea bass fillets or other firm white fish (2 to 3 pounds total)**

1. Melt butter in large skillet over medium-high heat. Add fennel, carrots and leeks. Cook and stir until beginning to soften and lightly brown. Season with salt and pepper.

2. Arrange half of vegetables in bottom of **CROCK-POT®** slow cooker.

3. Season fish with salt and pepper and place on vegetables in **CROCK-POT®** slow cooker. Top with remaining vegetables.

4. Cover and cook on LOW 2 to 3 hours or on HIGH 1 to 1½ hours or until fish is cooked through.

Makes 6 servings

Slow Cooker Fish Stock

- 2 **tablespoons olive oil**
- 1 **large onion, chopped**
- 2 **carrots, chopped**
- 2 **stalks celery, chopped**
- 1 **cup white wine**
- 2 **whole tilapia, scaled and gutted**
- 8 **cups water**
- 1 **sprig thyme**
- 4 **sprigs parsley**
- 4 **whole black peppercorns**
- 2 **teaspoons salt**

1. Heat olive oil in skillet over medium-high heat. Add onion, carrots and celery. Cook until tender and lightly browned, 6 to 8 minutes. Add wine and scrape browned bits off bottom of pan. Pour mixture into **CROCK-POT®** slow cooker. Stir in remaining ingredients. Cover and cook on HIGH 3½ hours.

2. Skim off any foam; strain and let cool. Chill stock in refrigerator and remove fat that rises to surface.

Makes about 8 cups stock

Shellfish and Chorizo Spanish Paella

  2   tablespoons extra-virgin olive oil
  1   pound chorizo, casings removed
2½   cups long grain white rice
  2   cups bottled clam juice
  1   can (11½ ounces) artichoke hearts, drained
  1   cup dry white wine
  1   cup tomato juice
  ½   cup water
  1   green bell pepper, cored, seeded and chopped
  1   medium red onion, chopped
  4   cloves garlic, minced
  1   teaspoon salt
  ½   teaspoon dried basil
  ½   teaspoon red pepper flakes
  ¼   teaspoon ground turmeric
  ¼   teaspoon black pepper
12   small clams, in shell, rinsed and scrubbed
  1   pound medium-size raw shrimp, peeled, deveined and cleaned
  1   pound cooked crab legs, in shell, cracked

1. Heat oil in skillet over medium heat until hot. Brown and crumble chorizo until lightly browned, about 10 minutes. Transfer to paper towel-lined plate with slotted spoon to drain excess fat. Place in **CROCK-POT**® slow cooker.

2. Add rice, clam juice, artichoke hearts, wine, tomato juice, water, bell pepper, onion, garlic, salt, basil, red pepper flakes, turmeric and black pepper. Stir well to combine. Cover; cook on HIGH 4 to 6 hours, stirring twice.

3. Thirty minutes before serving place clams and shrimp on top of paella. Arrange crab legs on top. Cover; cook about 20 to 30 minutes or until clams open. Discard any unopened clams. Serve hot.

Makes 6 to 8 servings

Creamy Crab Bisque

  4   cups heavy cream
  3   cups fresh crabmeat, flaked and picked over for shells
  3   tablespoons unsalted butter
  2   teaspoons grated lemon peel
  1   teaspoon lemon juice
  ½   teaspoon ground nutmeg
  ¼   teaspoon ground allspice
  3   tablespoons dry red wine
  ½   cup prepared mandlen* (soup nuts), ground into crumbs

*Or other crisp cracker-like saltines.

1. Combine cream, crabmeat, butter, lemon peel, lemon juice, nutmeg and allspice in **CROCK-POT**® slow cooker. Stir well to combine. Cover; cook on LOW 1 to 2 hours.

2. Stir in wine. Add mandlen crumbs to thicken soup and stir again. Continue cooking on LOW 10 minutes longer.

Makes 6 to 8 servings

Creamy Slow Cooker Seafood Chowder

1 quart (4 cups) half-and-half

2 cans (about 14 ounces each) whole white potatoes, drained and cubed

2 cans (10¾ ounces each) condensed cream of mushroom soup, undiluted

1 bag (16 ounces) frozen hash brown potatoes

1 medium onion, minced

½ cup (1 stick) butter, cubed

1 teaspoon salt

1 teaspoon black pepper

5 cans (about 8 ounces each) whole oysters, rinsed and drained

2 cans (about 6 ounces each) whole baby clams, rinsed and drained

2 cans (about 4 ounces each) cocktail shrimp, rinsed and drained

1. Combine half-and-half, canned potatoes, soup, frozen potatoes, onion, butter, salt and pepper in **CROCK-POT**® slow cooker. Mix well. Cover; cook on LOW 3½ to 4½ hours.

2. Add oysters, clams and shrimp; stir gently. Cover; cook on LOW 30 to 45 minutes or until done.

Makes 8 to 10 servings

Cod Fish Stew

½ pound bacon, coarsely chopped

1 large carrot, diced

1 large onion, diced

2 stalks celery, diced

2 cloves garlic, minced

Kosher salt and black pepper

1 can (28 ounces) plum tomatoes, drained

3 tablespoons tomato paste

½ cup white wine

3 tablespoons chopped flat-leaf parsley

3 cups water

2 cups clam juice or fish stock

3 saffron threads

2 potatoes, peeled and diced

2½ pounds fresh cod, skinned and cut into bite-size pieces

1. In skillet over medium-high heat, cook bacon until crisp. Remove with slotted spoon. Add carrot, onion, celery and garlic to skillet, season with salt and pepper and cook, stirring, until vegetables soften.

2. Place bacon and vegetables in **CROCK-POT**® slow cooker. Stir in tomatoes, tomato paste, wine, parsley, water, clam juice, saffron and potatoes. Cook on LOW 6 to 7 hours or on HIGH 3 to 4 hours, or until potatoes are tender.

3. Add cod and cook 10 to 20 minutes or until cod is just cooked through.

Makes 6 to 8 servings

Shrimp Louisiana-Style

1	pound shrimp, unpeeled, rinsed
½	cup (1 stick) butter, diced
⅓	cup lemon juice
1	tablespoon Worcestershire sauce
1	teaspoon minced garlic
1	teaspoon seafood seasoning
½	teaspoon salt
½	teaspoon coarsely ground black pepper
1½	teaspoons grated lemon peel, plus additional for garnish
	Hot cooked rice (optional)
4	lemon wedges (optional)

1. Coat **CROCK-POT®** slow cooker with nonstick cooking spray. Place shrimp in bottom. Add butter, lemon juice, Worcestershire sauce, garlic, seafood seasoning, salt and pepper. Stir well to combine. Cover; cook on HIGH 1¼ hours.

2. Turn off **CROCK-POT®** slow cooker. Stir in 1½ teaspoons lemon peel. Let stand, uncovered, 5 minutes. Serve in shallow soup bowl over rice, if desired. Garnish with grated lemon peel and serve with lemon wedge, if desired.

Makes 3 to 4 servings

Clam Chowder

5	cans (10¾ ounces each) condensed reduced-fat cream of potato soup, undiluted
2	cans (12 ounces each) evaporated skimmed milk
2	cans (10 ounces each) whole baby clams, rinsed and drained
1	can (14¾ ounces) cream-style corn
2	cans (4 ounces each) tiny shrimp, rinsed and drained
¾	cup crisp-cooked and crumbled bacon (about ½ pound)
	Lemon pepper, to taste
	Oyster crackers

Combine all ingredients except crackers in **CROCK-POT®** slow cooker. Cover; cook on LOW 3 to 4 hours, stirring occasionally. Serve with oyster crackers.

Makes 10 servings

Note

Chowder is a milk- or cream-based soup closely associated with New England. It is most often made with clams, but lobster and cod are other favored seafood ingredients.

patio
party foods

Campfired-Up Sloppy Joes

1½ pounds lean ground beef

½ cup chopped sweet onion

1 medium red bell pepper, cored, seeded and chopped

1 large clove garlic, crushed

½ cup ketchup

½ cup barbecue sauce

2 tablespoons cider vinegar

1 tablespoon Worcestershire sauce

1 tablespoon packed brown sugar

1 teaspoon chili powder

1 can (8 ounces) baked beans

6 kaiser rolls, split and warmed

Shredded sharp Cheddar cheese (optional)

1. Brown ground beef, onion, bell pepper and garlic 6 to 8 minutes in large skillet over medium-high heat, stirring to break up meat. Drain and discard excess fat. Transfer beef mixture to **CROCK-POT®** slow cooker.

2. Combine ketchup, barbecue sauce, vinegar, Worcestershire sauce, brown sugar and chili powder in small bowl. Transfer to **CROCK-POT®** slow cooker.

3. Add baked beans. Stir well to combine. Cover; cook on HIGH 3 hours.

4. To serve, fill each split roll with ½ cup sloppy joe mixture. Sprinkle with Cheddar cheese, if desired, before topping sandwich with roll top.

Makes 4 to 6 servings

Serving Suggestion

Serve with a side of coleslaw.

Vegetable Jollof Rice

1 medium eggplant (about 1¼ pounds), trimmed and cut into 1-inch cubes

1¾ teaspoons salt, divided

3 tablespoons vegetable oil, plus more as needed

1 medium onion, chopped

1 medium green bell pepper, seeded and chopped

3 medium carrots, cut into ½-inch-thick rounds

2 cloves garlic, minced

1½ cups converted rice

1 tablespoon plus ½ teaspoon chili powder

1 can (28 ounces) diced tomatoes in juice, undrained

1 can (14½ ounces) vegetable broth

1. Place eggplant cubes in colander. Toss with 1 teaspoon salt. Let stand in sink for 1 hour to drain. Rinse under cold water; drain and pat dry with paper towels.

2. Heat 1 tablespoon oil in large skillet over medium-high heat. Working in batches, add eggplant to skillet and cook, turning to brown on all sides. Remove eggplant to plate as it is browned. Add additional oil, 1 tablespoon at a time, to skillet as needed to prepare all remaining batches of eggplant.

3. Wipe out skillet with paper towels. Add another 1 tablespoon oil to skillet and heat. Add onion, bell pepper, carrots and garlic. Cook, stirring occasionally, until onion is soft but not brown. Add to **CROCK-POT®** slow cooker. Stir in rice, chili powder and remaining ¾ teaspoon salt.

4. Drain tomatoes over 1-quart measuring cup, reserving tomato juice. Add vegetable broth to tomato juice. Add additional water as needed to measure 4 cups total. Pour into **CROCK-POT®** slow cooker. Stir in drained tomatoes; top with eggplant. Cover; cook on LOW 3½ to 4 hours or until rice is tender and liquid is absorbed. Stir well; serve hot.

Makes 6 servings

Tip

Jollof Rice (also spelled "jolof" or sometimes "djolof") is an important dish in many West African cultures.

Asian Chicken Fondue

1 cup shiitake mushrooms, stems removed

2 cups chicken broth

1 tablespoon teriyaki sauce

1 small leek (white and green parts) cleaned, trimmed and chopped

1 head baby bok choy, trimmed and roughly chopped

2 tablespoons oyster sauce

1 tablespoon mirin

   Salt and black pepper

1 tablespoon canola oil

2 pounds boneless, skinless chicken breasts, cut into 1-inch cubes

1 cup peeled, seeded and cubed butternut squash

1 tablespoon cornstarch

2 tablespoons cold water

1 can (8 ounces) baby corn, drained

1 can (8 ounces) water chestnuts, drained

1. Combine mushrooms, chicken broth, teriyaki sauce, leek, bok choy, oyster sauce and mirin in **CROCK-POT®** slow cooker. Cover; cook on LOW while following remaining instructions.

2. Heat oil in large skillet over medium-high heat. Season chicken with salt and black pepper. Add to skillet; cook without stirring until browned on bottom, about 4 minutes. Turn and brown other side. Stir into sauce in **CROCK-POT®** slow cooker. Stir in butternut squash.

3. Cover; cook on LOW 4½ to 5 hours. Twenty minutes before end of cooking, stir cornstarch into cold water; set aside. Stir baby corn and water chestnuts into **CROCK-POT®** slow cooker, then stir in cornstarch mixture. Cover and continue cooking on LOW. Serve with bamboo skewers, fondue forks or tongs so guests may serve themselves as desired. Broth may also be served in small soup bowls.

Makes 6 to 8 servings

Chicken and Brie Sliders

1 red bell pepper, cut into chunks

1 to 2 carrots, sliced

½ cup sliced celery

1 small onion, chopped

1 clove garlic, minced

¼ teaspoon dried oregano

¼ teaspoon red pepper flakes

6 boneless, skinless chicken thighs or breasts

¼ cup all-purpose flour

1 teaspoon salt

½ teaspoon black pepper

1 tablespoon vegetable oil

1 can (about 14 ounces) chicken broth

6 sub rolls, split and toasted or 2 thin baguettes (about 12 ounces each), split and toasted

1 large wedge brie cheese, cut into 12 pieces

1. Place bell pepper, carrots, celery, onion, garlic, oregano and red pepper flakes in **CROCK-POT**® slow cooker.

2. Trim and discard visible fat from chicken. Combine flour, salt and black pepper in resealable food storage bag. Add chicken, 2 pieces at a time; shake to coat with flour mixture. Heat oil in large skillet over medium-high heat. Add chicken; brown about 2 minutes per side.

3. Place chicken over vegetables in **CROCK-POT**® slow cooker; add chicken broth. Cover; cook on LOW 5 to 6 hours.

4. Remove 1 piece of chicken from **CROCK-POT**® slow cooker, slice thinly and arrange on 1 sub roll. Spoon 1 to 2 tablespoons broth mixture over chicken and top with 2 slices cheese. Repeat with remaining chicken, bread and cheese. Slice each sandwich into 3 equal pieces, holding sandwiches together with cocktail picks, if desired. Serve immediately.

Makes 18 sliders

Spanish Paella-Style Rice

2 cans (about 14 ounces each) chicken broth

1½ cups uncooked converted long grain rice

1 small red bell pepper, diced

⅓ cup dry white wine or water

½ teaspoon saffron threads, crushed or ½ teaspoon ground turmeric

⅛ teaspoon red pepper flakes

½ cup frozen peas, thawed

Salt, to taste

1. Combine broth, rice, bell pepper, wine, saffron and red pepper flakes in **CROCK-POT®** slow cooker; mix well. Cover; cook on LOW 4 hours or until liquid is absorbed.

2. Stir in peas. Cover; cook 15 to 30 minutes or until peas are hot. Season with salt.

Makes 6 servings

Tip

Paella can contain a variety of meats as well. For more authenticity—and to turn this dish into a delicious main course—add ½ cup cooked ham, chicken, chorizo sausage or seafood when you add the peas.

196

Burgundy and Wild Cremini Mushroom Pilaf

2 tablespoons vegetable oil

2 cups converted long grain white rice

1 medium onion, chopped

1 cup sliced wild cremini mushrooms

1 small zucchini, thinly sliced

3½ cups beef or vegetable broth

½ cup burgundy or other red wine

½ teaspoon salt

¼ teaspoon black pepper

¼ cup (½ stick) butter, melted

1. Heat oil in skillet over medium heat until hot. Add rice, onion, mushrooms and zucchini. Cook and stir 4 to 5 minutes until rice is slightly browned and onion is soft. Transfer to **CROCK-POT®** slow cooker.

2. Add broth, burgundy, salt and pepper. Drizzle melted butter over all. Stir once. Cover; cook on LOW 6 to 8 hours.

Makes 6 servings

Best Beef Brisket Sandwich Ever

1 beef brisket (about 3 pounds)

2 cups apple cider, divided

1 head garlic, cloves separated, crushed and peeled

2 tablespoons whole peppercorns

⅓ cup chopped fresh thyme or 2 tablespoons dried thyme

1 tablespoon mustard seeds

1 tablespoon Cajun seasoning

1 teaspoon ground allspice

1 teaspoon ground cumin

1 teaspoon celery seeds

2 to 4 whole cloves

1 bottle (12 ounces) dark beer

10 to 12 sourdough sandwich rolls, sliced in half

1. Place brisket, ½ cup cider, garlic, peppercorns, thyme, mustard seeds, Cajun seasoning, allspice, cumin, celery seeds and cloves in large resealable food storage bag. Seal bag; marinate in refrigerator overnight.

2. Place brisket and marinade in **CROCK-POT®** slow cooker. Add remaining 1½ cups apple cider and beer. Cover; cook on LOW 10 hours or until brisket is tender.

3. Slice brisket and place on sandwich rolls. Strain sauce; drizzle over meat.

Makes 10 to 12 servings

Tip

Unless you have a 5-, 6- or 7-quart **CROCK-POT®** slow cooker, cut any roast larger than 2½ pounds in half so it cooks completely.

Hot Broccoli Cheese Dip

½ cup (1 stick) butter

6 stalks celery, sliced

2 onions, chopped

2 cans (4 ounces each) sliced mushrooms, drained

¼ cup plus 2 tablespoons all-purpose flour

2 cans (10¾ ounces each) condensed cream of celery soup

5 to 6 ounces garlic cheese, cut into cubes

2 packages (10 ounces each) frozen broccoli spears

French bread slices, bell pepper strips, cherry tomatoes

1. Melt butter in large skillet. Add celery, onions and mushrooms; cook and stir until translucent. Stir in flour and cook 2 to 3 minutes. Transfer to **CROCK-POT**® slow cooker.

2. Stir in soup, cheese and broccoli. Cover; cook on HIGH, stirring every 15 minutes, until cheese is melted. Turn **CROCK-POT**® slow cooker to LOW. Cover; cook 2 to 4 hours or until ready to serve.

3. Serve warm with bread slices and assorted vegetables.

Makes about 6 cups

Homestyle Apple Brown Betty

6 cups of your favorite cooking apples, peeled, cored and cut into eighths

1 cup bread crumbs

1 teaspoon ground cinnamon

1 teaspoon ground nutmeg

⅛ teaspoon salt

¾ cup packed brown sugar

½ cup (1 stick) butter or margarine, melted

¼ cup finely chopped walnuts

1. Lightly grease **CROCK-POT®** slow cooker. Place apples on bottom.

2. Combine bread crumbs, cinnamon, nutmeg, salt, brown sugar, butter and walnuts; spread over apples.

3. Cover; cook on LOW 3 to 4 hours or on HIGH 2 hours.

Makes 8 servings

 **Tip**

Expecting a crowd? Just double the amounts of all the ingredients and prepare in a 5-, 6- or 7-quart **CROCK-POT®** slow cooker.

Korean Barbecue Beef

4 to 4½ pounds beef short ribs

¼ cup chopped green onions (white and green parts)

¼ cup tamari or soy sauce

¼ cup beef broth or water

1 tablespoon packed brown sugar

2 teaspoons minced fresh ginger

2 teaspoons minced garlic

½ teaspoon black pepper

2 teaspoons dark sesame oil

Hot cooked rice or linguine pasta

2 teaspoons sesame seeds, toasted

1. Place ribs in **CROCK-POT®** slow cooker. Combine green onions, tamari, broth, brown sugar, ginger, garlic and pepper in medium bowl; mix well and pour over ribs. Cover; cook on LOW 7 to 8 hours or until ribs are fork-tender.

2. Remove ribs from cooking liquid. Cool slightly. Trim excess fat and discard. Cut rib meat into bite-size pieces, discarding bones and fat.

3. Let cooking liquid stand 5 minutes to allow fat to rise. Skim off fat and discard.

4. Stir sesame oil into cooking liquid. Return beef to **CROCK-POT®** slow cooker. Cover; cook on LOW 15 to 30 minutes or until hot. Serve over rice; garnish with sesame seeds.

Makes 6 servings

 Tip

Three pounds of boneless short ribs can be substituted for the beef short ribs.

Greek Rice

2　tablespoons butter

1¾　cups uncooked converted long grain rice

2　cans (14 ounces each) low-sodium, fat-free chicken broth

1　teaspoon Greek seasoning

1　teaspoon ground oregano

1　cup pitted kalamata olives, drained and chopped

¾　cup chopped roasted red peppers

Crumbled feta cheese (optional)

Chopped fresh Italian parsley (optional)

1. Melt butter in large nonstick skillet over medium-high heat. Add rice and sauté 4 minutes or until golden brown. Transfer to **CROCK-POT**® slow cooker. Stir in chicken broth, Greek seasoning and oregano.

2. Cover; cook on LOW 4 hours or until liquid is absorbed and rice is tender. Stir in olives and roasted red peppers; cook 5 minutes more. Garnish with feta and Italian parsley.

Makes 6 to 8 servings

Lemon Dilled Parsnips and Turnips

2 cups chicken broth

¼ cup chopped green onions

¼ cup dried dill

¼ cup lemon juice

1 teaspoon minced garlic

4 turnips, peeled and cut into ½-inch pieces

3 parsnips, peeled and cut into ½-inch pieces

¼ cup cornstarch

¼ cup cold water

1. Combine broth, green onions, dill, lemon juice and garlic in **CROCK-POT®** slow cooker.

2. Add turnips and parsnips; stir. Cover; cook on LOW 3 to 4 hours or on HIGH 1 to 3 hours.

3. Turn **CROCK-POT®** slow cooker to HIGH. Dissolve cornstarch in water. Add to **CROCK-POT®** slow cooker. Stir well to combine. Cover; continue cooking 15 minutes longer or until thickened.

Makes 8 to 10 servings

Fresh Berry Compote

2 cups fresh blueberries

4 cups fresh sliced
   strawberries

2 tablespoons orange juice

½ to ¾ cup sugar

4 slices (1½ × ½ inches)
   lemon peel with no white
   pith

1 cinnamon stick or
   ½ teaspoon ground
   cinnamon

1. Place blueberries in **CROCK-POT**® slow cooker. Cover; cook on HIGH 45 minutes or until blueberries begin to soften.

2. Add strawberries, orange juice, ½ cup sugar, lemon peel and cinnamon stick. Stir to blend. Cover; cook on HIGH 1 to 1½ hours or until strawberries soften and sugar dissolves. Check for sweetness and add more sugar if necessary, cooking until added sugar dissolves.

3. Remove insert from **CROCK-POT**® slow cooker to heatproof surface and let cool. Serve compote warm or chilled.

Makes 4 servings

 **Tip**

To turn this compote into a fresh fruit topping for cake, ice cream, waffles or pancakes, carefully spoon out fruit, leaving cooking liquid in **CROCK-POT**® slow cooker. Blend **1 to 2 tablespoons cornstarch** with ¼ cup cold water until smooth. Add to cooking liquid and cook on HIGH until thickened. Return fruit to sauce and blend in gently.

Chili Barbecue Beans

1 cup dried Great Northern beans

1 cup dried red beans or dried kidney beans

1 cup dried baby lima beans

3 to 4 cups water, plus additional for soaking

8 slices crisp-cooked bacon, crumbled or 8 ounces smoked sausage, sliced

¼ cup packed brown sugar

2 tablespoons minced onion

2 beef bouillon cubes

1 teaspoon dry mustard

1 teaspoon chili powder

1 teaspoon minced garlic

½ teaspoon black pepper

¼ teaspoon red pepper flakes

2 bay leaves

1 to 1½ cups barbecue sauce

1. Place beans in large bowl and add enough cold water to cover by at least 2 inches. Soak 6 to 8 hours or overnight.* Drain beans; discard water.

2. Combine soaked beans, 3 to 4 cups water, bacon, brown sugar, onion, bouillon cubes, mustard, chili powder, garlic, black pepper, red pepper flakes and bay leaves in **CROCK-POT®** slow cooker. Cover and cook on LOW 8 to 10 hours or until beans are tender.

3. Stir in barbecue sauce. Cover and cook 1 hour or until heated through. Remove and discard bay leaves. Serve hot.

Makes 8 to 10 servings

To quick soak beans, place beans in large saucepan; cover with water. Bring to a boil over high heat. Boil 2 minutes. Remove from heat; let soak, covered, 1 hour.

Asian Golden Barley with Cashews

2 tablespoons unsalted butter

1 cup hulled barley, sorted

3 cups vegetable broth

1 cup chopped celery

1 green bell pepper, cored, seeded and chopped

1 yellow onion, peeled and minced

1 clove garlic, minced

¼ teaspoon black pepper

¼ cup finely chopped cashews

1. Heat skillet over medium heat until hot. Add butter and barley. Cook and stir about 10 minutes or until barley is slightly browned. Transfer to **CROCK-POT®** slow cooker.

2. Add broth, celery, bell pepper, onion, garlic and black pepper. Stir well to combine. Cover; cook on LOW 4 to 5 hours or on HIGH 2 to 3 hours, or until barley is tender and liquid is absorbed.

3. To serve, garnish with cashews.

Makes 4 servings

Arizona Ranch Beans

1 pound uncooked, dried pinto beans

8 cups cool water, plus more for soaking

½ pound bacon, cooked and drained, reserving 2 tablespoons drippings

1 can (14½ ounces) tomatoes, undrained and coarsely chopped

2 medium onions, chopped

2 cloves garlic, minced

1 can (4 ounces) diced green chiles

1 teaspoon chili powder

½ teaspoon dried oregano

¼ teaspoon ground cumin

Salt

2 limes, cut into wedges

1. Place beans in large bowl and add enough cool water to cover by at least 2 inches. Soak 6 to 8 hours or overnight.* Drain beans; discard water.

2. Place drained beans and 8 cups water in **CROCK-POT**® slow cooker. Crumble bacon into **CROCK-POT**® slow cooker and add reserved drippings. Stir in tomatoes with juice, onions, garlic, green chiles, chili powder, oregano and cumin. Cover and cook on LOW 8 to 10 hours or until beans are tender.

3. Season to taste with salt. Serve hot with lime wedges to squeeze over each serving.

Makes 6 to 8 servings

To quick soak beans, place beans in large saucepan; cover with water. Bring to a boil over high heat. Boil 2 minutes. Remove from heat; let soak, covered, 1 hour.

Strawberry Rhubarb Crisp

Fruit

- **4 cups sliced hulled strawberries**
- **4 cups diced rhubarb (about 5 stalks), cut into ½-inch dice**
- **1½ cups granulated sugar**
- **2 tablespoons lemon juice**
- **1½ tablespoons cornstarch, plus water (optional)**

Topping

- **1 cup all-purpose flour**
- **1 cup old-fashioned oats**
- **½ cup granulated sugar**
- **½ cup packed brown sugar**
- **½ teaspoon ground ginger**
- **½ teaspoon ground nutmeg**
- **½ cup (1 stick) butter, cut into pieces**
- **½ cup sliced almonds, toasted***

*To toast almonds, spread in single layer on baking sheet. Bake in preheated 350°F oven 8 to 10 minutes or until golden brown, stirring frequently.

1. Coat **CROCK-POT®** slow cooker with nonstick cooking spray. Place strawberries, rhubarb, 1½ cups granulated sugar and lemon juice in **CROCK-POT®** slow cooker and mix well. Cook on HIGH 1½ hours or until fruit is tender.

2. If fruit is dry after cooking, add a little water. If fruit has too much liquid, mix cornstarch with 2 tablespoons water and stir into liquid. Cook on HIGH an additional 15 minutes or until cooking liquid is thickened.

3. Preheat oven to 375°F. For topping, combine flour, oats, sugars, ginger and nutmeg in medium bowl. Cut in butter using pastry cutter or two knives until mixture resembles coarse crumbs. Stir in almonds.

4. Remove lid from **CROCK-POT®** slow cooker and gently sprinkle topping onto fruit. Transfer stoneware to oven. Bake 15 to 20 minutes or until topping begins to brown.

Makes 8 servings

Asian-Spiced Chicken Wings

3   pounds chicken wings

1   cup packed brown sugar

1   cup soy sauce

½   cup ketchup

2   teaspoons fresh ginger, minced

2   cloves garlic, minced

¼   cup dry sherry

½   cup hoisin sauce

1   tablespoon fresh lime juice

3   tablespoons sesame seeds, toasted

¼   cup thinly sliced green onions

1. Broil the chicken wings 10 minutes on each side or until browned. Transfer chicken wings to **CROCK-POT®** slow cooker. Add next 6 ingredients; stir thoroughly. Cover; cook on LOW 5 to 6 hours or on HIGH 2 to 3 hours or until wings are no longer pink, stirring once halfway through the cooking time to baste the wings with sauce.

2. Remove wings from stoneware. Remove ¼ cup of cooking liquid (discard the rest). Combine reserved liquid with hoisin sauce and lime juice. Drizzle mixture over wings.

3. Before serving, sprinkle wings with sesame seeds and green onions.

Makes 10 to 16 servings

Note

Chicken wings are always crowd pleasers. Garnishing them with toasted sesame seeds and green onions gives these appetizers added crunch and contrasting color.

Fresh Bosc Pear Granita

- 1 **pound fresh Bosc pears, cored, peeled and cubed**
- 1¼ **cups water**
- ¼ **cup sugar**
- ½ **teaspoon ground cinnamon**
- 1 **tablespoon lemon juice**

1. Place pears, water, sugar and cinnamon in **CROCK-POT®** slow cooker. Cover; cook on HIGH 2½ to 3½ hours, or until pears are very soft and tender. Stir in lemon juice.

2. Transfer pears and syrup to blender or food processor and process mixture until smooth. Strain mixture through sieve. Discard any pulp. Pour liquid into 11×9-inch baking pan. Cover tightly with plastic wrap. Place pan in freezer.

3. Stir every hour while freezing, tossing granita with fork. Crush any lumps in mixture as it freezes. Freeze 3 to 4 hours or until firm. You may keep granita in freezer up to 2 days before serving; toss granita every 6 to 12 hours.

Makes 6 servings

Bananas Foster

- 12 **bananas, cut into quarters**
- 1 **cup flaked coconut**
- 1 **cup dark corn syrup**
- ⅔ **cup butter, melted**
- ¼ **cup lemon juice**
- 2 **teaspoons grated lemon peel**
- 2 **teaspoons rum**
- 1 **teaspoon ground cinnamon**
- ½ **teaspoon salt**
- 12 **slices pound cake**
- 1 **quart vanilla ice cream**

Combine bananas and coconut in **CROCK-POT®** slow cooker. Stir together corn syrup, butter, lemon juice, lemon peel, rum, cinnamon and salt in medium bowl; pour over bananas. Cover; cook on LOW 1 to 2 hours. To serve, arrange bananas on pound cake slices. Top with ice cream and warm sauce.

Makes 12 servings

Lemon and Tangerine Glazed Carrots

- **6 cups sliced carrots**
- **1½ cups apple juice**
- **6 tablespoons butter**
- **¼ cup packed brown sugar**
- **2 tablespoons grated lemon peel**
- **2 tablespoons grated tangerine peel**
- **½ teaspoon salt**
- **Fresh parsley, chopped (optional)**

1. Combine all ingredients except parsley in **CROCK-POT®** slow cooker.

2. Cover; cook on LOW 4 to 5 hours or on HIGH 1 to 3 hours. Garnish with chopped parsley.

Makes 10 to 12 servings

Sweet and Spicy Sausage Rounds

- **1 pound kielbasa sausage, cut into ¼-inch-thick rounds**
- **⅔ cup blackberry jam**
- **⅓ cup steak sauce**
- **1 tablespoon prepared yellow mustard**
- **½ teaspoon ground allspice**

1. Place all ingredients in **CROCK-POT®** slow cooker; toss to coat completely. Cook on HIGH 3 hours or until richly glazed.

2. Serve with decorative cocktail picks.

Makes about 16 servings

Creamy Curried Spinach

3 **packages (10 ounces each) frozen spinach, thawed**

1 **onion, chopped**

4 **teaspoons minced garlic**

2 **tablespoons curry powder**

2 **tablespoons butter, melted**

¼ **cup chicken broth**

¼ **cup heavy cream**

1 **teaspoon lemon juice**

1. Combine spinach, onion, garlic, curry powder, butter and broth in **CROCK-POT®** slow cooker.

2. Cover; cook on LOW 3 to 4 hours or on HIGH 2 hours or until done. Stir in cream and lemon juice 30 minutes before end of cooking time.

Makes 6 to 8 servings

Barley with Currants and Pine Nuts

1 **tablespoon unsalted butter**

1 **small onion, finely chopped**

½ **cup uncooked pearled barley**

2 **cups chicken broth**

½ **teaspoon salt, or to taste**

¼ **teaspoon black pepper**

⅓ **cup currants**

¼ **cup pine nuts**

1. Melt butter in small skillet over medium-high heat. Add onion. Cook and stir until lightly browned, about 2 minutes. Transfer to **CROCK-POT®** slow cooker. Add barley, broth, salt and pepper. Stir in currants. Cover; cook on LOW 3 hours.

2. Stir in pine nuts and serve immediately.

Makes 4 servings

Easy Dirty Rice

½ pound bulk Italian sausage

2 cups water

1 cup uncooked long grain rice

1 large onion, finely chopped

1 large green bell pepper, finely chopped

½ cup finely chopped celery

1½ teaspoons salt

½ teaspoon ground red pepper

½ cup chopped fresh parsley

1. Brown sausage in skillet 6 to 8 minutes over medium-high heat, stirring to break up meat. Drain fat. Place sausage in **CROCK-POT®** slow cooker.

2. Stir in all remaining ingredients except parsley. Cover; cook on LOW 2 hours. Stir in parsley.

Makes 4 servings

Barbecue Roast Beef

2 pounds boneless cooked roast beef

1 bottle (12 ounces) barbecue sauce

1½ cups water

10 to 12 sandwich rolls, halved

1. Combine roast beef, barbecue sauce and water in **CROCK-POT®** slow cooker. Cover; cook on LOW 2 hours.

2. Remove beef from **CROCK-POT®** slow cooker. Shred with 2 forks. Return beef to sauce; mix well. Serve on rolls.

Makes 10 to 12 sandwiches

 Tip
Freeze leftovers as individual portions; just reheat in a microwave for fast meals!

213

Spicy Sweet & Sour Cocktail Franks

- **2 packages (8 ounces each) cocktail franks**
- **½ cup ketchup or chili sauce**
- **½ cup apricot preserves**
- **1 teaspoon hot pepper sauce plus additional hot pepper sauce (optional)**

1. Combine all ingredients in 1½-quart **CROCK-POT®** slow cooker; mix well. Cover; cook on LOW 2 to 3 hours.

2. Serve warm or at room temperature with additional hot pepper sauce to taste.

Makes 16 servings

Boston Baked Beans

- **2 pounds small dry white beans**
- **12 cups water**
-   **Olive oil**
- **¼ cup finely chopped salt pork or thick-sliced bacon**
- **1 cup molasses**
- **½ cup chopped onions**
- **½ cup packed dark brown sugar**
- **2 tablespoons dry mustard**
- **2 teaspoons salt**

1. Soak beans in water in uncovered **CROCK-POT®** slow cooker overnight (or a minimum of 8 hours). After soaking, cover; cook on LOW 3 hours. Drain liquid, reserving 1 cup. Remove beans; set aside.

2. Heat oil in skillet over medium heat until hot. Add salt pork. Cook and stir 5 to 10 minutes to render fat. Remove with slotted spoon and drain on paper towels. Transfer to **CROCK-POT®** slow cooker.

3. Add reserved 1 cup cooking liquid, beans and remaining ingredients; stir well to combine. Cover; cook on LOW 10 to 12 hours or on HIGH 6 to 8 hours.

Makes 8 servings

Blueberry Cobbler

- ¾ cup biscuit mix
- ½ cup packed brown sugar
- ⅓ cup granulated sugar
- 2 large eggs
- 1 teaspoon vanilla
- ½ teaspoon almond extract
- 1 can (5 ounces) evaporated milk
- 2 teaspoons melted butter
- 3 cups fresh or frozen blueberries

  Vanilla ice cream, for serving

1. Spray inside of **CROCK-POT**® slow cooker with nonstick cooking spray. In large bowl, combine biscuit mix and sugars. Add eggs, vanilla and almond extract. Stir to combine. Add evaporated milk and butter. Stir until fully combined.

2. Pour about one fourth of batter into prepared **CROCK-POT**® slow cooker. Place blueberries on top. Pour remaining batter over blueberries. Cover and cook on LOW 5 to 6 hours. Serve warm with ice cream.

Makes 4 to 6 servings

Spicy Fruit Dessert

- 2 cups canned pears, drained and diced
- 2 cups carambola (star fruit), sliced and seeds removed
- 1 can (6 ounces) frozen orange juice concentrate
- ¼ cup orange marmalade
- ¼ teaspoon pumpkin pie spice

1. Combine pears, carambola, orange juice concentrate, marmalade and pumpkin pie spice in **CROCK-POT**® slow cooker.

2. Cover; cook on LOW 4 to 6 hours or on HIGH 2 to 3 hours or until done. Serve warm over pound cake or ice cream.

Makes 4 to 6 servings

Best Asian-Style Ribs

2 full racks baby back pork ribs, split into
  3 sections each

6 ounces hoisin sauce

2 tablespoons minced fresh ginger

½ cup maraschino cherries

½ cup rice wine vinegar

  Water

4 green onions, chopped (optional)

1. Combine ribs, hoisin sauce, ginger, cherries and
vinegar in **CROCK-POT**® slow cooker. Add water to
cover ribs.

2. Cover; cook on LOW 6 to 7 hours or on HIGH 3 to
3½ hours or until ribs are done. Sprinkle with green
onions before serving, if desired.

Makes 6 to 8 servings

Teriyaki Chicken Wings

3 to 4 pounds chicken wings

¼ cup soy sauce

¼ cup sherry

¼ cup honey

1 tablespoon hoisin sauce

1 tablespoon orange juice

2 cloves garlic, minced

1 fresh red chile pepper, finely chopped*
  (optional)

*Chile peppers can sting and irritate the skin, so wear
rubber gloves when handling and do not touch your
eyes.*

1. Place wings in **CROCK-POT**® slow cooker.
Combine remaining ingredients in mixing bowl.
Pour mixture over wings.

2. Cover; cook on LOW 3 to 3½ hours or on HIGH
1½ to 2 hours.

Makes 6 to 8 servings

Corn on the Cob with Garlic Herb Butter

½ cup (1 stick) unsalted butter, softened

3 to 4 cloves garlic, minced

2 tablespoons finely minced fresh parsley

4 to 5 ears of corn, husked

Salt and freshly ground black pepper

1. Thoroughly mix butter, garlic and parsley in small bowl.

2. Place each ear of corn on a piece of aluminum foil and generously spread with butter mixture. Season with salt and pepper and tightly seal foil. Place in **CROCK-POT®** slow cooker; overlap ears, if necessary. Add enough water to come one fourth of the way up each ear.

3. Cover; cook on LOW 4 to 5 hours or on HIGH 2 to 2½ hours or until done.

Makes 4 to 5 servings

Easy Cheesy BBQ Chicken

6 boneless, skinless chicken breasts (about 1½ pounds)

1 bottle (26 ounces) barbecue sauce

6 slices cooked bacon

6 slices Swiss cheese

1. Place chicken in **CROCK-POT®** slow cooker. Cover with barbecue sauce. Cover; cook on LOW 8 to 9 hours. (If sauce becomes too thick during cooking, add a little water.)

2. Before serving, cut bacon slices in half. Place 2 pieces cooked bacon on each chicken breast in **CROCK-POT®** slow cooker. Top with cheese. Cover; cook on HIGH until cheese melts.

Makes 6 servings

Cherry Delight

1 can (21 ounces) cherry pie filling

1 package (about 18 ounces) yellow cake mix

½ cup (1 stick) butter, melted

⅓ cup chopped walnuts

Whipped topping or vanilla ice cream (optional)

1. Place pie filling in **CROCK-POT®** slow cooker. Mix together cake mix and butter in medium bowl. Spread evenly over pie filling. Sprinkle walnuts on top.

2. Cover; cook on LOW 3 to 4 hours or on HIGH 1½ to 2 hours. Spoon into serving dishes. Serve warm with whipped topping or ice cream, if desired.

Makes 8 to 10 servings

Brownie Bottoms

¾ cup water

½ cup packed brown sugar

2 tablespoons unsweetened cocoa powder

2½ cups packaged brownie mix

1 package (2¾ ounces) instant chocolate pudding mix

½ cup milk chocolate chips

2 eggs, beaten

3 tablespoons butter or margarine, melted

1. Lightly grease **CROCK-POT®** slow cooker with nonstick cooking spray. Combine water, brown sugar and cocoa powder in small saucepan over medium heat; bring to a boil over medium-high heat.

2. Meanwhile, combine brownie mix, pudding mix, chocolate chips, eggs and butter in medium bowl; stir until well blended. Spread batter in bottom of **CROCK-POT®** slow cooker; pour boiling sugar mixture over batter. Cover; cook on HIGH 1½ hours.

3. Turn off and let stand for 30 minutes before serving. Serve warm.

Makes 6 servings

Garlic and Herb Polenta

3 tablespoons butter, divided

8 cups water

2 cups yellow cornmeal

2 teaspoons finely minced garlic

2 teaspoons salt

3 tablespoons chopped fresh herbs such as parsley, chives, thyme or chervil (or a combination of any of these)

1. Butter inside of **CROCK-POT®** slow cooker with 1 tablespoon butter. Add water, cornmeal, garlic, salt and remaining 2 tablespoons butter; stir.

2. Cover; cook on LOW 4 hours or on HIGH 3 hours, stirring occasionally. Stir in chopped herbs just before serving.

Makes 6 servings

Tip

Polenta may also be poured into a greased pan and allowed to cool until set. Cut into squares (or slice as desired) to serve. For even more great flavor, chill polenta slices until firm, then grill or fry until golden brown.

Mexican-Style Rice and Cheese

1 can (about 15 ounces) Mexican-style beans, rinsed and drained

1 can (about 14 ounces) diced tomatoes with jalapeños, undrained

2 cups (8 ounces) shredded Monterey Jack or Colby cheese, divided

1½ cups uncooked converted long grain rice

1 large onion, finely chopped

½ (8-ounce) package cream cheese

3 cloves garlic, minced

1. Spray inside of **CROCK-POT®** slow cooker with nonstick cooking spray. Combine beans, tomatoes with juice, 1 cup cheese, rice, onion, cream cheese and garlic in **CROCK-POT®** slow cooker; mix well.

2. Cover; cook on LOW 6 to 8 hours or until rice is tender but not overcooked.

3. Sprinkle with remaining 1 cup cheese just before serving.

Makes 6 to 8 servings

fall
favorites

Simple Shredded Pork Tacos

2 pounds boneless pork roast

1 cup salsa

1 can (4 ounces) chopped green chiles

½ teaspoon garlic salt

½ teaspoon black pepper

12 corn or flour tortillas

Optional toppings: salsa, sour cream, diced tomatoes, shredded cheese, shredded lettuce

1. Place pork, salsa, chiles, garlic salt and pepper in **CROCK-POT**® slow cooker. Cover; cook on LOW 8 hours or until meat is tender.

2. Remove pork from **CROCK-POT**® slow cooker; shred with two forks. Serve on tortillas with sauce. Top as desired.

Makes 6 servings

Tip

Cut the pork roast to fit in the bottom of your **CROCK-POT**® slow cooker in one or two layers.

Harvest Ham Supper

6   carrots, cut into 2-inch pieces

3   medium sweet potatoes, quartered

1   to 1½ pounds boneless ham

1   cup maple syrup

1. Arrange carrots and potatoes in bottom of **CROCK-POT®** slow cooker to form rack.

2. Place ham on top of vegetables. Pour syrup over ham and vegetables. Cover; cook on LOW 6 to 8 hours.

Makes 6 servings

Country-Style Steak

4   to 6 beef cube steaks (about 1½ to 3 pounds total)

    All-purpose flour

1   tablespoon vegetable oil

1   package (about 1 ounce) dry onion soup mix

1   package (about 1 ounce) brown gravy mix

    Water

1. Dust steaks with flour. Heat oil in large skillet over medium-low heat. Brown steaks on both sides. Drain fat. Transfer steaks to **CROCK-POT®** slow cooker.

2. Add soup and gravy mixes and enough water to cover meat. Cover; cook on LOW 6 to 8 hours.

Makes 4 to 6 servings

Serving Suggestion
Serve with mashed potatoes.

Harvest Ham Supper

Spicy Sausage Bolognese Sauce

2 tablespoons olive oil, divided

1 pound ground beef

1 pound hot Italian sausage, casings removed

¼ pound pancetta, diced

1 large onion, finely diced

2 medium carrots, peeled and finely diced

1 large stalk celery, finely diced

½ teaspoon salt

½ teaspoon ground black pepper

3 tablespoons tomato paste

1 tablespoon minced garlic

2 cans (28 ounces each) diced tomatoes, drained

¾ cup whole milk

¾ cup dry red wine

1 pound hot cooked spaghetti (optional)

½ cup grated Parmesan cheese (optional)

1. Heat 1 tablespoon olive oil in large skillet over medium-high heat. Add ground beef and Italian sausage and cook until no longer pink, stirring often to break up meat. Transfer to **CROCK-POT®** slow cooker with slotted spoon. Discard drippings and wipe out pan with paper towels; return pan to heat.

2. Add remaining 1 tablespoon olive oil to pan. Add pancetta and cook until crisp and brown, stirring occasionally. Transfer to **CROCK-POT®** slow cooker with slotted spoon.

3. Reduce heat to medium and add onion, carrots, celery, salt and pepper. Cook, stirring occasionally, until onion is translucent and carrots and celery are just tender. Stir in tomato paste and garlic. Cook 1 minute, stirring constantly, then add to **CROCK-POT®** slow cooker. Stir in tomatoes, milk and wine. Cover and cook on LOW 6 hours. Reserve 5 cups sauce for another use. Toss remaining 6 cups sauce with hot cooked spaghetti and sprinkle with Parmesan cheese, if desired, just before serving.

Makes 6 servings

Tip

Don't add water to the **CROCK-POT®** slow cooker unless the recipe specifically says to do so. Foods don't lose as much moisture during slow cooking as they do during conventional cooking, so follow recipe guidelines for best results.

Peppered Beef Tips

- **1 pound beef round tip roast or round steak, cut into 1- to 1½-inch pieces**
- **2 cloves garlic, minced**

  Black pepper
- **1 can (10¾ ounces) condensed French onion soup, undiluted**
- **1 can (10¾ ounces) condensed cream of mushroom soup, undiluted**

  Hot cooked rice or noodles

1. Place beef in **CROCK-POT®** slow cooker. Season with garlic and pepper. Pour soups over beef.

2. Cover; cook on LOW 8 to 10 hours. Serve over rice or noodles.

Makes 2 to 3 servings

Dad's Dill Beef Roast

- **1 beef chuck roast (3 to 4 pounds)**
- **1 large jar whole dill pickles, undrained**

Place beef in **CROCK-POT®** slow cooker. Pour pickles with juice over top of beef. Cover; cook on LOW 8 to 10 hours. Remove beef to platter and shred with two forks.

Makes 6 to 8 servings

Serving Suggestion

Pile this beef onto toasted rolls or buns or, for an easy dinner variation, serve it with mashed potatoes.

Peppered Beef Tips

Golden Pork with Cinnamon-Sugar Apples

1 pork sirloin roast (about 3 pounds)

1 can condensed golden mushroom soup, undiluted

½ cup water

¼ cup packed brown sugar

2 tablespoons soy sauce

¼ cup granulated sugar

3 tablespoons ground cinnamon

2 Granny Smith apples, cored and sliced

Hot cooked egg noodles or rice

1. Place pork in **CROCK-POT®** slow cooker.

2. Combine soup, water, brown sugar and soy sauce in medium bowl; stir to mix well. Pour over pork. Cover; cook on LOW 8 hours.

3. About 1 hour before serving, combine granulated sugar and cinnamon in medium resealable plastic food storage bag. Add apples; shake to coat well. Place apples on top of pork. Cover; cook 1 hour longer. Serve with egg noodles or rice.

Makes 6 servings

Fall-Apart Pork Roast with Mole

⅔ cup whole almonds

⅔ cup raisins

3 tablespoons vegetable oil, divided

½ cup chopped onion

4 cloves garlic, chopped

2¾ pounds lean boneless pork shoulder roast, well trimmed

1 can (14½ ounces) diced fire-roasted tomatoes or diced tomatoes, undrained

1 cup cubed bread, any variety

½ cup chicken broth

2 ounces Mexican chocolate, chopped

2 tablespoons chipotle peppers in adobo sauce, chopped

1 teaspoon salt

Fresh cilantro, coarsely chopped (optional)

1. Heat large skillet over medium-high heat until hot. Add almonds and toast 3 to 4 minutes, stirring frequently, until fragrant. Add raisins. Cook 1 to 2 minutes longer, stirring constantly, until raisins begin to plump. Place half of almond mixture in large mixing bowl. Reserve remaining half for garnish.

2. Heat 1 tablespoon oil in same skillet. Add onion and garlic. Cook and stir 2 to 3 minutes until softened. Add to almond mixture; set aside.

3. Heat remaining 2 tablespoons oil in same skillet. Add pork roast and brown on all sides. Transfer to **CROCK-POT®** slow cooker.

4. Combine tomatoes with juice, bread, broth, chocolate, chipotle peppers and salt with almond mixture. Purée mixture in blender, in 2 to 3 batches, until smooth. Pour purée over pork roast in **CROCK-POT®** slow cooker. Cover; cook on LOW 7 to 8 hours or on HIGH 3 to 4 hours or until pork is done.

5. Remove pork roast from **CROCK-POT®** slow cooker. Whisk sauce until smooth before spooning over pork roast. Garnish with reserved almond mixture and chopped cilantro.

Makes 6 servings

Turkey Paprikash

2 tablespoons all-purpose flour

¼ teaspoon salt, or to taste

¼ teaspoon black pepper, or to taste

¼ teaspoon sweet paprika

⅛ teaspoon crushed red pepper flakes

1 pound turkey breast meat, cut into bite-size pieces

2 tablespoons olive oil

1 small onion, chopped

1 clove garlic, minced

1 can (14½ ounces) diced tomatoes, undrained

12 ounces egg noodles

¼ cup sour cream

Sliced green olives

1. Place flour, salt, black pepper, paprika and red pepper flakes in resealable plastic food storage bag. Add turkey and shake well to coat. Heat oil in large skillet over medium-high heat until hot. Add turkey in single layer. Brown on all sides, about 3 minutes per side. Arrange turkey in single layer in **CROCK-POT®** slow cooker.

2. Add onion and garlic to skillet. Cook and stir over medium-high heat 2 minutes or until onion begins to turn golden. Transfer to **CROCK-POT®** slow cooker. Stir in tomatoes with juice. Cover; cook on LOW 1 to 2 hours or until turkey is tender.

3. Meanwhile, cook noodles until tender. Drain and place in large shallow bowl. Spoon turkey and sauce over noodles. Top with sour cream and olives.

Makes 4 servings

Roast Chicken with Peas, Prosciutto and Cream

1 **whole roasting chicken (about 2½ pounds), cut up**

   Salt and black pepper, to taste

5 **ounces prosciutto, diced**

1 **small white onion, finely chopped**

½ **cup dry white wine**

1 **package (10 ounces) frozen peas**

½ **cup heavy cream**

1½ **tablespoons cornstarch**

2 **tablespoons water**

4 **cups farfalle pasta, cooked al dente**

1. Season chicken pieces with salt and pepper. Combine chicken, prosciutto, onion and wine in **CROCK-POT®** slow cooker. Cover; cook on LOW 8 to 10 hours or on HIGH 3½ to 4 hours.

2. During last 30 minutes of cooking, add frozen peas and heavy cream to cooking liquid.

3. Remove chicken when done and no pink remains. Carve meat and set aside on a warmed platter.

4. Combine cornstarch and water. Add to cooking liquid in **CROCK-POT®** slow cooker. Cover; cook on HIGH 10 to 15 minutes or until thickened.

5. To serve, spoon pasta onto individual plates. Place chicken on pasta and top each portion with sauce.

Makes 6 servings

Braised Italian Chicken with Tomatoes and Olives

2 pounds boneless, skinless chicken thighs

1 teaspoon kosher salt

½ teaspoon black pepper

½ cup all-purpose flour

Olive oil

1 can (14½ ounces) diced tomatoes, drained

⅓ cup dry red wine

⅓ cup pitted quartered kalamata olives

1 clove garlic, minced

1 teaspoon chopped fresh rosemary

½ teaspoon red pepper flakes

Cooked linguini or spaghetti

Grated or shredded Parmesan cheese (optional)

1. Season chicken with salt and black pepper. Spread flour on plate, and lightly dredge chicken in flour, coating both sides.

2. Heat oil in skillet over medium heat until hot. Sear chicken in two or three batches until well browned on both sides. Use additional oil as needed to prevent sticking. Transfer to **CROCK-POT®** slow cooker.

3. Add tomatoes, wine, olives and garlic. Cover; cook on LOW 4 to 5 hours.

4. Add rosemary and red pepper flakes; stir in. Cover; cook on LOW 1 hour longer. Serve over linguini. Garnish with cheese.

Makes 4 servings

Sticky Caramel Pumpkin Cake

2 cups all-purpose flour

2 teaspoons baking powder

1 teaspoon baking soda

½ teaspoon pumpkin pie spice or ground cinnamon

½ teaspoon salt

1 cup (2 sticks) unsalted butter, at room temperature

1⅓ cups sugar

4 eggs, at room temperature

1 can (15 ounces) solid-pack pumpkin

1 jar (16 ounces) caramel sauce or caramel ice cream topping, divided

Vanilla ice cream (optional)

1. Coat 4½-quart **CROCK-POT®** slow cooker with nonstick cooking spray.

2. Whisk together flour, baking powder, baking soda, pumpkin pie spice and salt in large bowl. Beat butter and sugar in separate bowl with electric mixer on high speed until light, about 3 minutes. Add eggs one at a time, beating with mixer to incorporate each egg before adding another. Beat in pumpkin. With mixer running on low speed, carefully add flour mixture and beat until smooth. Spread evenly in stoneware insert.

3. Cover; cook on HIGH 2 to 2½ hours or until toothpick inserted into center of cake comes out clean. Drizzle ½ cup caramel sauce over cake. Spoon into bowls and serve warm with ice cream, if desired, and drizzle with additional caramel sauce.

Makes 8 servings

Asian Short Ribs

½ cup beef broth

¼ cup soy sauce

¼ cup dry sherry

1 tablespoon honey

1 tablespoon grated fresh ginger*

2 teaspoons minced garlic

3 pounds boneless beef short ribs

1 teaspoon salt

½ teaspoon black pepper

½ cup chopped green onions (optional)

Hot cooked rice

To mince ginger quickly, cut a small chunk, remove the skin and put through a garlic press. Store remaining unpeeled ginger in a plastic food storage bag in the refrigerator for up to 3 weeks.

1. Stir together beef broth, soy sauce, sherry, honey, ginger and garlic in **CROCK-POT**® slow cooker.

2. Season short ribs with salt and pepper. Place in **CROCK-POT**® slow cooker, turning to coat all sides with sauce.

3. Cover and cook on LOW 7 to 8 hours or until meat is fork-tender.

4. Remove beef and place on serving dish. Garnish with green onions. Serve over rice.

Makes 4 to 6 servings

Autumn Herbed Chicken with Fennel and Squash

3 to 4 pounds chicken thighs

Salt and black pepper, to taste

All-purpose flour, as needed

2 tablespoons olive oil

1 fennel bulb, thinly sliced

½ butternut squash, peeled, seeded and cut into ¾-inch cubes

1 teaspoon dried thyme

¾ cup walnuts (optional)

¾ cup chicken broth

½ cup apple cider or juice

Cooked rice or pasta

¼ cup fresh basil, sliced into ribbons

2 teaspoons fresh rosemary, finely minced

1. Season chicken on all sides with salt and pepper, then lightly coat with flour. Heat oil in skillet over medium heat until hot. Brown chicken in batches to prevent crowding. Brown on each side 3 to 5 minutes, turning once. Remove with slotted spoon. Transfer to **CROCK-POT®** slow cooker.

2. Add fennel, squash and thyme. Stir well to combine. Add walnuts, if desired, broth and cider. Cover; cook on LOW 5 to 7 hours or on HIGH 2½ to 4½ hours.

3. Serve over rice or pasta and garnish with basil and fresh rosemary.

Makes 6 servings

Jambalaya

1 can (28 ounces) whole tomatoes, undrained

1 pound cooked andouille sausage, sliced*

2 cups boiled ham, diced

2 cups water

1 cup uncooked rice

2 onions, chopped

2 stalks celery, sliced

½ green bell pepper, diced

¼ cup tomato paste

2 tablespoons olive or canola oil

1 tablespoon minced garlic

1 tablespoon minced flat-leaf parsley

1 to 2 teaspoons hot pepper sauce, to taste

½ teaspoon dried thyme

2 whole cloves

1 pound medium to large shrimp, peeled, deveined and cleaned

*Or substitute 1 pound cooked smoked sausage or kielbasa.

1. Place all ingredients except shrimp in **CROCK-POT®** slow cooker. Stir well to combine. Cover; cook on LOW 8 to 10 hours or on HIGH 4 to 6 hours.

2. Thirty minutes before serving, turn **CROCK-POT®** slow cooker to HIGH. Add shrimp and continue cooking until shrimp are done. Adjust seasonings, as desired.

Makes 6 to 8 servings

Five-Bean Casserole

2 medium onions, chopped

8 ounces bacon, diced

2 cloves garlic, minced

½ cup packed brown sugar

½ cup cider vinegar

1 teaspoon salt

1 teaspoon dry mustard

¼ teaspoon black pepper

2 cans (about 15 ounces each) kidney beans, rinsed and drained

1 can (about 15 ounces) chickpeas, rinsed and drained

1 can (about 15 ounces) butter beans, rinsed and drained

1 can (about 15 ounces) Great Northern or cannellini beans, rinsed and drained

1 can (about 15 ounces) baked beans

Chopped green onions (optional)

1. Cook and stir onions, bacon and garlic in large skillet over medium heat until onions are tender; drain. Stir in brown sugar, vinegar, salt, mustard and pepper. Simmer over low heat 15 minutes.

2. Combine all beans in **CROCK-POT®** slow cooker. Spoon onion mixture evenly over top. Cover; cook on LOW 6 to 8 hours or on HIGH 3 to 4 hours. Serve hot, garnished with green onions.

Makes 16 servings

New England Baked Beans

4 slices uncooked bacon, chopped

3 cans (about 15 ounces each) Great Northern beans, rinsed and drained

¾ cup water

1 small onion, chopped

⅓ cup canned diced tomatoes, well drained

3 tablespoons packed light brown sugar

3 tablespoons maple syrup

3 tablespoons unsulphured molasses

2 cloves garlic, minced

½ teaspoon salt

½ teaspoon dry mustard

⅛ teaspoon black pepper

½ bay leaf

1. Cook bacon in large skillet until almost cooked but not crispy. Drain on paper towels.

2. Combine bacon and all remaining ingredients in **CROCK-POT®** slow cooker. Cover and cook on LOW 6 to 8 hours or until mixture is thickened. Remove and discard bay leaf before serving.

Makes 4 to 6 servings

Harvest Beef Stew

1	tablespoon olive oil
1½	pounds beef for stew
1	quart (32 ounces) canned or stewed tomatoes, undrained
6	carrots, cut into 1-inch pieces
3	medium potatoes, cut into 1-inch pieces
3	stalks celery, chopped (about 1 cup)
1	medium onion, sliced
1	cup apple juice
2	tablespoons dried parsley flakes
1	tablespoon dried basil
2	teaspoons salt
1	clove garlic, minced
½	teaspoon black pepper
2	bay leaves
¼	cup all-purpose flour (optional)
½	cup warm water (optional)

1. Heat oil in large skillet over medium-low heat. Brown stew meat on all sides. Drain excess fat.

2. Place browned meat and remaining ingredients except flour and water in **CROCK-POT®** slow cooker. Mix well. Cover; cook on HIGH 6 to 7 hours.

3. Before serving, thicken gravy, if desired. Combine flour and warm water in small bowl, stirring well until all lumps are gone. Add mixture to liquid in **CROCK-POT®** slow cooker; mix well. Cook 10 to 20 minutes or until sauce thickens. Remove and discard bay leaves before serving.

Makes 6 servings

Wild Rice with Fruit & Nuts

2 cups wild rice (or wild rice blend), rinsed*

½ cup dried cranberries

½ cup chopped raisins

½ cup chopped dried apricots

½ cup almond slivers, toasted**

5 to 6 cups chicken broth

1 cup orange juice

2 tablespoons butter, melted

1 teaspoon ground cumin

2 green onions, thinly sliced

2 to 3 tablespoons chopped fresh parsley

Salt and black pepper, to taste

*Do not use parboiled rice or a blend containing parboiled rice.

**To toast almonds, spread in single layer in heavy-bottomed skillet. Cook over medium heat 1 to 2 minutes, stirring frequently, until nuts are lightly browned. Remove from skillet immediately. Cool before using.

1. Combine wild rice, cranberries, raisins, apricots and almonds in **CROCK-POT®** slow cooker.

2. Combine broth, orange juice, butter and cumin in medium bowl. Pour mixture over rice and stir to mix.

3. Cover; cook on LOW 7 hours or on HIGH 2½ to 3 hours. Stir once, adding more hot broth if necessary.

4. When rice is soft, add green onions and parsley. Adjust seasonings, if desired. Cook 10 minutes longer and serve.

Makes 6 to 8 servings

Sweet & Spicy Pork Picadillo

1 tablespoon olive oil

1 yellow onion, cut into ¼-inch dice

2 cloves garlic, minced

1 pound boneless pork country-style ribs, trimmed of excess fat and cut into 1-inch cubes

1 can (14½ ounces) diced tomatoes, undrained

3 tablespoons cider vinegar

2 chipotle peppers in adobo sauce, chopped*

½ cup raisins, chopped

½ teaspoon cumin

½ teaspoon ground cinnamon

Salt and black pepper, to taste

Substitute dried chipotles, soaked in warm water about 20 minutes to soften before chopping.

1. Heat oil in skillet over medium-low heat until hot. Cook and stir onion and garlic until translucent, about 4 minutes.

2. Add pork to skillet and brown. Transfer to **CROCK-POT®** slow cooker.

3. Combine tomatoes with juice, vinegar, chipotle peppers, raisins, cumin and cinnamon in medium bowl. Pour over pork. Cover; cook on LOW 5 hours or on HIGH 3 hours or until pork is fork-tender. Shred pork using 2 forks. Cook 30 minutes longer. Adjust seasonings before serving, if desired.

Makes 4 servings

Saucy Tropical Turkey

3 to 4 turkey thighs (about 2½ pounds), skin removed

2 tablespoons vegetable oil

1 small onion, sliced

1 can (20 ounces) pineapple chunks, drained

1 red bell pepper, cubed

⅔ cup apricot preserves

3 tablespoons soy sauce

1 teaspoon grated lemon peel

1 teaspoon ground ginger

2 tablespoons cornstarch

¼ cup cold water

Hot cooked rice

1. Rinse turkey and pat dry. Heat oil in large skillet over medium-high heat until hot. Brown turkey on all sides. Place onion in **CROCK-POT®** slow cooker. Transfer turkey to **CROCK-POT®** slow cooker; top with pineapple and bell pepper.

2. Combine preserves, soy sauce, lemon peel and ginger in small bowl; mix well. Spoon over turkey. Cover; cook on LOW 6 to 7 hours.

3. Transfer turkey to serving platter; cover with foil to keep warm. Blend cornstarch and water until smooth; stir into cooking liquid. Cook, uncovered, on HIGH 15 minutes or until sauce is slightly thickened. Adjust seasonings, if necessary. Return turkey to **CROCK-POT®** slow cooker; cook until hot. Serve over rice.

Makes 6 servings

Hearty Cassoulet

- **1 tablespoon olive oil**
- **1 large onion, finely chopped**
- **4 boneless, skinless chicken thighs, chopped**
- **¼ pound smoked turkey sausage, finely chopped**
- **3 cloves garlic, minced**
- **1 teaspoon dried thyme**
- **½ teaspoon black pepper**
- **4 tablespoons tomato paste**
- **2 tablespoons water**
- **3 cans (about 15 ounces each) Great Northern beans, rinsed and drained**
- **½ cup plain dry bread crumbs**
- **3 tablespoons minced fresh parsley**

1. Heat oil in large skillet over medium heat. Add onion; cook and stir 5 minutes or until tender. Stir in chicken, sausage, garlic, thyme and pepper. Cook 5 minutes or until chicken and sausage are browned.

2. Remove skillet from heat; stir in tomato paste and water until blended. Place beans and chicken mixture in **CROCK-POT**® slow cooker. Cover; cook on LOW 4 to 4½ hours.

3. Before serving, combine bread crumbs and parsley in small bowl. Sprinkle over top of cassoulet.

Makes 6 servings

Mexican Corn Bread Pudding

- 1 can (14¾ ounces) cream-style corn
- 2 eggs
- 1 can (4 ounces) diced mild green chilies
- 2 tablespoons vegetable oil
- ¾ cup yellow cornmeal
- 2 tablespoons sugar
- 2 teaspoons baking powder
- ¾ teaspoon salt
- ½ cup shredded Cheddar cheese

Coat 2-quart **CROCK-POT®** slow cooker with nonstick cooking spray. Combine corn, eggs, chilies, oil, cornmeal, sugar, baking powder and salt in medium bowl. Stir well to blend. Pour into **CROCK-POT®** slow cooker. Cover; cook on LOW 2 to 2½ hours or until center is set. Sprinkle cheese over top. Cover and let stand 5 minutes or until cheese is melted.

Makes 8 servings

Warm Spiced Apples and Pears

- ½ cup (1 stick) unsalted butter
- 1 vanilla bean
- 1 cup packed brown sugar
- ½ cup water
- ½ lemon, sliced
- 1 cinnamon stick, broken in half
- ½ teaspoon ground cloves
- 5 pears, quartered and cored
- 5 small Granny Smith apples, quartered and cored

1. Melt butter in saucepan over medium heat. Cut vanilla bean in half and scrape out seeds. Add seeds and pod to pan with brown sugar, water, lemon slices, cinnamon stick and cloves. Bring to a boil; cook and stir 1 minute. Remove from heat.

2. Combine pears, apples and butter mixture in **CROCK-POT®** slow cooker; mix well. Cover; cook on LOW 3½ to 4 hours or on HIGH 2 hours. Stir every 45 minutes to ensure even cooking. Remove vanilla pod before serving.

Makes 6 servings

Bacon-Wrapped Fingerling Potatoes with Thyme

- 1 pound fingerling potatoes
- 2 tablespoons olive oil
- 1 tablespoon minced fresh thyme
- ½ teaspoon black pepper
- ¼ teaspoon paprika
- ½ pound bacon strips
- ¼ cup chicken broth

1. Toss potatoes with oil, thyme, pepper and paprika in large bowl.

2. Cut each bacon slice in half lengthwise; wrap half slice bacon tightly around each potato.

3. Heat large skillet over medium heat; add potatoes. Reduce heat to medium-low; cook until lightly browned and bacon has tightened around potatoes.

4. Place potatoes in **CROCK-POT®** slow cooker. Add broth. Cover; cook on HIGH 3 hours.

Makes 4 to 6 servings

Knockwurst and Cabbage

- Olive oil
- 8 to 10 knockwurst sausages
- 1 head red cabbage, cut into ¼-inch slices
- ½ cup thinly sliced white onion
- 2 teaspoons caraway seeds
- 1 teaspoon salt
- 4 cups chicken broth

1. Heat oil in skillet over medium heat until hot. Brown knockwursts on all sides, turning as they brown. Transfer to **CROCK-POT®** slow cooker.

2. Add cabbage and onion to **CROCK-POT®** slow cooker. Sprinkle with caraway seeds and salt. Add broth. Cover; cook on LOW 4 hours or on HIGH about 2 hours, or until knockwursts are cooked through and cabbage and onion are soft.

Makes 8 servings

Spinach Gorgonzola Corn Bread

- 2 boxes (8½ ounces each) corn bread mix
- 3 eggs
- ½ cup cream
- 1 box (10 ounces) frozen chopped spinach, thawed and drained
- 1 cup crumbled Gorgonzola
- 1 teaspoon black pepper
  Paprika (optional)

1. Coat 4½-quart **CROCK-POT®** slow cooker with nonstick cooking spray.

2. Mix all ingredients in medium bowl. Place batter in **CROCK-POT®** slow cooker. Cover; cook on HIGH 1½ hours. Sprinkle top with paprika for more colorful crust, if desired. Let bread cool completely before inverting onto serving platter.

Makes 10 to 12 servings

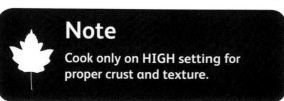

Note

Cook only on HIGH setting for proper crust and texture.

Fall-Off-the-Bone BBQ Ribs

- ½ cup paprika
- ⅜ cup sugar
- ¼ cup onion powder
- 1½ teaspoons salt
- 1½ teaspoons black pepper
- 2½ pounds pork baby back ribs, silver skin removed
- 1 can (20 ounces) beer or beef broth
- 1 quart barbecue sauce
- ½ cup honey
  Sesame seeds and chopped chives (optional)

1. Preheat grill. Lightly oil grill grate.

2. Meanwhile, combine paprika, sugar, onion powder, salt and pepper in small bowl. Generously season ribs with dry rub mixture. Place ribs on grate. Cook for 3 minutes on each side or until ribs have grill marks.

3. Portion ribs into sections of 3 to 4 bones. Place in **CROCK-POT®** slow cooker. Pour beer over ribs. Cover; cook on HIGH 2 hours. Combine barbecue sauce and honey in medium bowl and add to **CROCK-POT®** slow cooker. Cover; cook 1½ hours longer. Sprinkle with sesame seeds and chives, if desired. Serve with extra sauce on the side.

Makes 6 to 8 servings

Risotto-Style Peppered Rice

1 cup uncooked converted long grain rice

1 medium green bell pepper, chopped

1 medium red bell pepper, chopped

1 cup chopped onion

½ teaspoon ground turmeric

⅛ teaspoon ground red pepper (optional)

1 can (about 14 ounces) fat-free chicken broth

4 ounces Monterey Jack cheese with jalapeño peppers, cubed

½ cup milk

¼ cup butter, cut into small pieces

1 teaspoon salt

1. Place rice, bell peppers, onion, turmeric and ground red pepper, if desired, in **CROCK-POT®** slow cooker. Stir in broth. Cover; cook on LOW 4 to 5 hours or until rice is tender and broth is absorbed.

2. Stir in cheese, milk, butter and salt; fluff rice with fork. Cover; cook on LOW 5 minutes or until cheese melts.

Makes 4 to 6 servings

Autumn Chicken

1 can (14 ounces) whole artichoke hearts, drained

1 can (14 ounces) whole mushrooms, divided

12 boneless, skinless chicken breasts

1 jar (6½ ounces) marinated artichoke hearts, undrained

¾ cup white wine

½ cup balsamic vinaigrette

Hot cooked egg noodles

Paprika (optional)

Spread whole artichokes over bottom of **CROCK-POT®** slow cooker. Top with half of mushrooms. Layer chicken over mushrooms. Add marinated artichoke hearts with liquid. Add remaining mushrooms. Pour in wine and vinaigrette. Cover; cook on LOW 4 to 5 hours. Serve over noodles. Garnish with paprika.

Makes 10 to 12 servings

Pizza Fondue

½ pound bulk Italian sausage

1 cup chopped onion

2 jars (26 ounces each) meatless pasta sauce

4 ounces thinly sliced ham, finely chopped

1 package (3 ounces) sliced pepperoni, finely chopped

¼ teaspoon red pepper flakes

1 pound mozzarella cheese, cut into ¾-inch cubes

1 loaf Italian or French bread, cut into 1-inch cubes

1. Cook and stir sausage and onion in large skillet over medium-high heat until sausage is browned. Drain and discard fat.

2. Transfer sausage mixture to **CROCK-POT®** slow cooker. Stir in pasta sauce, ham, pepperoni and red pepper flakes. Cover; cook on LOW 3 to 4 hours. Serve warm fondue with mozzarella cheese and bread cubes.

Makes 20 to 25 servings

Sauerkraut Pork Ribs

1 tablespoon vegetable oil

3 to 4 pounds pork country-style ribs

1 large onion, thinly sliced

1 teaspoon caraway seeds

½ teaspoon garlic powder

¼ to ½ teaspoon black pepper

¾ cup water

2 jars (about 28 ounces each) sauerkraut

12 medium red potatoes, quartered

1. Heat oil in large skillet over medium-low heat. Brown ribs on all sides. Transfer to **CROCK-POT®** slow cooker. Drain excess fat and discard.

2. Add onion to skillet; cook until tender. Add caraway seeds, garlic powder and pepper; cook 15 minutes. Transfer onion mixture to **CROCK-POT®** slow cooker.

3. Add water to skillet, stirring to scrape up any brown bits. Pour pan juices into **CROCK-POT®** slow cooker. Partially drain sauerkraut, leaving some liquid; pour over meat. Top with potatoes. Cover; cook on LOW 6 to 8 hours or until potatoes are tender, stirring once during cooking.

Makes 12 servings

Chorizo and Corn Bread Dressing

½ pound chorizo sausage, casings removed

1 can (10¾ ounces) condensed cream of chicken soup, undiluted

1 can (14 ounces) reduced-sodium chicken broth

1 box (6 ounces) corn bread stuffing mix

1 cup chopped onions

1 cup diced red bell pepper

1 cup chopped celery

3 large eggs, lightly beaten

1 cup frozen corn

1. Lightly spray inside of **CROCK-POT®** slow cooker with nonstick cooking spray.

2. Cook chorizo in large skillet over medium-high heat until browned, stirring frequently to break up meat. Transfer to **CROCK-POT®** slow cooker with slotted spoon and return skillet to heat.

3. Whisk cream of chicken soup and chicken broth into drippings in skillet. Add remaining ingredients and stir until well blended. Stir into **CROCK-POT®** slow cooker. Cover and cook on LOW 7 hours or on HIGH 3½ hours.

Makes 4 to 6 servings

Mango Ginger Pork Roast

1 pork shoulder roast (about 4 pounds)

½ to 1 teaspoon ground ginger, or to taste
Salt and black pepper, to taste

2 cups mango salsa

2 tablespoons honey

¼ cup apricot preserves
Hot cooked rice

1. Season roast with ginger, salt and pepper. Transfer to **CROCK-POT®** slow cooker.

2. Combine salsa, honey and preserves. Pour over roast. Cover; cook on LOW 6 to 8 hours. Turn **CROCK-POT®** slow cooker to HIGH and cook 3 to 4 hours longer, or until roast is tender. Serve with rice.

Makes 4 to 6 servings

Harvest Time Turkey Loaf

- 2 pounds ground turkey meat
- 2 beaten eggs
- ¾ cup bread crumbs
- 1 apple, peeled, cored and coarsely grated
- ¼ cup apple juice
- ¼ cup minced onion
- ½ cup shredded Cheddar cheese
- ¼ cup minced fresh parsley
- ¼ cup ground walnuts
- ½ teaspoon ground allspice

  Parsley sprigs and cranberry sauce (optional)

Combine all ingredients, except parsley sprigs and cranberry sauce, in large mixing bowl; mix well. Shape mixture into 7-inch round loaf. Place loaf in round **CROCK-POT®** slow cooker. Cover; cook on LOW 5 to 6 hours. Slice loaf and garnish with parsley and cranberry sauce.

Makes 6 servings

Polenta-Style Corn Casserole

- 1 can (14½ ounces) chicken broth
- ½ cup cornmeal
- 1 can (7 ounces) corn, drained
- 1 can (4 ounces) diced green chiles, drained
- ¼ cup diced red bell pepper
- ½ teaspoon salt
- ¼ teaspoon black pepper
- 1 cup (4 ounces) shredded Cheddar cheese

1. Pour broth into **CROCK-POT®** slow cooker. Whisk in cornmeal. Add corn, chiles, bell pepper, salt and black pepper. Cover; cook on LOW 4 to 5 hours or on HIGH 2 to 3 hours.

2. Stir in cheese. Continue cooking, uncovered, 15 to 30 minutes or until cheese melts.

Makes 6 servings

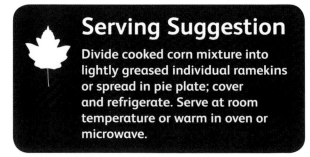

Serving Suggestion

Divide cooked corn mixture into lightly greased individual ramekins or spread in pie plate; cover and refrigerate. Serve at room temperature or warm in oven or microwave.

Chicken with Italian Sausage

10 ounces bulk mild or hot Italian sausage

6 boneless, skinless chicken thighs

1 can (about 15 ounces) white beans, rinsed and drained

1 can (about 15 ounces) red beans, rinsed and drained

1 cup chicken broth

1 medium onion, chopped

1 teaspoon black pepper

½ teaspoon salt

Chopped fresh parsley

1. Brown sausage in large skillet over medium-high heat, stirring to break up meat. Drain fat and discard. Spoon sausage into **CROCK-POT**® slow cooker.

2. Trim fat from chicken and discard. Place chicken, beans, broth, onion, pepper and salt in **CROCK-POT**® slow cooker. Cover; cook on LOW 5 to 6 hours.

3. Adjust seasonings, if desired. Slice each chicken thigh on the diagonal. Serve with sausage and beans. Garnish with parsley.

Makes 6 servings

Polska Kielbasa with Beer & Onions

⅓ cup honey mustard

⅓ cup packed dark brown sugar

18 ounces beer or brown ale

2 kielbasa sausages (16 ounces each), cut into 4-inch pieces

2 onions, quartered

Combine honey mustard and brown sugar in **CROCK-POT**® slow cooker. Whisk in beer. Add sausage pieces. Top with onions. Cover; cook on LOW 4 to 5 hours, stirring occasionally.

Makes 6 to 8 servings

veggie variety

Bean and Vegetable Burritos

2 tablespoons chili powder

2 teaspoons dried oregano

1½ teaspoons ground cumin

1 large sweet potato, peeled and diced

1 can (15 ounces) black beans, rinsed and drained

4 cloves garlic, minced

1 medium onion, halved and thinly sliced

1 jalapeño pepper, seeded and minced*

1 green bell pepper, chopped

1 cup frozen corn, thawed and drained

3 tablespoons lime juice

1 tablespoon chopped fresh cilantro

¾ cup (3 ounces) shredded Monterey Jack cheese

4 (10-inch) flour tortillas

Jalapeño peppers can sting and irritate the skin, so wear rubber gloves when handling peppers and do not touch your eyes.

1. Combine chili powder, oregano and cumin in small bowl. Set aside.

2. Layer sweet potato, beans, half of chili powder mixture, garlic, onion, jalapeño pepper, bell pepper, remaining half of chili powder mixture and corn in **CROCK-POT®** slow cooker. Cover; cook on LOW 5 hours or until sweet potato is tender. Stir in lime juice and cilantro.

3. Preheat oven to 350°F. Spoon 2 tablespoons cheese into center of each tortilla. Top with 1 cup filling. Fold up bottom edges of tortillas over filling; fold in sides and roll to enclose filling. Place burritos seam-side down on baking sheet. Cover with foil and bake 20 to 30 minutes or until heated through.

Makes 4 servings

Autumn Apple and Squash Soup

5 tablespoons butter

2½ pounds butternut squash, peeled, seeded and cut into ½-inch pieces (about 6 cups)

2 large red onions

3 to 4 large stalks celery

3 large green apples, peeled, cored and coarsely chopped

2 to 3 sprigs fresh thyme, stemmed

10 fresh sage leaves, minced

4 cups vegetable stock

Kosher salt and black pepper

½ cup pepitas*

1 tablespoon honey

1 tablespoon water

Crumbled blue cheese (optional)

Extra-virgin olive oil (optional)

Pepitas, or shelled pumpkin seeds, are available at specialty and Latin food stores and make a great garnish to almost any soup or salad. They can be sweetened and spiced as desired and lightly toasted in a skillet on the stovetop.

1. Melt butter in large, heavy saucepan over medium-high heat. Add squash, onions and celery; cook and stir until slightly softened, about 15 minutes. Place vegetables in **CROCK-POT**® slow cooker. Mix in apples, thyme and sage. Add stock and cook on LOW 12 hours or on HIGH 8 hours.

2. Working in batches, purée soup in blender, pulsing to achieve a coarser or smoother texture as desired. Return soup to **CROCK-POT**® slow cooker; set to WARM. (If soup has cooled considerably, set to HIGH.) Taste and adjust seasonings.

3. Combine pepitas with honey and water in small skillet over medium heat. Toast lightly. Ladle soup into bowls. Top with honeyed pepitas and blue cheese, and drizzle with olive oil.

Makes 6 to 8 servings

Variations

Add lump crabmeat or serve with cinnamon and butter toasted croutons.

Curried Potatoes, Cauliflower and Peas

1   tablespoon vegetable oil

1   large onion, chopped

2   tablespoons peeled and minced fresh ginger

2   cloves garlic, chopped

2   pounds red-skinned potatoes, scrubbed, cut into ½-inch-thick rounds

1   teaspoon garam masala*

1   teaspoon salt, plus more to taste

1   small (about 1¼ pounds) head cauliflower, trimmed and broken into florets

1   cup vegetable broth or water

2   ripe plum (Roma) tomatoes, seeded and chopped

1   cup thawed frozen peas

     Hot cooked basmati or long grain rice

Garam masala is a blend of Asian spices available in the spice aisle of many supermarkets. If garam masala is unavailable substitute ½ teaspoon ground cumin and ½ teaspoon ground coriander seeds.

1. Heat oil in large skillet over medium heat. Add onion, ginger and garlic. Cook, stirring occasionally, until onion softens. Remove from heat and set aside.

2. Put potatoes in **CROCK-POT**® slow cooker. Mix garam masala and salt in small bowl. Sprinkle half of spice mixture over potatoes. Top with onion mixture, then cauliflower. Sprinkle remaining spice mixture over cauliflower. Pour in broth. Cover; cook on HIGH 3½ hours.

3. Remove cover and gently stir in tomatoes and peas. Cover; cook for 30 minutes more or until potatoes are tender. Stir gently. Adjust seasoning with more salt, if desired. Spoon over rice in bowls and serve.

Makes 6 servings

Corn Chowder with Basil Oil

3 tablespoons butter

3 leeks, cleaned well and sliced or 2 onions, peeled and diced

4 cups vegetable stock

5 cups frozen corn

3 sprigs fresh thyme, stemmed

Kosher salt and black pepper

½ cup heavy cream

Basil Oil (recipe follows)

1. Melt butter in skillet over medium-high heat. Add leeks; cook and stir until softened and just beginning to brown.

2. Place leeks in **CROCK-POT®** slow cooker and add stock, corn, thyme, salt and pepper. Cover; cook on LOW 8 to 10 hours or on HIGH 4 to 6 hours.

3. Stir in cream and cook until just heated through.

4. Ladle into individual soup bowls and drizzle with Basil Oil as desired.

Makes 6 to 8 servings

Basil Oil

3 cups fresh basil

1 cup olive oil

1. Place basil and oil in blender and process until smooth. Place purée in saucepan and bring to a simmer over medium heat; simmer 30 seconds. Remove from heat.

2. Strain oil through a fine mesh sieve suspended over a bowl. Do not stir or push paste through sieve. Discard solids.

3. Store Basil Oil in refrigerator up to 3 days.

Lentil and Portobello Soup

2   portobello mushrooms (about 8 ounces total), cleaned

1   tablespoon olive oil

1   medium onion, chopped

2   medium carrots, cut into ½-inch-thick rounds

2   cloves garlic, minced

1   cup dried lentils

1   can (28 ounces) diced tomatoes in juice, undrained

1   can (14½ ounces) vegetable broth

1   teaspoon dried rosemary

1   bay leaf

   Salt

   Black pepper

1. Remove stems from mushrooms; coarsely chop stems. Cut each cap in half, then cut each half into ½-inch pieces. Set aside.

2. Heat oil in large skillet over medium heat. Add onion, carrots and garlic; cook, stirring occasionally, until onion softens. Transfer to **CROCK-POT**® slow cooker. Layer lentils, tomatoes with juice, vegetable broth, mushrooms caps and stems, dried rosemary and bay leaf on top of carrots and onion. Cover; cook on HIGH 5 to 6 hours or until lentils are tender. Remove bay leaf and season to taste with salt and pepper before serving. Serve hot.

Makes 6 servings

Black Bean and Mushroom Chilaquiles

2 tablespoons olive oil

1 medium onion, chopped

1 medium green bell pepper, seeded, cored and chopped

1 jalapeño or serrano pepper, seeded and minced*

2 cans (about 15 ounces each) black beans, rinsed and drained

1 can (14½ ounces) diced tomatoes, undrained

10 ounces white mushrooms, cut into quarters

1½ teaspoons ground cumin

1½ teaspoons dried oregano

1 cup (about 2 ounces) shredded sharp white Cheddar cheese, plus additional for garnish

6 cups baked tortilla chips

*Jalapeño and serrano peppers can sting and irritate the skin, so wear rubber gloves when handling peppers and do not touch your eyes.

1. Heat oil in medium skillet over medium heat. Add onion, bell pepper and jalapeño pepper. Cook, stirring occasionally, until onion softens. Transfer to **CROCK-POT**® slow cooker. Add beans, tomatoes with juice, mushrooms, cumin and oregano. Cover; cook on LOW 6 hours or on HIGH 3 hours.

2. Remove cover and sprinkle 1 cup Cheddar cheese over beans and mushrooms. Cover again and cook until cheese melts; stir to combine melted cheese.

3. For each serving, coarsely crush 1 cup tortilla chips in individual serving bowl. Top with black bean mixture; sprinkle with additional cheese, if desired.

Makes 6 servings

Southwestern Corn and Beans

1　tablespoon olive oil

1　large onion, diced

1　or 2 jalapeño peppers, diced*

1　clove garlic, minced

2　cans (15 ounces each) light red kidney beans, rinsed and drained

1　bag (16 ounces) frozen corn, thawed

1　can (14½ ounces) diced tomatoes, undrained

1　green bell pepper, cut into 1-inch pieces

2　teaspoons medium-hot chili powder

¾　teaspoon salt

½　teaspoon ground cumin

½　teaspoon black pepper

　　Sour cream or plain yogurt (optional)

　　Sliced black olives (optional)

*Jalapeño peppers can sting and irritate the skin, so wear rubber gloves when handling peppers and do not touch your eyes.

1. Heat oil in medium skillet over medium heat. Add onion, jalapeño pepper and garlic; cook and stir 5 minutes. Combine onion mixture, beans, corn, tomatoes with juice, bell pepper, chili powder, salt, cumin and black pepper in **CROCK-POT**® slow cooker; mix well. Cover; cook on LOW 7 to 8 hours or on HIGH 2 to 3 hours.

2. Serve with sour cream and black olives, if desired.

Makes 6 servings

Asian Sweet Potato and Corn Stew

1 tablespoon vegetable oil

1 large onion, chopped

2 tablespoons peeled and minced fresh ginger

½ jalapeño or serrano pepper, seeded and minced*

2 cloves garlic, minced

1 cup drained canned or thawed frozen corn kernels

2 teaspoons curry powder

1 can (13½ ounces) coconut milk, well shaken

1 teaspoon cornstarch

1 can (14½ ounces) vegetable broth

1 tablespoon soy sauce, plus more to taste

4 sweet potatoes, peeled and cut into ¾-inch cubes

Hot cooked jasmine or long grain rice

Chopped cilantro (optional)

*Jalapeño and serrano peppers can sting and irritate the skin, so wear rubber gloves when handling peppers and do not touch your eyes.

1. Heat oil in large skillet over medium heat. Add onion, ginger, jalapeño pepper and garlic. Cook, stirring occasionally, until onion softens, about 5 minutes. Remove from heat and stir in corn and curry powder.

2. Whisk coconut milk and cornstarch together in **CROCK-POT**® slow cooker. Stir in broth and soy sauce. Carefully add sweet potatoes then top with curried corn. Cover; cook on LOW 5 to 6 hours or until sweet potatoes are tender. Stir gently to smooth cooking liquid (coconut milk may look curdled) without breaking up sweet potatoes. Adjust seasoning to taste with additional soy sauce. Spoon over rice in serving bowls and sprinkle with cilantro, if desired.

Makes 6 servings

Vegetarian Lasagna

1 small eggplant, sliced into ½-inch rounds

½ teaspoon salt

2 tablespoons olive oil, divided

1 tablespoon butter

8 ounces mushrooms, sliced

1 small onion, diced

1 can (26 ounces) pasta sauce

1 teaspoon dried basil

1 teaspoon dried oregano

2 cups part-skim ricotta cheese

1½ cups (6 ounces) shredded Monterey Jack cheese

1 cup grated Parmesan cheese, divided

1 package (8 ounces) whole wheat lasagna noodles, cooked and drained

1 medium zucchini, thinly sliced

1. Sprinkle eggplant with salt; let stand 10 to 15 minutes. Rinse off excess salt and pat dry; brush with 1 tablespoon olive oil. Brown on both sides in medium skillet over medium heat. Transfer to plate.

2. Heat remaining 1 tablespoon olive oil and butter in same skillet over medium heat; cook and stir mushrooms and onion until softened. Stir in pasta sauce, basil and oregano; set aside.

3. Combine ricotta cheese, Monterey Jack cheese and ½ cup Parmesan cheese in medium bowl; set aside.

4. Spread one third of sauce mixture in bottom of **CROCK-POT**® slow cooker. Layer with one third of lasagna noodles, half of eggplant and half of cheese mixture. Repeat layers. For last layer, use remaining one third of lasagna noodles, zucchini, remaining one third of sauce mixture and top with remaining ½ cup Parmesan cheese.

5. Cover; cook on LOW 6 hours. Let stand 15 to 20 minutes before serving.

Makes 4 to 6 servings

Italian Escarole and White Bean Stew

1 tablespoon olive oil

1 medium onion, chopped

3 medium carrots, cut into ½-inch-thick rounds

2 cloves garlic, minced

1 can (14½ ounces) vegetable broth

1 head (about 12 ounces) escarole

¼ teaspoon red pepper flakes

2 cans (15½ ounces each) Great Northern beans, rinsed and drained

Salt

Grated Parmesan cheese (optional)

1. Heat oil in medium skillet over medium-high heat. Add onion and carrots. Cook, stirring occasionally, until onion softens. Add garlic and stir until fragrant, about 1 minute. Transfer to **CROCK-POT®** slow cooker. Top with vegetable broth.

2. Trim off base of escarole. Roughly cut crosswise into 1-inch-wide strips. Wash well in large bowl of cold water. Lift out by handfuls, leaving sand or dirt in bottom of bowl. Shake to remove excess water, but do not dry. Add to vegetable mixture in **CROCK-POT®** slow cooker. Sprinkle with red pepper flakes. Top with beans.

3. Cover; cook on LOW 7 to 8 hours or on HIGH 3½ to 4 hours, until escarole is wilted and very tender. Season with salt. Serve in bowls and sprinkle with Parmesan cheese, if desired.

Makes 4 servings

 Tip

Escarole is very leafy and easily fills a 4½-quart **CROCK-POT®** slow cooker when raw, but it shrinks dramatically as it cooks down. This recipe makes 4 servings, but it can easily be doubled. Simply double the quantities of all the ingredients listed and be sure to use a 6-quart (or larger) **CROCK-POT®** slow cooker.

Vegetarian Paella

2	tablespoons olive oil
1	medium onion, chopped
1	medium red bell pepper, seeded and chopped
2	cloves garlic, minced
1½	cups uncooked converted rice
2	cans (14½ ounces each) vegetable broth
½	cup dry white wine
½	teaspoon crushed saffron threads, smoked paprika or ground turmeric
¾	teaspoon salt
¼	teaspoon red pepper flakes
1	can (about 15 ounces) garbanzo beans, rinsed and drained
1	package (11 ounces) frozen artichoke hearts, thawed
½	cup frozen peas, thawed

1. Heat oil in medium skillet over medium heat. Add onion, bell pepper and garlic. Cook, stirring occasionally, until onion softens. Transfer to **CROCK-POT®** slow cooker. Stir in rice, broth, wine, saffron, salt and red pepper flakes. Cover; cook on LOW 3 hours.

2. Add garbanzo beans, artichoke hearts and peas to **CROCK-POT®** slow cooker. Do not stir. Cover; cook on LOW about 30 minutes or until rice is tender and liquid is absorbed. Stir well; serve hot.

Makes 6 servings

French Lentil Rice Soup

6 cups vegetable or chicken broth

1 cup lentils, picked over and rinsed

2 medium carrots, peeled and finely diced

1 small onion, finely chopped

2 stalks celery, finely diced

3 tablespoons uncooked white rice

2 tablespoons minced garlic

1 teaspoon herbes de Provence or dried thyme

½ teaspoon salt

⅛ teaspoon ground white pepper or black pepper

¼ cup heavy cream or sour cream (optional)

¼ cup chopped parsley (optional)

1. Stir together broth, lentils, carrots, onion, celery, rice, garlic, herbes de Provence, salt and pepper in **CROCK-POT®** slow cooker. Cover; cook on LOW 8 hours or on HIGH 4 to 5 hours.

2. Remove 1½ cups soup and purée in food processor or blender until almost smooth.* Stir puréed soup back into **CROCK-POT®** slow cooker.

3. Divide soup evenly among 4 serving bowls. Garnish each serving with 1 tablespoon cream and 1 tablespoon chopped parsley.

Makes 4 servings

Use caution when processing hot liquids in blender. Vent lid of blender and cover with clean kitchen towel as directed by manufacturer.

Vegetarian Sausage Rice

2 cups chopped green bell peppers

1 can (15 ounces) dark kidney beans, rinsed and drained

1 can (14½ ounces) diced tomatoes with green bell peppers and onions, undrained

1 cup chopped onion

1 cup sliced celery

1 cup water, divided

¾ cup uncooked converted long grain rice

1¼ teaspoons salt

1 teaspoon hot pepper sauce, plus additional for garnish

½ teaspoon dried thyme

½ teaspoon red pepper flakes

3 bay leaves

1 package (8 ounces) vegetable-protein breakfast patties, thawed

2 tablespoons olive oil

½ cup chopped fresh parsley

1. Combine bell peppers, beans, tomatoes with juice, onion, celery, ½ cup water, rice, salt, hot sauce, thyme, red pepper flakes and bay leaves in **CROCK-POT**® slow cooker. Cover; cook on LOW 4 to 5 hours. Remove and discard bay leaves.

2. Dice breakfast patties. Heat oil in large nonstick skillet over medium-high heat until hot. Add patties; cook 2 minutes or until lightly browned, scraping bottom of skillet occasionally.

3. Place patties in **CROCK-POT**® slow cooker. Do not stir. Add remaining ½ cup water to skillet; bring to a boil over high heat 1 minute, scraping up browned bits on bottom of skillet. Add liquid and parsley to **CROCK-POT**® slow cooker; stir gently to blend. Serve immediately with additional hot sauce, if desired.

Makes 8 cups

Black Bean Chipotle Soup

- 1 **pound dry black beans**
- 2 **stalks celery, cut into ¼-inch dice**
- 2 **carrots, cut into ¼-inch dice**
- 1 **yellow onion, cut into ¼-inch dice**
- 2 **chipotle peppers in adobo sauce, chopped**
- 1 **cup crushed tomatoes**
- 1 **can (4 ounces) chopped mild green chilies, drained**
- 6 **cups vegetable or chicken stock**
- 2 **teaspoons cumin**

  Salt and black pepper, to taste

  Optional toppings: sour cream, chunky-style salsa, fresh chopped cilantro

1. Rinse and sort beans and place in large bowl; cover completely with water. Soak 6 to 8 hours or overnight. (To quick-soak beans, place beans in large saucepan; cover with water. Bring to a boil over high heat. Boil 2 minutes. Remove from heat; let soak, covered, 1 hour.) Drain beans; discard water.

2. Place beans in **CROCK-POT**® slow cooker. Add celery, carrots and onion.

3. Combine chipotles, tomatoes, chilies, stock and cumin in medium bowl. Add to **CROCK-POT**® slow cooker. Cover; cook on LOW 7 to 8 hours or on HIGH 4½ to 5 hours or until beans are tender. Season with salt and pepper.

4. If desired, process mixture in blender, in 2 or 3 batches, to desired consistency. Serve with sour cream, salsa and cilantro, if desired.

Makes 4 to 6 servings

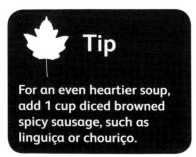

Tip

For an even heartier soup, add 1 cup diced browned spicy sausage, such as linguiça or chouriço.

Baked Beans

2 cans (16 ounces each) baked beans

1 cup ketchup

½ cup barbecue sauce

½ cup packed brown sugar

5 slices bacon, chopped

½ green bell pepper, chopped

½ onion, chopped

1½ teaspoons prepared mustard

Fresh parsley (optional)

1. Place all ingredients except parsley in **CROCK-POT®** slow cooker. Stir well to combine.

2. Cover; cook on LOW 8 to 12 hours or on HIGH 3 to 4 hours. Garnish with fresh parsley.

Makes 6 to 8 servings

Slow Cooker Veggie Stew

1 tablespoon vegetable oil

⅔ cup carrot slices

½ cup diced onion

2 cloves garlic, chopped

2 cans (about 14 ounces each) vegetable broth

1½ cups chopped green cabbage

½ cup cut green beans

½ cup diced zucchini

1 tablespoon tomato paste

½ teaspoon dried basil

½ teaspoon dried oregano leaves

¼ teaspoon salt

1. Heat oil in medium skillet over medium-high heat. Add carrot, onion and garlic. Cook and stir until tender.

2. Transfer carrot mixture to **CROCK-POT®** slow cooker. Add remaining ingredients and stir to combine. Cover; cook on LOW 8 to 10 hours or on HIGH 4 to 5 hours.

Makes 4 to 6 servings

Lentil Stew over Couscous

3 cups dried lentils (1 pound), sorted and rinsed

3 cups water

1 can (about 14 ounces) vegetable or chicken broth

1 can (about 14 ounces) diced tomatoes

1 large onion, chopped

1 green bell pepper, chopped

4 stalks celery, chopped

1 medium, halved lengthwise and sliced

2 cloves garlic, chopped

1 teaspoon marjoram

¼ teaspoon black pepper

1 tablespoon olive oil

1 tablespoon cider vinegar

4½ to 5 cups hot cooked couscous

1. Combine all ingredients except olive oil, cider vinegar and couscous in **CROCK-POT®** slow cooker; stir. Cover; cook on LOW 8 to 9 hours or until vegetables are tender.

2. Stir in oil and vinegar. Serve over couscous.

Makes 12 servings

Caponata

1 medium eggplant (about 1 pound), peeled and cut into ½-inch pieces

1 can (about 14 ounces) diced Italian plum tomatoes, undrained

1 medium onion, chopped

1 red bell pepper, cut into ½-inch pieces

½ cup medium-hot salsa

¼ cup extra-virgin olive oil

2 tablespoons capers, drained

2 tablespoons balsamic vinegar

3 cloves garlic, minced

1 teaspoon dried oregano

¼ teaspoon salt

⅓ cup packed fresh basil, cut into thin strips

Toasted sliced Italian or French bread

1. Mix eggplant, tomatoes with juice, onion, bell pepper, salsa, oil, capers, vinegar, garlic, oregano and salt in **CROCK-POT®** slow cooker.

2. Cover; cook on LOW 7 to 8 hours or until vegetables are crisp-tender.

3. Stir in basil. Serve at room temperature with toasted bread.

Makes about 5¼ cups

Arroz con Queso

- 1 can (16 ounces) whole tomatoes, crushed
- 1 can (15 ounces) black beans, rinsed and drained
- 1½ cups uncooked converted long grain rice
- 1 onion, chopped
- 1 cup cottage cheese
- 1 can (4 ounces) chopped green chilies
- 2 tablespoons vegetable oil
- 3 teaspoons minced garlic
- 2 cups grated Monterey Jack cheese, divided

1. Combine tomatoes, beans, rice, onion, cottage cheese, chilies, oil, garlic and 1 cup cheese in **CROCK-POT®** slow cooker; mix thoroughly.

2. Cover; cook on LOW 6 to 9 hours or until liquid is absorbed. Sprinkle with remaining cheese before serving.

Makes 8 to 10 servings

Southwestern Stuffed Peppers

- 4 green bell peppers
- 1 can (15 ounces) black beans, rinsed and drained
- 1 cup (4 ounces) shredded pepper jack cheese
- ¾ cup medium salsa
- ½ cup frozen corn
- ½ cup chopped green onions
- ⅓ cup uncooked long grain white rice
- 1 teaspoon chili powder
- ½ teaspoon ground cumin
  Sour cream (optional)

1. Cut thin slice off top of each bell pepper. Carefully remove seeds and membrane, leaving pepper whole.

2. Combine beans, cheese, salsa, corn, green onions, rice, chili powder and cumin in medium bowl. Spoon filling evenly into each pepper. Place peppers in **CROCK-POT®** slow cooker.

3. Cover; cook on LOW 4 to 6 hours. Serve with sour cream, if desired.

Makes 4 servings

Spring Pea and Mint Broth Soup

- 8 cups water
- 3 carrots, cut into chunks
- 2 onions, coarsely chopped
- 2 to 3 leeks, cleaned well and coarsely chopped
- 2 stalks celery, cut into chunks
- 1 bunch fresh mint
- 3 to 4 cups fresh spring peas or 1 bag (32 ounces) frozen peas
- 1 tablespoon fresh lemon juice
  Kosher salt and black pepper
  Creme fraîche or sour cream

1. Combine water, carrots, onions, leeks, celery and mint in **CROCK-POT®** slow cooker. Cover and cook on HIGH 5 hours.

2. Strain broth and return to **CROCK-POT®** slow cooker. Discard solids. Add peas and lemon juice. Cover and cook on LOW 4 to 5 hours or on HIGH 2 to 3 hours.

3. Season with salt and pepper. Ladle soup into bowls and garnish with dollop of creme fraîche.

Makes 6 to 8 servings

Red Hot Applesauce

- 10 to 12 apples, peeled, cored and chopped
- ¾ cup hot cinnamon candies
- ½ cup apple juice or water

1. Combine apples, candies and apple juice in **CROCK-POT®** slow cooker.

2. Cover; cook on LOW 7 to 8 hours or on HIGH 4 hours or until desired consistency. Serve warm or chilled.

Makes 6 servings

Artichoke and Tomato Paella

- 4 cups vegetable broth
- 2 cups converted white rice
- 5 ounces (½ of 10-ounce package) frozen chopped spinach, thawed and drained
- 1 green bell pepper, cored, seeded and chopped
- 1 medium ripe tomato, sliced into wedges
- 1 medium yellow onion, chopped
- 1 medium carrot, peeled and diced
- 3 cloves garlic, minced
- 1 tablespoon minced flat-leaf parsley
- 1 teaspoon salt
- ½ teaspoon black pepper
- 1 can (about 14 ounces) quartered artichoke hearts, rinsed and well-drained
- ½ cup frozen peas

1. Combine broth, rice, spinach, bell pepper, tomato, onion, carrot, garlic, parsley, salt and black pepper in **CROCK-POT®** slow cooker. Mix thoroughly. Cover; cook on LOW 4 hours or on HIGH 2 hours.

2. Add artichoke hearts and peas. Cover; cook on HIGH 15 minutes. Mix well before serving.

Makes 8 servings

Vegetable Curry

- 4 baking potatoes, diced
- 1 large onion, chopped
- 1 red bell pepper, chopped
- 2 carrots, diced
- 2 tomatoes, chopped
- 1 can (6 ounces) tomato paste
- ¾ cup water
- 2 teaspoons cumin seeds
- ½ teaspoon garlic powder
- ½ teaspoon salt
- 3 cups cauliflower
- 1 package (10 ounces) frozen peas, thawed

1. Combine potatoes, onion, bell pepper, carrots and tomatoes in **CROCK-POT®** slow cooker. Stir in tomato paste, water, cumin seeds, garlic powder and salt. Add cauliflower; stir well.

2. Cover; cook on LOW 8 to 9 hours or until vegetables are tender. Stir in peas before serving.

Makes 6 servings

Macaroni and Cheese

6 cups cooked macaroni

2 tablespoons butter

4 cups evaporated milk

6 cups (24 ounces) shredded Cheddar cheese

2 teaspoons salt

½ teaspoon black pepper

1. Toss macaroni with butter in large bowl. Stir in evaporated milk, cheese, salt and pepper; place in **CROCK-POT**® slow cooker.

2. Cover; cook on HIGH 2 to 3 hours.

Makes 6 to 8 servings

Tip

Make this mac and cheese recipe more fun. Add some tasty mix-ins: diced green or red bell pepper, peas, hot dog slices, chopped tomato, browned ground beef or chopped onion. Be creative!

Cuban Black Beans and Rice

3¾ cups vegetable or chicken broth

1½ cups uncooked brown rice

1 large onion, chopped

1 jalapeño pepper, seeded and chopped*

3 cloves garlic, minced

2 teaspoons ground cumin

1 teaspoon salt

2 cans (15 ounces each) black beans, rinsed and drained

1 tablespoon fresh lime juice

Sour cream (optional)

Chopped green onions (optional)

Jalapeño peppers can sting and irritate the skin, so wear rubber gloves when handling peppers and do not touch your eyes.

1. Place broth, rice, onion, jalapeño pepper, garlic, cumin and salt in **CROCK-POT**® slow cooker; mix well. Cover; cook on LOW 7½ hours or until rice is tender.

2. Stir in beans and lime juice. Cover; cook 15 to 20 minutes more or until beans are heated through. Garnish with sour cream and green onions.

Makes 4 to 6 servings

Artichoke and Nacho Cheese Dip

2 cans (10¾ ounces each) condensed nacho cheese soup, undiluted

1 can (about 14 ounces) quartered artichoke hearts, drained and coarsely chopped

1 cup (4 ounces) shredded or thinly sliced pepper jack cheese

1 can (4 ounces) evaporated milk

2 tablespoons minced chives, divided

½ teaspoon paprika

Crackers or chips

1. Combine soup, artichoke hearts, cheese, evaporated milk, 1 tablespoon chives and paprika in **CROCK-POT®** slow cooker. Cover; cook on LOW 2 hours.

2. Stir well. Sprinkle with remaining 1 tablespoon chives and serve with crackers.

Makes about 4 cups

Black Bean Stuffed Peppers

Nonstick cooking spray

1 medium onion, finely chopped

¼ teaspoon ground red pepper

¼ teaspoon dried oregano

¼ teaspoon ground cumin

¼ teaspoon chili powder

1 can (15 ounces) black beans, rinsed and drained

6 tall green bell peppers, tops removed, cored and seeded

1 cup (4 ounces) shredded Monterey Jack cheese

1 cup tomato salsa

½ cup sour cream

1. Spray medium skillet with nonstick cooking spray; add onion and cook until golden. Add ground red pepper, oregano, cumin and chili powder.

2. Mash half of black beans with cooked onion in medium bowl. Stir in remaining beans. Place bell peppers in **CROCK-POT®** slow cooker; spoon black bean mixture into bell peppers. Sprinkle cheese over peppers. Pour salsa over cheese. Cover; cook on LOW 6 to 8 hours or on HIGH 3 to 4 hours.

3. Serve each pepper with a dollop of sour cream.

Makes 6 servings

autumn

Asiago and Asparagus Risotto-Style Rice

- 2 cups chopped onion
- 1 can (about 14 ounces) vegetable broth
- 1 cup uncooked converted rice
- 2 medium cloves garlic, minced
- ½ pound asparagus spears, trimmed and broken into 1-inch pieces
- 1 to 1¼ cups half-and-half, divided
- ½ cup shredded Asiago cheese, plus additional for garnish
- ¼ cup (½ stick) butter, cut into small pieces
- 2 ounces pine nuts or slivered almonds, toasted
- 1 teaspoon salt

1. Combine onion, broth, rice and garlic in **CROCK-POT®** slow cooker. Stir until well blended. Cover; cook on HIGH 2 hours or until rice is tender.

2. Stir in asparagus and ½ cup half-and-half. Cover; cook 20 to 30 minutes more or until asparagus is crisp-tender.

3. Stir in remaining ingredients; cover and let stand 5 minutes to allow cheese to melt slightly. Fluff with fork and garnish with additional Asiago cheese before serving.

Makes 4 servings

Orange Soup

- 2 tablespoons olive oil
- 1 small onion, minced
- ¼ cup peeled, minced fresh ginger
- 4 to 5 cups peeled, sliced carrots (about 1½ pounds)
- 3 to 4 cups vegetable stock, divided
- 1½ cups orange juice
- ½ cup half-and-half
- Salt and black pepper

1. Heat oil in large, heavy saucepan over medium-high heat. Add onion and ginger; cook and stir until onion is translucent, about 5 minutes.

2. Place onion and ginger in **CROCK-POT®** slow cooker; add carrots and 3 cups stock. Cover; cook on LOW 7 to 8 hours or on HIGH 3 to 4 hours.

3. Using an immersion blender, regular blender or food processor, purée soup; return to **CROCK-POT®** slow cooker. Stir in orange juice and half-and-half; cook on HIGH 15 to 20 minutes or until heated through. Do not simmer. Season soup to taste with salt and pepper. Thin with remaining stock as desired.

Makes 6 to 8 servings

Creamy Red Pepper Polenta

- ¼ cup (½ stick) butter, melted
- ¼ teaspoon paprika, plus additional for garnish
- ⅛ teaspoon ground red pepper
- ⅛ teaspoon ground cumin
- 6 cups boiling water
- 2 cups yellow cornmeal
- 1 small red bell pepper, cored, seeded and finely chopped
- 2 teaspoons salt

1. Combine butter, paprika, red pepper and cumin in **CROCK-POT**® slow cooker. Add hot water, cornmeal, bell pepper and salt. Stir well to combine.

2. Cover; cook on LOW 3 to 4 hours or on HIGH 1 to 2 hours, stirring occasionally. Garnish with additional paprika.

Makes 4 to 6 servings

Ziti Ratatouille

- 1 large eggplant, peeled and cut into ½-inch cubes (about 1½ pounds)
- 2 medium zucchini, cut into ½-inch cubes
- 1 green or red bell pepper, seeded and cut into ½-inch pieces
- 1 large onion, chopped
- 4 cloves garlic, minced
- 1 jar (about 24 ounces) marinara sauce
- 2 cans (about 14 ounces each) diced tomatoes with garlic and onions, undrained
- 1 can (6 ounces) pitted black olives, drained
- 1 package (8 ounces) ziti pasta
  Lemon juice (optional)
  Shredded Parmesan cheese (optional)

1. Combine eggplant, zucchini, bell pepper, onion, garlic, marinara sauce and tomatoes with juice in **CROCK-POT**® slow cooker. Cover; cook on LOW 4½ hours.

2. Stir in olives and pasta. Cover; cook 25 minutes. Drizzle with lemon juice and sprinkle with Parmesan cheese, if desired.

Makes 6 to 8 servings

Pesto Rice and Beans

1 can (15 ounces) Great Northern beans, rinsed and drained

1 can (about 14 ounces) vegetable or chicken broth

¾ cup uncooked converted long grain rice

1½ cups frozen cut green beans, thawed and drained

½ cup prepared pesto

Grated Parmesan cheese (optional)

1. Combine Great Northern beans, broth and rice in **CROCK-POT®** slow cooker. Cover; cook on LOW 2 hours.

2. Stir in green beans. Cover; cook 1 hour or until rice and beans are tender.

3. Turn off **CROCK-POT®** slow cooker and transfer stoneware to heatproof surface. Stir in pesto and Parmesan cheese, if desired. Let stand, covered, 5 minutes or until cheese is melted. Serve immediately.

Makes 8 servings

Double Thick Baked Potato-Cheese Soup

2 pounds baking potatoes, peeled and cut into ½-inch cubes

2 cans (10½ ounces each) condensed cream of mushroom soup

1½ cups finely chopped green onions, divided

¼ teaspoon garlic powder

⅛ teaspoon ground red pepper

1½ cups (6 ounces) shredded sharp Cheddar cheese

1 cup (8 ounces) sour cream

1 cup milk

Black pepper

1. Combine potatoes, cream of mushroom soup, 1 cup green onions, garlic powder and red pepper in **CROCK-POT®** slow cooker. Cover; cook on LOW 8 hours or on HIGH 4 hours.

2. Add cheese, sour cream and milk; stir until cheese has completely melted. Cover; cook on HIGH 10 minutes. Season to taste with black pepper. Garnish with remaining green onions.

Makes 6 servings

Meatless Sloppy Joes

2 cups thinly sliced onions

2 cups chopped green bell peppers

1 can (about 15 ounces) kidney beans, drained and mashed

1 can (8 ounces) tomato sauce

2 tablespoons ketchup

1 tablespoon yellow mustard

2 cloves garlic, finely chopped

1 teaspoon chili powder

Cider vinegar (optional)

4 sandwich rolls

1. Combine onions, bell peppers, beans, tomato sauce, ketchup, mustard, garlic and chili powder in **CROCK-POT**® slow cooker.

2. Cover; cook on LOW 5 to 5½ hours or until vegetables are tender. Season to taste with cider vinegar, if desired. Serve on rolls.

Makes 4 servings

Caribbean Sweet Potato and Bean Stew

2 medium sweet potatoes (about 1 pound), peeled and cut into 1-inch cubes

2 cups frozen cut green beans

1 can (about 15 ounces) black beans, rinsed and drained

1 can (about 14 ounces) vegetable broth

1 small onion, sliced

2 teaspoons Caribbean jerk seasoning

½ teaspoon dried thyme

¼ teaspoon salt

¼ teaspoon ground cinnamon

⅓ cup slivered almonds, toasted*

To toast almonds, spread in single layer on baking sheet. Bake in preheated 350°F oven 8 to 10 minutes or until golden brown, stirring frequently.

1. Combine sweet potatoes, beans, broth, onion, jerk seasoning, thyme, salt and cinnamon in **CROCK-POT**® slow cooker.

2. Cover; cook on LOW 5 to 6 hours or until vegetables are tender. Serve with almonds.

Makes 4 servings

Slow Cooker Vegetable Stock

- 3 carrots, coarsely chopped
- 3 parsnips, coarsely chopped
- 3 onions, quartered
- 3 leeks, coarsely chopped
- 3 stalks celery, coarsely chopped
- 3 bay leaves
- 2 sprigs thyme
- 4 sprigs parsley
- 8 whole peppercorns
  Water
  Kosher salt, to taste

1. Add all ingredients to **CROCK-POT®** slow cooker and fill three quarters full with water. Season with salt. Cook on LOW 10 to 12 hours or on HIGH 6 to 8 hours.

2. Strain stock and discard solids. Allow stock to cool to room temperature. Refrigerate, freeze or use immediately.

Makes 10 to 12 cups stock

Note

This recipe calls for bay leaves, thyme and parsley, but any combination of herbs and spices can be used to create a signature broth for a special soup such as Vietnamese Pho. Try a variety of classic herbs and spices such as rosemary, sage, parsley and chives, or experiment with more exotic varieties such as Thai basil, mint, cilantro, ginger, lemongrass and star anise. Varying the vegetables to suit the soup also offers limitless possibilities with additions such as turnip, sweet potato and mushrooms.

Broccoli and Cheese Strata

- 2 cups chopped broccoli florets
- 4 slices firm white bread, ½ inch thick
- 4 teaspoons butter
- 1½ cups (6 ounces) shredded Cheddar cheese
- 1½ cups milk
- 3 eggs
- ½ teaspoon salt
- ½ teaspoon hot pepper sauce
- ⅛ teaspoon black pepper

1. Butter 1-quart casserole or soufflé dish that will fit in **CROCK-POT®** slow cooker. Cook broccoli in boiling water 10 minutes or until tender. Drain. Spread one side of each bread slice with 1 teaspoon butter. Arrange 2 slices bread, buttered sides up, in prepared casserole dish. Layer cheese, broccoli and remaining 2 bread slices, buttered sides down.

2. Beat milk, eggs, salt, hot pepper sauce and black pepper in medium bowl. Slowly pour over bread.

3. Place small wire rack in **CROCK-POT®** slow cooker. Pour in 1 cup water. Place casserole on rack. Cover; cook on HIGH 3 hours.

Makes 4 servings

soup
for supper

Beef Fajita Soup

1 pound beef stew meat

1 can (15 ounces) pinto beans, rinsed and drained

1 can (15 ounces) black beans, rinsed and drained

1 can (about 14 ounces) diced tomatoes with roasted garlic, undrained

1 can (about 14 ounces) beef broth

1 small green bell pepper, thinly sliced

1 small red bell pepper, thinly sliced

1 small onion, thinly sliced

1½ cups water

2 teaspoons ground cumin

1 teaspoon seasoned salt

1 teaspoon black pepper

1. Combine beef, beans, tomatoes with juice, broth, bell peppers, onion, water, cumin, salt and black pepper in **CROCK-POT®** slow cooker.

2. Cover; cook on LOW 8 hours.

Makes 8 servings

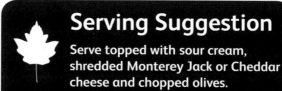

Serving Suggestion

Serve topped with sour cream, shredded Monterey Jack or Cheddar cheese and chopped olives.

Middle Eastern Beef and Eggplant Stew

1 teaspoon olive oil

1 small eggplant, trimmed and cut into 1-inch chunks

2 cups shiitake or cremini mushrooms, quartered

1 can (about 14 ounces) no-salt-added diced tomatoes

½ pound beef top round steak, trimmed of fat and cut into 1-inch pieces

1 medium onion, chopped

1 cup reduced-sodium beef broth

1 clove garlic, minced

½ teaspoon salt

⅓ teaspoon ground cumin

¼ teaspoon red pepper flakes

¼ teaspoon ground cinnamon

Grated peel of 1 lemon

⅛ teaspoon black pepper

1. Heat oil in large nonstick skillet over medium-high heat. Add eggplant and cook 3 to 5 minutes, stirring frequently or until lightly browned on all sides. Transfer to **CROCK-POT®** slow cooker.

2. Stir in remaining ingredients. Cover; cook on LOW 6 hours.

Makes 4 servings

Tip

To remove any bitterness from the eggplant, draw off moisture and reduce the amount of oil absorbed during cooking, try salting it. Cut the eggplant as the recipe directs, place it in a colander and sprinkle cut sides with salt. Allow the eggplant to drain for 30 minutes. Rinse it and pat dry with paper towels. Cook eggplant as directed in recipe.

Chuck and Stout Soup

2 tablespoons olive oil

3 pounds beef chuck, cut into 1-inch cubes

Kosher salt and black pepper

8 cups beef stock

3 large onions, thinly sliced

3 stalks celery, diced

6 carrots, peeled and diced

4 cloves garlic, peeled and minced

2 packages (10 ounces each) cremini mushrooms, thinly sliced

1 package (about 1 ounce) dried porcini mushrooms, processed to a fine powder (see Note)

4 sprigs fresh thyme

1 bottle (12 ounces) stout beer

Flat-leaf parsley (optional)

1. Heat oil in large skillet over medium-high heat until hot. Season meat with salt and pepper. In two batches, brown beef on all sides, taking care to not crowd meat. Meanwhile, in large saucepan, bring beef stock to a boil and reduce by half.

2. Remove beef and place in **CROCK-POT®** slow cooker. Add reduced stock and all remaining ingredients except parsley. Cover; cook on LOW 10 hours or on HIGH 6 hours.

3. Garnish with parsley and serve.

Makes 6 to 8 servings

Note

A coffee grinder works best for processing dried mushrooms, but a food processor or blender can also be used.

Italian Sausage Soup

Sausage Meatballs

- 1 pound mild Italian sausage, casings removed
- ½ cup dried bread crumbs
- ¼ cup grated Parmesan cheese
- ¼ cup milk
- 1 egg
- ½ teaspoon dried basil
- ½ teaspoon black pepper
- ¼ teaspoon garlic salt

Soup

- 4 cups hot chicken broth
- 1 tablespoon tomato paste
- 1 clove garlic, minced
- ¼ teaspoon red pepper flakes
- ½ cup uncooked mini pasta shells*
- 1 bag (10 ounces) baby spinach leaves

  Grated Parmesan cheese

Or use other tiny pasta, such as ditalini (mini tubes) or farfallini (mini bowties).

1. Combine all meatball ingredients. Roll into marble-size balls.

2. Combine broth, tomato paste, garlic and red pepper flakes in **CROCK-POT**® slow cooker. Add meatballs. Cover; cook on LOW 5 to 6 hours.

3. Thirty minutes before serving, add pasta. When pasta is tender, stir in spinach leaves. Ladle into bowls and sprinkle with Parmesan cheese; serve immediately.

Makes 4 to 6 servings

Tip

To quickly shape uniform meatballs, place meat mixture on cutting board; pat evenly into large square, 1 inch thick. With sharp knife, cut meat into 1-inch squares; shape each square into a ball.

Chicken Tortilla Soup

4 boneless, skinless chicken thighs

2 cans (15 ounces each) diced tomatoes, undrained

1 can (4 ounces) chopped mild green chilies, drained

½ to 1 cup chicken broth

1 yellow onion, diced

2 cloves garlic, minced

1 teaspoon ground cumin

Salt and black pepper, to taste

4 corn tortillas, sliced into ¼-inch strips

2 tablespoons chopped fresh cilantro

½ cup (2 ounces) shredded Monterey Jack cheese

1 avocado, peeled, diced and tossed with lime juice to prevent browning

Lime wedges

1. Place chicken in **CROCK-POT**® slow cooker. Combine tomatoes with juice, chilies, ½ cup broth, onion, garlic and cumin in small bowl. Pour mixture over chicken.

2. Cover; cook on LOW 6 hours or on HIGH 3 hours or until chicken is tender. Remove chicken from **CROCK-POT**® slow cooker. Shred with two forks. Return to cooking liquid. Adjust seasonings, adding salt and pepper and more broth, if necessary.

3. Just before serving, add tortillas and cilantro to **CROCK-POT**® slow cooker. Stir to blend. Ladle soup into bowls; top each serving with cheese, avocado and a squeeze of lime juice.

Makes 4 to 6 servings

Northwest Beef and Vegetable Soup

2 tablespoons olive oil

1 pound lean stew beef, fat removed and cut into 1-inch cubes

1 medium onion, chopped

1 clove garlic, minced

3½ cups canned crushed tomatoes, undrained

1 can (15 ounces) white beans, rinsed and drained

1 buttercup squash, peeled and diced

1 turnip, peeled and diced

1 large potato, peeled and diced

2 stalks celery, sliced

2 tablespoons minced fresh basil

1½ teaspoons salt

1 teaspoon black pepper

8 cups water

1. Heat oil in skillet over medium heat until hot. Sear beef on all sides, turning as it browns. Add onion and garlic during last few minutes of searing. Transfer to **CROCK-POT®** slow cooker.

2. Add remaining ingredients. Gently stir well to combine. Cover; cook on HIGH 2 hours. Turn **CROCK-POT®** slow cooker to LOW. Cook on LOW 4 to 6 hours longer, stirring occasionally and adjusting seasonings to taste.

Makes 6 to 8 servings

Russian Borscht

4 cups thinly sliced green cabbage

1½ pounds fresh beets, shredded

5 small carrots, halved lengthwise then cut into 1-inch pieces

1 parsnip, peeled, halved lengthwise then cut into 1-inch pieces

1 cup chopped onion

4 cloves garlic, minced

1 pound beef stew meat, cut into ½-inch cubes

1 can (about 14 ounces) diced tomatoes

3 cans (about 14 ounces each) reduced-sodium beef broth

¼ cup lemon juice, or more to taste

1 tablespoon sugar, or more to taste

1 teaspoon black pepper

Sour cream (optional)

Fresh parsley (optional)

1. Layer ingredients in **CROCK-POT®** slow cooker in following order: cabbage, beets, carrots, parsnip, onion, garlic, beef, tomatoes, broth, lemon juice, sugar and pepper. Cover; cook on LOW 7 to 9 hours or until vegetables are crisp-tender.

2. Season with additional lemon juice and sugar, if desired. Dollop each serving with sour cream and sprinkle with parsley, if desired.

Makes 12 servings

Smoked Sausage and Navy Bean Soup

8 cups chicken broth

1 pound dried navy beans, sorted and rinsed

2 ham hocks (about 1 pound total)

2 onions, diced

1 cup diced carrots

1 cup diced celery

1 can (about 14 ounces) diced tomatoes

2 tablespoons tomato paste

2 cloves garlic, minced

1 bay leaf

1 teaspoon dried thyme

1 smoked sausage (1 pound), cut into ½-inch rounds

1. Bring broth to a boil in large saucepan over medium-high heat. Cover; reduce heat to low.

2. Place beans in **CROCK-POT**® slow cooker. Add ham hocks, onions, carrots, celery, tomatoes, tomato paste, garlic, bay leaf and thyme. Carefully pour in hot broth. Cover; cook on HIGH 8 to 9 hours or until beans are tender.

3. Remove and discard bay leaf. Remove ham hocks from **CROCK-POT**® slow cooker; let stand until cool enough to handle. Remove ham from hocks, chop and return to **CROCK-POT**® slow cooker. Stir in sausage. Cover; cook 15 to 30 minutes or until sausage is heated through.

Makes 8 servings

Tuscan Bean and Prosciutto Soup

2 tablespoons unsalted butter

4 slices prosciutto*

3 cups water

1 cup dried navy beans, sorted and rinsed

½ cup dried lima beans, sorted and rinsed

1 medium yellow onion, finely chopped

1 tablespoon chopped fresh cilantro

1 teaspoon salt

1 teaspoon ground cumin

1 teaspoon ground black pepper

½ teaspoon ground paprika

2 cans (15 ounces each) diced tomatoes, undrained

*Substitute 4 slices bacon, if desired.

1. Melt butter in large skillet over medium-high heat. Add prosciutto and cook until crisp. Remove to paper towels to cool.

2. Crumble prosciutto into small pieces in **CROCK-POT®** slow cooker. Add water, navy beans, lima beans, onion, cilantro, salt, cumin, black pepper and paprika. Stir well to combine. Cover; cook on LOW 10 to 12 hours.

3. Add tomatoes and juice; stir well. Cover; cook on HIGH 30 to 40 minutes or until soup is heated through.

Makes 6 servings

Simmering Hot and Sour Soup

2 cans (about 14 ounces each) chicken broth

1 cup chopped cooked chicken or pork

4 ounces fresh shiitake mushroom caps, thinly sliced

½ cup thinly sliced bamboo shoots

3 tablespoons rice wine vinegar

2 tablespoons soy sauce

1½ teaspoons chili paste or 1 teaspoon hot chili oil

4 ounces firm tofu, well drained and cut into ½-inch pieces

2 teaspoons sesame oil

2 tablespoons cornstarch

2 tablespoons cold water

Chopped cilantro or sliced green onions

1. Combine broth, chicken, mushrooms, bamboo shoots, vinegar, soy sauce and chili paste in **CROCK-POT**® slow cooker. Cover; cook on LOW 3 to 4 hours or on HIGH 2 to 3 hours.

2. Stir in tofu and sesame oil. Whisk cornstarch into water in small bowl; stir into soup. Cover; cook on HIGH 10 minutes or until soup has thickened. To serve, sprinkle with cilantro.

Makes 4 servings

Cannellini Minestrone Soup

4 cups chicken broth

1 can (14½ ounces) diced tomatoes, undrained

1 can (12 ounces) tomato-vegetable juice

2 cups escarole, cut into ribbons

1 cup chopped green onions

1 cup chopped carrots

1 cup chopped celery

1 cup chopped potatoes

¼ cup dried cannellini beans, sorted and rinsed

2 tablespoons chopped fresh chives

1 tablespoon chopped fresh flat-leaf parsley

¼ teaspoon salt

¼ teaspoon black pepper

2 ounces uncooked ditalini pasta

1. Place all ingredients except pasta in **CROCK-POT®** slow cooker. Stir well to combine. Cover; cook on LOW 6 to 8 hours or on HIGH 4 to 6 hours.

2. Stir in pasta. Cover; cook 20 minutes or until pasta is tender.

Makes 6 servings

Double Corn Chowder

2 small celery stalks, trimmed and chopped

6 ounces Canadian bacon, chopped

1 small onion

1 serrano pepper, seeded and diced*

1 cup frozen corn, thawed

1 cup canned hominy

¼ teaspoon salt

¼ teaspoon dried thyme

¼ teaspoon black pepper, or to taste

1 cup chicken broth

1 tablespoon all-purpose flour

1½ cups milk, divided

Serrano peppers can sting and irritate the skin, so wear rubber gloves when handling peppers and do not touch your eyes.

1. Combine celery, bacon, onion, serrano pepper, corn, hominy, salt, thyme and black pepper in **CROCK-POT®** slow cooker. Pour in broth. Cover; cook on LOW 5 to 6 hours or on HIGH 3 to 3½ hours.

2. Stir together flour and 2 tablespoons milk in small bowl. Stir into corn mixture. Add remaining milk. Cover; cook on LOW 20 minutes.

Makes 4 servings

Tip

For richer chowder, use ¾ cup milk and ¾ cup half-and-half.

Plantation Peanut Soup

6 cups chicken broth

2 cups light cream

1 cup chunky peanut butter

1 cup chopped peanuts, divided

½ cup chopped onion

½ cup chopped celery

¼ cup (½ stick) butter

½ teaspoon salt

½ cup all-purpose flour

½ cup water

1. Combine broth, cream, peanut butter, ½ cup peanuts, onion, celery, butter and salt in **CROCK-POT®** slow cooker. Cover; cook on LOW 4 hours.

2. Turn **CROCK-POT®** slow cooker to HIGH. Whisk together flour and water; stir into soup. Cover; cook on HIGH 20 to 25 minutes or until thickened, stirring occasionally.

3. To serve, garnish with remaining chopped peanuts.

Makes 8 servings

Chicken Fiesta Soup

4 **boneless, skinless chicken breasts, cooked and shredded**

1 **can (14½ ounces) stewed tomatoes, drained**

2 **cans (4 ounces each) chopped green chilies**

1 **can (28 ounces) enchilada sauce**

1 **can (14½ ounces) chicken broth**

1 **cup finely chopped onion**

2 **cloves garlic, minced**

1 **teaspoon ground cumin**

1 **teaspoon chili powder**

1 **teaspoon salt**

¾ **teaspoon black pepper**

¼ **cup finely chopped fresh cilantro**

1 **cup frozen whole kernel corn**

1 **yellow squash, diced**

1 **zucchini, diced**

8 **tostada shells, crumbled**

8 **ounces shredded Cheddar cheese**

1. Combine chicken, tomatoes, chilies, enchilada sauce, broth, onion, garlic, cumin, chili powder, salt, pepper, cilantro, corn, squash and zucchini, in **CROCK-POT®** slow cooker.

2. Cover; cook on LOW 8 hours. Ladle soup into bowls. Garnish with crumbled tostada shells and cheese.

Makes 8 servings

Butternut Squash-Apple Soup

3 packages (12 ounces each) frozen cooked winter squash, thawed and drained or about 4½ cups mashed cooked butternut squash

2 cans (about 14 ounces each) chicken broth

1 medium Golden Delicious apple, peeled, cored and chopped

2 tablespoons minced onion

1 tablespoon packed brown sugar

1 teaspoon minced fresh sage or ½ teaspoon ground sage

¼ teaspoon ground ginger

½ cup whipping cream or half-and-half

1. Combine squash, broth, apple, onion, brown sugar, sage and ginger in **CROCK-POT®** slow cooker.

2. Cover; cook on LOW 6 hours or on HIGH 3 hours or until squash is tender.

3. Purée soup in food processor or blender. Stir in cream just before serving.

Makes 6 to 8 servings

Leek and Potato Soup

6 slices bacon, chopped

5 cups shredded frozen hash brown potatoes

3 leeks (white and light green parts) cut into ¾-inch pieces

1 can (10¾ ounces) condensed cream of potato soup, undiluted

1 can (about 14 ounces) reduced-sodium chicken broth

2 ribs celery, sliced

1 can (5 ounces) evaporated milk

½ cup sour cream

1. Cook bacon in large skillet over medium-high heat, stirring occasionally, until crisp and browned. Remove with slotted spoon and drain on paper towel-lined plate.

2. Set aside 2 tablespoons bacon. Combine remaining bacon, potatoes, leeks, soup, broth, celery and evaporated milk in **CROCK-POT®** slow cooker. Cover; cook on LOW 6 to 7 hours. Stir in sour cream. Sprinkle each serving with reserved bacon.

Makes 4 to 6 servings

Spicy Thai Coconut Soup

2 cups chicken broth

1 can (13½ ounces) light coconut milk

1 tablespoon minced fresh ginger

½ to 1 teaspoon red curry paste

3 cups coarsely shredded cooked chicken
(about 12 ounces)

1 can (15 ounces) straw mushrooms, drained

1 can (about 8 ounces) baby corn, drained

2 tablespoons lime juice

¼ cup chopped fresh cilantro

1. Combine broth, coconut milk, ginger and red curry paste in **CROCK-POT®** slow cooker. Add chicken, mushrooms and corn.

2. Cover; cook on HIGH 2 to 3 hours. Stir in lime juice and sprinkle with cilantro just before serving.

Makes 4 servings

Note

Red curry paste is available in the ethnic section of large supermarkets. Spice levels vary so start with ½ teaspoon and add more to taste.

Cauliflower Soup

2 heads cauliflower, cut into small florets

8 cups chicken broth

¾ cup chopped celery

¾ cup chopped onion

2 teaspoons salt

2 teaspoons black pepper

2 cups milk or light cream

1 teaspoon Worcestershire sauce

1. Combine cauliflower, broth, celery, onion, salt and pepper in **CROCK-POT®** slow cooker. Cover; cook on LOW 7 to 8 hours or on HIGH 3 to 4 hours.

2. Using a hand mixer or hand blender, purée soup until smooth. Mix in milk and Worcestershire sauce until smooth. Cover; cook on HIGH 15 to 20 minutes before serving.

Makes 8 servings

Lentil Soup with Ham and Bacon

- 8 ounces chopped bacon
- 8 cups beef broth
- 1½ pounds dried lentils
- 2 cups chopped ham
- 1 cup chopped carrots
- ¾ cup chopped celery
- ¾ cup chopped tomatoes
- ½ cup chopped onion
- 2 teaspoons salt
- 2 teaspoons black pepper
- ½ teaspoon dried marjoram

1. Heat skillet over medium heat until hot. Add bacon. Cook and stir until crisp. Transfer to **CROCK-POT®** slow cooker using slotted spoon.

2. Add remaining ingredients. Cover; cook on LOW 8 to 10 hours or on HIGH 6 to 8 hours or until lentils are tender.

Makes 8 servings

Hearty Mushroom and Barley Soup

- 9 cups chicken broth
- 1 package (16 ounces) sliced fresh button mushrooms
- 1 large onion, chopped
- 2 carrots, chopped
- 2 stalks celery, chopped
- ½ cup uncooked pearl barley
- ½ ounce dried porcini mushrooms
- 3 cloves garlic, minced
- 1 teaspoon salt
- ½ teaspoon dried thyme
- ½ teaspoon black pepper

Combine all ingredients in **CROCK-POT®** slow cooker; stir until well blended. Cover; cook on LOW 4 to 6 hours.

Makes 8 to 10 servings

Variation

For even more flavor, add a beef or ham bone to the CROCK-POT® slow cooker with the rest of the ingredients.

Tuscan White Bean Soup

10 cups chicken broth

1 package (16 ounces) dried Great Northern beans, sorted and rinsed

1 can (about 14 ounces) diced tomatoes

1 large onion, chopped

3 carrots, chopped

6 ounces bacon, crisp-cooked and diced

4 cloves garlic, minced

1 fresh rosemary sprig or 1 teaspoon dried rosemary

1 teaspoon black pepper

1. Combine broth, beans, tomatoes, onion, carrots, bacon, garlic, rosemary and pepper in **CROCK-POT**® slow cooker.

2. Cover; cook on LOW 8 hours. Remove and discard rosemary sprigs before serving.

Makes 8 to 10 servings

Serving Suggestion

Place slices of toasted Italian bread in bottom of individual soup bowls. Drizzle with olive oil. Ladle soup over bread and serve.

Nana's Mini Meatball Soup

1 pound ground beef

1 pound ground pork

1½ cups finely grated Pecorino Romano or Parmesan cheese

1 cup Italian bread crumbs

2 eggs

1 bunch flat-leaf parsley

Kosher salt and black pepper

3 quarts chicken stock

1 bunch escarole, coarsely chopped

½ box (8 ounces) ditalini pasta, cooked

1. Combine beef, pork, cheese, bread crumbs, eggs, parsley, salt and pepper in large bowl. Mix well by hand and roll into ¾-inch meatballs.

2. Add meatballs and chicken stock to **CROCK-POT**® slow cooker. Cook on LOW 9 hours or on HIGH 5 hours.

3. Add escarole and cook until wilted, bright green and tender, about 15 minutes. Add cooked ditalini to soup and serve.

Makes 6 to 8 servings

Mother's Sausage and Vegetable Soup

- 1 can (15 ounces) black beans, rinsed and drained
- 1 can (about 14 ounces) diced tomatoes
- 1 can (10¾ ounces) condensed cream of mushroom soup, undiluted
- ½ pound smoked turkey sausage, cut into ½-inch slices
- 2 cups diced potato
- 1 cup chopped onion
- 1 cup chopped red bell pepper
- ½ cup water
- 2 teaspoons extra-hot prepared horseradish
- 2 teaspoons honey
- 1 teaspoon dried basil

1. Combine all ingredients in **CROCK-POT®** slow cooker; mix well.

2. Cover; cook on LOW 7 to 8 hours or until potato is tender.

Makes 6 to 8 servings

Greek Lemon and Rice Soup

- 3 cans (14 ounces each) chicken broth
- ½ cup uncooked long grain white rice (not converted or instant rice)
- 3 egg yolks
- ¼ cup fresh lemon juice
- ¼ teaspoon salt
- ⅛ teaspoon ground white pepper*
- 4 thin slices lemon (optional)
- 4 teaspoons finely chopped parsley (optional)

Or substitute ground black pepper.

1. Stir chicken broth and rice together in **CROCK-POT®** slow cooker. Cover; cook on HIGH 2 to 3 hours or until rice is cooked.

2. Turn to LOW. Whisk egg yolks and lemon juice together in medium bowl. Whisk large spoonful of hot rice mixture into egg yolk mixture. Whisk back into **CROCK-POT®** slow cooker.

3. Cook on LOW 10 minutes. Season with salt and pepper. Ladle soup into serving bowls and garnish each bowl with thin slice of lemon and 1 teaspoon chopped parsley.

Makes 4 servings

Tortilla Soup

- 2 cans (about 14 ounces each) chicken broth
- 1 can (about 14 ounces) diced tomatoes with jalapeño peppers
- 2 cups chopped carrots
- 2 cups frozen corn, thawed
- 1½ cups chopped onions
- 1 can (8 ounces) tomato sauce
- 1 tablespoon chili powder
- 1 teaspoon ground cumin
- ¼ teaspoon garlic powder
- 2 cups chopped cooked chicken (optional)

1. Combine broth, tomatoes, carrots, corn, onions, tomato sauce, chili powder, cumin and garlic powder in **CROCK-POT®** slow cooker. Cover; cook on LOW 6 to 8 hours.

2. Stir in chicken, if desired. Ladle into bowls. Top each serving with cheese and tortilla chips.

Makes 6 servings

Serving Suggestion
Top with shredded Monterey Jack cheese and crushed tortilla chips.

Chicken Soup

- 6 cups chicken broth
- 1½ pounds boneless, skinless chicken breasts, cubed
- 2 cups sliced carrots
- 1 cup sliced mushrooms
- 1 red bell pepper, chopped
- 1 onion, chopped
- 2 tablespoons grated fresh ginger
- 3 teaspoons minced garlic
- ½ teaspoon crushed red pepper
  Salt and black pepper, to taste

Place all ingredients in **CROCK-POT®** slow cooker. Cover; cook on LOW 6 to 7 hours or on HIGH 3 to 3½ hours.

Makes 4 to 6 servings

Chicken and Vegetable Chowder

- 1 pound boneless, skinless chicken breasts, cut into 1-inch pieces
- 1 can (about 14 ounces) reduced-sodium chicken broth
- 1 can (10¾ ounces) condensed cream of potato soup, undiluted
- 1 package (10 ounces) frozen broccoli florets, thawed
- 1 cup sliced carrots
- 1 jar (4½ ounces) sliced mushrooms, drained
- ½ cup chopped onion
- ½ cup whole kernel corn
- 2 cloves garlic, minced
- ½ teaspoon dried thyme leaves
- ⅓ cup half-and-half

1. Combine chicken, broth, soup, broccoli, carrots, mushrooms, onion, corn, garlic and thyme in **CROCK-POT®** slow cooker; mix well. Cover; cook on LOW 5 to 6 hours.

2. Stir in half-and-half. Cover; cook on HIGH 15 minutes or until heated through.

Makes 6 servings

Pizza Soup

- 2 cans (14½ ounces each) stewed tomatoes with Italian seasonings, undrained
- 2 cups beef broth
- 1 cup sliced mushrooms
- 1 small onion, chopped
- 1 tablespoon tomato paste
- ¼ teaspoon salt, or to taste
- ¼ teaspoon black pepper, or to taste
- ½ pound turkey Italian sausage, casings removed
    Shredded mozzarella cheese

1. Combine tomatoes with juice, broth, mushrooms, onion, tomato paste, salt and pepper in **CROCK-POT®** slow cooker.

2. Shape sausage into marble-size balls. Gently stir into soup mixture. Cover; cook on LOW 6 to 7 hours. Adjust salt and pepper, if necessary. Serve with cheese.

Makes 4 servings

Winter's Best Bean Soup

6 ounces bacon, diced

10 cups chicken broth

3 cans (about 15 ounces each) Great Northern beans, drained

1 can (about 14 ounces) diced tomatoes, undrained

1 large onion, chopped

1 package (10 ounces) frozen sliced or diced carrots

2 teaspoons bottled minced garlic

1 fresh rosemary sprig or 1 teaspoon dried rosemary

1 teaspoon black pepper

1. Cook bacon in medium skillet over medium-high heat until just cooked; drain and transfer to **CROCK-POT®** slow cooker. Add remaining ingredients.

2. Cover; cook on LOW 8 hours or until beans are tender. Remove rosemary sprig. Mince leaves and add to soup before serving.

Makes 8 to 10 servings

Serving Suggestion

Place slices of toasted Italian bread in bottom of individual soup bowls. Drizzle with olive oil. Pour soup over bread and serve.

Mexican Cheese Soup

1 pound pasteurized processed cheese product, cubed

1 pound ground beef, cooked and drained

1 can (about 15 ounces) kidney beans, undrained

1 can (about 14 ounces) diced tomatoes with green chilies, undrained

1 can (about 14 ounces) stewed tomatoes, undrained

1 can (8¾ ounces) whole kernel corn, undrained

1 envelope taco seasoning

1 jalapeño pepper, seeded and diced* (optional)

Corn chips (optional)

Jalapeño peppers can sting and irritate the skin, so wear rubber gloves when handling peppers and do not touch your eyes. Wash hands after handling.

1. Coat inside of **CROCK-POT®** slow cooker with nonstick cooking spray. Add cheese, beef, beans, tomatoes with chilies, tomatoes with juice, corn, taco seasoning and jalapeño pepper, if desired. Mix well.

2. Cover; cook on LOW 4 to 5 hours or on HIGH 3 hours or until done. Serve with corn chips.

Makes 6 to 8 servings

Old-Fashioned Split Pea Soup

4 quarts chicken broth

2 pounds dried split peas

1 cup chopped ham

½ cup chopped onion

½ cup chopped celery

2 teaspoons salt

2 teaspoons black pepper

1. Place all ingredients in **CROCK-POT®** slow cooker. Stir well to combine. Cover; cook on LOW 8 to 10 hours or on HIGH 4 to 6 hours, or until peas are soft.

2. Mix with hand mixer or hand blender on LOW speed until smooth.

Makes 8 servings

Linguiça & Green Bean Soup

1 large yellow onion, chopped

3 cloves garlic, minced

2 tablespoons olive oil

1 cup tomato juice

4 cups water

1 tablespoon Italian seasoning

2 teaspoons garlic salt

1 teaspoon ground cumin

1 bay leaf

2 cans (16 ounces each) cut green beans, drained

1 can (16 ounces) kidney beans, drained

1 pound linguiça sausage, fried until cooked through then cut into bite-size pieces

1. Place all ingredients in **CROCK-POT®** slow cooker. Cover; cook on LOW 8 to 10 hours or on HIGH 4 to 6 hours. Add more boiling water during cooking, if necessary.

2. Serve with warm corn bread.

Makes 6 servings

Roasted Corn and Red Pepper Chowder

2   tablespoons extra-virgin olive oil

2   cups fresh corn kernels or frozen corn, thawed

1   red bell pepper, cored, seeded and diced

2   green onions, sliced

4   cups chicken broth

2   baking potatoes, peeled and diced

1   teaspoon salt

½   teaspoon black pepper

1   can (13 ounces) evaporated milk

2   tablespoons minced flat-leaf parsley

1. Heat oil in skillet over medium heat until hot. Add corn, bell pepper and onions. Cook and stir until vegetables are tender and lightly browned, about 7 to 8 minutes. Transfer to **CROCK-POT®** slow cooker.

2. Add broth, potatoes, salt and black pepper. Stir well to combine. Cover; cook on LOW 7 to 9 hours or on HIGH 4 to 5 hours.

3. Thirty minutes before serving, add evaporated milk. Stir well to combine and continue cooking. To serve, garnish with parsley.

Makes 4 servings

Slow Cooker Chicken Stock

1   large chicken (4 to 6 pounds), cut into pieces

1   package (16 ounces) celery, cut into large pieces

1   large carrot, peeled and cut into 2- to 3-inch pieces

2   onions or leeks, quartered

2   large parsnips, peeled and coarsely chopped

½   cup loosely packed fresh herbs such as flat-leaf parsley, dill, thyme, chervil or a combination

Kosher salt and black pepper, to taste

1. Place all ingredients in **CROCK-POT®** slow cooker and add enough water to fill three quarters full. Cook on LOW 12 hours or on HIGH 8 hours.

2. Strain out solids, cool and refrigerate 12 hours. Skim off and discard any fat.

Makes about 10 cups stock

Tip

Make this stock in the fall so that you have homemade stock on hand for all of your winter soups. Freeze stock in 2-cup portions (one 14-ounce can of chicken broth contains 2 cups). Simply thaw one 2-cup portion for each can of broth called for in the recipe.

Parsnip and Carrot Soup

Nonstick cooking spray

1 medium leek, thinly sliced

4 medium parsnips, peeled and diced

4 medium carrots, peeled and diced

4 cups chicken broth or stock

1 bay leaf

½ teaspoon salt

½ teaspoon freshly ground pepper

½ cup small pasta, cooked and drained

1 tablespoon chopped Italian parsley

1 cup low-fat croutons

1. Spray small nonstick skillet with cooking spray; add leek and cook over medium heat until golden. Place in **CROCK-POT®** slow cooker.

2. Add parsnips, carrots, broth, bay leaf, salt and pepper. Cover; cook on LOW 6 to 9 hours or on HIGH 2 to 4 hours or until vegetables are tender. Add pasta during last hour of cooking.

3. Remove bay leaf. Sprinkle each serving with parsley and croutons.

Makes 4 servings

Veggie Soup with Beef

2 cans (15 ounces each) mixed vegetables

1 pound beef stew meat

1 can (8 ounces) tomato sauce

2 cloves garlic, minced

   Water

1. Combine mixed vegetables, beef, tomato sauce and garlic in **CROCK-POT®** slow cooker.

2. Add enough water to fill **CROCK-POT®** slow cooker to within ½ inch of top. Cover; cook on LOW 8 to 10 hours.

Makes 4 servings

Tip

For a heartier soup, add cooked brown rice, barley or orzo just before serving and heat through. Serve with garlic bread or Texas toast and a quick salad.

Vietnamese Chicken Pho

8 cups chicken stock

2 to 3 cups shredded cooked chicken

8 ounces bean sprouts

Rice stick noodles

1 bunch Thai basil, chopped

Hoisin sauce (optional)

Lime wedges (optional)

1. Combine stock and chicken in **CROCK-POT®** slow cooker. Cover; cook on LOW 6 to 7 hours or on HIGH 3 hours.

2. Add bean sprouts, noodles and Thai basil. Cover; cook until noodles are softened.

3. Spoon soup into individual serving bowls and serve with hoisin sauce and lime wedges.

Makes 4 to 6 servings

Note

A simple soup to prepare with leftover shredded chicken, this classic Asian chicken noodle soup packs tons of flavor.

Black Bean Soup

3 cans (15 ounces each) black beans, rinsed and drained

3½ cups beef stock

4 plum tomatoes, diced

2 jalapeño peppers, minced*

½ pound bacon, cooked and crumbled

1 large onion, chopped

⅓ cup red wine vinegar

1 teaspoon dried oregano leaves

1½ teaspoons ground cumin

1 teaspoon dried thyme leaves

Kosher salt and black pepper, to taste

Optional toppings: diced avocado, lime juice and Cheddar cheese

*Jalapeño peppers can sting and irritate the skin, so wear rubber gloves when handing peppers and do not touch your eyes.

1. Combine beans, stock, tomatoes, jalapeño peppers, bacon, onion, vinegar, oregano, cumin and thyme in **CROCK-POT®** slow cooker and stir well. Cover; cook on LOW 8 to 10 hours or on HIGH 4 to 5 hours.

2. Adjust seasoning with salt and black pepper to taste; serve with desired toppings.

Makes 4 to 6 servings

recipe index

recipe index

recipe index

metric
conversion chart

VOLUME MEASUREMENTS (dry)

1/8 teaspoon = 0.5 mL
1/4 teaspoon = 1 mL
1/2 teaspoon = 2 mL
3/4 teaspoon = 4 mL
1 teaspoon = 5 mL
1 tablespoon = 15 mL
2 tablespoons = 30 mL
1/4 cup = 60 mL
1/3 cup = 75 mL
1/2 cup = 125 mL
2/3 cup = 150 mL
3/4 cup = 175 mL
1 cup = 250 mL
2 cups = 1 pint = 500 mL
3 cups = 750 mL
4 cups = 1 quart = 1 L

VOLUME MEASUREMENTS (fluid)

1 fluid ounce (2 tablespoons) = 30 mL
4 fluid ounces (1/2 cup) = 125 mL
8 fluid ounces (1 cup) = 250 mL
12 fluid ounces (1 1/2 cups) = 375 mL
16 fluid ounces (2 cups) = 500 mL

WEIGHTS (mass)

1/2 ounce = 15 g
1 ounce = 30 g
3 ounces = 90 g
4 ounces = 120 g
8 ounces = 225 g
10 ounces = 285 g
12 ounces = 360 g
16 ounces = 1 pound = 450 g

DIMENSIONS

1/16 inch = 2 mm
1/8 inch = 3 mm
1/4 inch = 6 mm
1/2 inch = 1.5 cm
3/4 inch = 2 cm
1 inch = 2.5 cm

OVEN TEMPERATURES

250°F = 120°C
275°F = 140°C
300°F = 150°C
325°F = 160°C
350°F = 180°C
375°F = 190°C
400°F = 200°C
425°F = 220°C
450°F = 230°C

BAKING PAN AND DISH EQUIVALENTS

Utensil	Size in Inches	Size in Centimeters	Volume	Metric Volume
Baking or Cake Pan (square or rectangular)	8×8×2	20×20×5	8 cups	2 L
	9×9×2	23×23×5	10 cups	2.5 L
	13×9×2	33×23×5	12 cups	3 L
Loaf Pan	8½×4½×2½	21×11×6	6 cups	1.5 L
	9×9×3	23×13×7	8 cups	2 L
Round Layer Cake Pan	8×1½	20×4	4 cups	1 L
	9×1½	23×4	5 cups	1.25 L
Pie Plate	8×1½	20×4	4 cups	1 L
	9×1½	23×4	5 cups	1.25 L
Baking Dish or Casserole			1 quart/4 cups	1 L
			1½ quart/6 cups	1.5 L
			2 quart/8 cups	2 L
			3 quart/12 cups	3 L